Becoming a
Strategic Leader

Join us at josseybass.com

Register at **www.josseybass.com/email**
for more information on our publications,
authors, and to receive special offers.

Becoming a Strategic Leader

Your Role in Your Organization's Enduring Success

Second Edition

Richard L. Hughes

Katherine Colarelli Beatty

David L. Dinwoodie

Center for
Creative
Leadership
www.ccl.org

JB JOSSEY-BASS™
A Wiley Brand

Published by Jossey-Bass
A Wiley Imprint
One Montgomery Street, Suite 1200, San Francisco, CA 94104-4594
www.josseybass.com

Jossey-Bass books and products are available through most bookstores. To contact Jossey-Bass directly call our Customer Care Department within the U.S. at 800-956-7739, outside the U.S. at 317-572-3986, or fax 317-572-4002.

Wiley publishes in a variety of print and electronic formats and by print-on-demand. Some material included with standard print versions of this book may not be included in e-books or in print-on-demand. If this book refers to media such as a CD or DVD that is not included in the version you purchased, you may download this material at http://booksupport.wiley.com. For more information about Wiley products, visit www.wiley.com.

Library of Congress Cataloging-in-Publication Data

Hughes, Richard L.
    Becoming a strategic leader : your role in your organization's enduring success / Richard L. Hughes, Katherine Colarelli Beatty, David L. Dinwoodie. — Second edition.
    "A joint publication of The Jossey-Bass Business & Management Series And The Center for Creative Leadership."
    Includes bibliographical references and index.
    ISBN 978-1-118-57313-6 (pdf) — ISBN 978-1-118-57315-0 (epub) — ISBN 978-1-118-56723-4 (cloth)
        1. Leadership.   2. Strategic planning.   3. Organizational effectiveness.   4. Success in business.   I. Beatty, Katherine Colarelli, 1965–   II. Dinwoodie, David L.   III. Title.
    HD57.7
    658.4'092—dc23

                                                                                2013034738

Printed in the United States of America
SECOND EDITION
HB Printing   10 9 8 7 6 5 4

A Joint Publication of

The Jossey-Bass

Business & Management Series

and

The Center for Creative Leadership

Contents

Preface

We've worked together for over fifteen years at the Center for Creative Leadership (CCL), and the focus of our work has been developing the strategic leadership of individual executives, their teams, and their organizations at large. During that time, we have worked personally with over two thousand different managers and executives—sometimes with heterogeneous groups from different companies and sometimes with groups from the same organization.

Frequently that work has been in the context of Developing the Strategic Leader, a program that has recently been revised and relaunched as Leading Strategically. We've had the opportunity to work with the executives who participate in the program as they've struggled to become better strategic leaders. As we've weathered this challenge alongside them, we have deepened our own understanding about how to become more strategic. We have also had the opportunity to facilitate customized versions of strategic leadership programs for corporate clients in many parts of the world. From Europe to North America to South America to the Middle East to Asia, we have been in a position to assist leaders as they foster a strategic leadership mind-set throughout their organizations. In a general sense, this book reflects our attempt to put some of the lessons of that program and what we have learned through our work in it into a more explicit and accessible format.

One thing we have gained from this work is greater clarity about the challenges managers and executives face in becoming more effective strategic leaders. Our understanding has come in part from what executives themselves tell us about their challenges, which typically fall into the following broad categories: spanning organizational boundaries to influence others more effectively, thinking strategically with a broader organizational perspective, achieving a better balance in handling short-term and long-term priorities, and actually leading the formulation and execution of strategic change initiatives across different parts of the organization.

We've gained from this work an appreciation of how the nature of strategic leadership in organizations is changing, which is reflected in the people who describe these challenges to us. Managers and executives at many levels and across many functions participate in the Leading Strategically program to improve their effectiveness as strategic leaders. For example, about 14 percent of participants in the program represent the top leadership of their organizations, 42 percent are executives, 35 percent are from upper-middle management, and 5 percent are from middle management.

What does it mean to find such a broad spectrum of managers and executives intent on developing their effectiveness as strategic leaders? We believe it's more than just preparation for future responsibilities. We believe it reflects something fundamental about how strategic leadership itself is changing: strategic leadership increasingly is the responsibility of many people, not just those at the top. More and more we see that leaders at different levels in the organization are charged with contributing to strategy formulation and leading strategy execution.

The challenges we address are not theoretical; rather they reflect what managers and executives are struggling with now as they prepare their organizations to move toward their desired futures. In that regard, the list presents to us a fairly reasonable outline of what it means to be strategic. True, it is only a rather sparse outline. An important part of what we have learned over the years is how to help managers and executives add depth as well as breadth to this outline, in ways tailored to their unique development needs and circumstances. We've also learned a lot about what facilitates the development of strategic leadership, especially how the understanding and practice of strategic leadership evolve in an environment that plays host to an ongoing interplay of action, observation, and reflection.

Over time, we have also come to appreciate a certain connectedness between the kinds of experiences that facilitate the development of strategic leadership and those that facilitate the ongoing development, implementation, and refinement of organizational strategy itself. Both have everything to do with viewing strategy as a learning process, an idea that is central to this book. Part of becoming an effective strategic leader involves facilitating that process throughout the organization (or one's part of it).

This book's title, *Becoming a Strategic Leader*, underscores a central lesson we've learned in this work: that strategic leadership is about *becoming*. It's about a process of never-ending individual, team, and organizational learning. Working at CCL and with the participants of the Leading Strategically program has been a privilege, in particular because of the opportunity we have had to help so many individuals play a more effective role in the strategic leadership of their organizations. We hope our insights from that work, captured here as best we can, will help them continue that process and will reach new audiences as well.

Colorado Springs, Colorado   Richard L. Hughes
November 2013   Katherine Colarelli Beatty
                                         David L. Dinwoodie

Acknowledgments

This book represents the contributions of many people over many years, and we acknowledge our debt to them here. Even as we began work on the second edition of this book, we continued to be indebted to those within the Center for Creative Leadership (CCL) who played such a significant role at the outset related to the development of our own thinking about strategic leadership.

Our ideas about strategic leadership have been largely formulated in the context of our work in CCL's Developing the Strategic Leader (DSL) and Leading Strategically programs. We've learned much from executives participating in the programs, and we've learned equally from our colleagues on the faculty, who have enriched our understanding of the nature of strategic leadership. We are particularly indebted to fellow faculty members Kevin Asbjörnson, Stephanie Trovas, Laura Quinn, Pam Shipp, Ted Grubb, Dennis Lindoerfer, Gary Rhodes, Bruce Byington, Jessica Baltes, Chuck Hinkle, Jamie Gurley, Tom Turney, Paul Stames, Gayle Magee, Cindy McLaughlin, Kristen Kramer, Russ McCallian, and Tasha Eurich for their insight, savvy, generosity, and comradeship.

The work of Stephanie Trovas, Tom Turney, Paul Stames, David Horth, Diane Reinhold, Heather Champion, Laura Quinn, Cindy McLaughlin, Harold Scharlatt, Leigh Allen, Barbara Fly-Dierks, Renée Hultin, Lisa DesRochers, Mark Jones, and Lori Spaulding to redesign the DSL program had a profound impact on this book. We also appreciate CCL's portfolio action team, whose foresight and championing of CCL's leader development road map provided a foundation for creating the Leading Strategically program. Members of this team include Renée Hultin, Jennifer Martineau, Emily Hoole, Kris Downing, Susan Smith, and Jeff Howard.

We are particularly indebted to alumni of the program who participated in interviews conducted by Tom Francis to help us ascertain areas to focus on as we updated and revised the chapters: Alan Smart, Beth Jackson, Beth Meyers, Clay McBride, Grace H. Li, Herman Williams, Jan Walstrom, Loan T. Ng, Jeff Palla, Kevin Hart, Paul Goeffy, Paul Testa, Paula Littlewood, Rory Sexton, Stephen Park, and Trevor Dierdorff.

Some of our colleagues contributed in unique ways. John Ryan pushed us to explore the changing nature of strategic leadership challenges and revise our training programs and management publications to reflect today's organizational realities. Bruce Byington was an indispensable collaborator in helping us formulate and refine our understanding of strategy as a learning process, the framework on which this book is based. Jessica Baltes had many responsibilities in the DSL training programs, including an invaluable role in guiding the early research efforts cited throughout the book. Judith Steed, Dennis Lindoerfer, Laura Quinn, and Cory Stern also contributed significantly in the research efforts.

We are indebted to John McGuire for his contributions to our appreciating the role of culture in leadership strategy, and Bill Pasmore, who brought a wealth of knowledge and experience related to strategic organizational design. Roland Smith, Michael Campbell, and Cindy McCauley helped shape our approach to talent systems. We are indebted to Patricia O'Connor, Jennifer Martineau, and Davida Sharpe, whose impressive work with Catholic Healthcare Partners is highlighted in the book. We are similarly indebted to Laura Santana, Rosa Belzer, Montse Auso, and Enrique Alvarez for their contribution to the Credicorp Group case study. Chuck Palus and David Horth's work on creative competencies had a significant impact on our own approach to strategic thinking. Sara King and Bill Drath's support for the first edition of this book took many forms, not the least of which was their continuing personal and institutional encouragement for the project. Their contributions remain in this new edition.

We owe a particular debt of gratitude to CCL's leadership strategy services team members—Edward Marshall, Diane Reinhold, Jennifer Martineau, Bill Pasmore, Laura Quinn, John McGuire, and Gary Adkins—for their tireless work converting leadership strategy theory into practical frameworks. We also appreciate and acknowledge our CCL colleagues and partners who applied boundary-spanning leadership principles with the teams transitioning from a military operation to a civilian operation in Iraq: Bill Adams, Chris Ernst, John Ferguson, George Houston, Jennifer Martineau, Harold Scharlatt, and Clemson Turregano.

In the journey from the first to the second edition of this book, we could not have had more supportive or able collaborators than Peter Scisco, our editor at CCL, and the professionals at Jossey-Bass, notably Kathe Sweeney and Alison Hankey.

Many organizations and many individuals are featured in stories throughout the book, and some in particular gave of their time to assist in providing relevant examples. We are grateful to those organizations for the opportunity to mention them here and to those individuals for sharing their experiences so generously and publicly. The organizations include Torstar, Harlequin, Verizon, Starbucks, Xerox, American Power Conversion (now part of Schneider Electric), Catholic Healthcare Partners, Procter & Gamble Company, Credicorp Group, Banco de Credito de Bolivia, Intermón-Oxfam, Juniper Networks, La Quinta Inn & Suites, Kaiser Permanente, Aegon USA Investment Management, LLC, and The Wendy's Company. Those individuals include Rob Prichard, Karen Hanna, and Kim Eckel at Torstar; Donna Hayes, Trish Hewitt, and Isabel Swift at Harlequin; Marilyn O'Connell at Verizon; Margaret Wheeler at Starbucks; Tim Conlon and Jim Firestone at Xerox; Andrew Cole at American Power Conversion; Jon Abeles at Catholic Healthcare Partners; Bob McDonald at Procter & Gamble; Walter Bayly and Ursula Alvarez at Credicorp

Group; Miguel Solis at Banco de Credito de Bolivia; Francesc Mateu, Pilar Orenes, and Jose María Vera at Intermón-Oxfam; Courtney Harrision at Juniper Networks; Jeff Palla at La Quinta Inn & Suites; Kevin Hart at Kaiser Permanente; Clay McBride at for Aegon USA Investment Management, LLC; and Kaye O'Neal at Wendy's.

Several individuals gave us useful and detailed feedback on earlier drafts of the book, including Mark Edwards, Amy Edmondson, Bill Clover, and Nick Colarelli (Kate's dad).

We are particularly grateful for the help of Grant Smith for graphics work on the strategic leadership model and Karen Andrews, who has supported this effort administratively during its development. Their creativity, patience, good humor, and attention to quality have made all the difference.

Finally, our deepest appreciation goes to those closest in our lives, whose understanding and support made our work on this long project possible: Chris, Mark, and Thomas Beatty; Georgeann Hughes; Marta Palmés Fàbregas; and Arianna and Natàlia Dinwoodie Palmés. You're the best!

About the Authors

Richard L. Hughes recently retired from his position as Transformation Chair at the US Air Force Academy. In that role, he worked with senior leaders across the academy to help guide organizational transformation of the academy in ways to ensure it is meeting its mission of producing leaders of character. He served previously on the academy faculty as full professor and head of the Department of Behavioral Sciences and Leadership. From 1995 until 2007, he worked at the Center for Creative Leadership in various management, research, and teaching capacities. His work at CCL focused on senior executive leadership, and he helped create CCL's practice in organizational leadership development. He is senior author of the textbook *Leadership: Enhancing the Lessons of Experience*, now in its eighth edition. He received his BS from the US Air Force Academy, his MA from the University of Texas, and his PhD in clinical psychology from the University of Wyoming. He holds the rank of brigadier general, USAF (ret.).

• • •

Katherine Colarelli Beatty is the managing director for the Colorado Springs campus of the Center for Creative Leadership, where she is responsible for all operations to meet the needs of the clients served from this campus. Previously she was the director of global portfolio management for CCL, responsible for ensuring a high-quality, relevant, and scalable portfolio to meet the demands of clients across the globe. She has a long history with

CCL's organization leadership practice, of which strategic leadership is one component. Her expertise in strategic leadership is reflected in her many research, writing, public speaking, and training activities. She joined CCL in 1996. Formerly she was a consultant to organizations in the areas of change leadership and team development. She also worked for Anheuser-Busch in its efforts to develop future company leaders and was a member of a leadership training program for engineers at GE Medical Systems. She earned her BS in electrical engineering from the University of Illinois. She holds MS and PhD degrees in organizational psychology from Saint Louis University.

• • •

David L. Dinwoodie is the regional director of Latin America for the Center for Creative Leadership. He coordinates the design of leadership solutions and faculty development for CCL's activities in the Spanish- and Portuguese-speaking Americas. As a senior faculty at CCL, he serves as lead trainer for the Leading Strategically program, as well as delivering custom leadership development solutions for corporate clients. He is a member of CCL's organizational leadership practice team and a research associate on the CCL research project Leadership Across Differences. Before joining CCL, he lived and worked throughout Europe and North and South America. He held senior positions with pan-European and global responsibilities in Ernst & Young, BICC General Cable, Planeta de Agostini, and Bristol-Myers Squibb. In the field of executive education, he held the post of general manager of EADA Business School in Barcelona. He studied political science at the University of Colorado, holds a master of international management from the Thunderbird School of Global Management, and earned an MBA from ESADE Business School in Barcelona. His doctoral degree is from Aston University (UK) in the area of work group and organizational psychology.

Becoming a
Strategic Leader

Introduction

What if you could turn your organization into an engine of maximum performance potential, with the agility to weather uncertainty and success with equal measure? What if you could transform your personal and technical skills into a leadership practice with the power to build an organization capable of ever-deepening insight and high performance? What if you could have adaptive, effective strategic leadership throughout all levels, functions, and regions of your organization? This book is your guide.

The Changing Nature of Strategic Leadership

Have you noticed how it seems more challenging to get work done in organizations today? Garnering resources for a project, for example, now often requires conversations and coordination among people and groups inside and outside your organization who did not have to interact before. In general, work has become more complex and more interdependent in most organizations.

Consider the evidence. CEO turnover happens at a more rapid rate than before, organizations develop new products faster, new competitors spring up from unexpected quarters, and governments continue to set and change regulatory requirements. In addition, organizations and their leaders are increasingly interdependent. Prior to the global financial crises of 2008, some leaders we talked to doubted the need to truly lead and work interdependently. These days, however, we find that most leaders, if not all, fully resonate with a desire to develop leadership for a truly interdependent world.

Change has become so fast and so pervasive that it has an impact on virtually every organization everywhere, and everyone in them. And appropriate to our times, an acronym has been given to this condition: VUCA. As imagined by the US Army War College and popularized by Bob Johansen in *Leaders Make the Future* (2012), VUCA describes a world that is volatile, uncertain, complex, and ambiguous. Correspondingly, today's strategic leaders must be able think, act, and influence in that environment.

Johansen describes several forces that are contributing to the VUCA nature of our world. Underpinning these forces are some fundamental trends, such as the widening rich-poor gap. For example, in 2012, the richest 1 percent of the population worldwide earned as much as the bottom 57 percent of the population. And while there has always been some degree of a rich-poor gap, Johansen argues it will widen further and increasingly be a source of conflict in the world (especially over food production and distribution).

Climate change and ecosystems in general signify another trend of a VUCA world. Decisions that leaders make today will have an impact on the future of ecosystems ten or more years from now. Are contemporary leaders skilled (or even rewarded) for attending to factors that are measured on such a long time frame? People may sense that their actions will affect generations to come, but can leaders adapt mind-sets and practices that attend to long-term impacts? Climate and ecosystem changes can affect food production and distribution, which can make it more difficult for some populations to feed themselves. This will exacerbate the rich-poor divide. What will be the effect?

Neither can leaders ignore another trend: the move toward cloud computing and mobile device access that fuels the ability of social networking to significantly influence local, regional, and global events, as evidenced by the 2011 overturn of Egyptian president Hosni Mubarak. As individuals are connected to others through global communications, they have a huge potential to extend their reach and impact. To the extent that we think of leaders as nodes in a variety of social networks, how might those nodes work together to create collective intention for something that is of broader benefit to the globe? How might leaders organize and harness this trend? Or will they be in a state only to react when others do?

Johansen points out that society used to look to government, science, and large companies to think about the future. People trusted those in positions of authority to shape the future for them. This allowed a level of perceived control regarding the impact the future might have. But now, with the power of social media and connectivity, the potential to shape the future belongs to us all, and with that comes a sense of unpredictability. Johansen notes that in the year 2012, everyone under the age of twenty-five came of age in the era of social media and are digital natives. Their power, amplified by new technologies, will be quite different from anything we've experienced in the past. According to Johansen, "Economies of scale give way to economies of organization—you are what you organize" (p. 19).

All of these forces and changes create a new competitive environment that has led to more complex and interdependent work in organizations and requires them to be more agile and resilient. But being both agile and resilient at the same time is not easy. As a result, organizations may strive to meet competing sets of external and internal demands by trying to be all things to all people. As the tension between internal needs and external needs increases, it becomes increasingly difficult for leaders to create direction, alignment, and commitment throughout the organization.

This situation calls for more people, not fewer, in organizations to be engaged in strategic leadership. To be sure, certain individuals have greater opportunity and responsibility to affect their organization than others. But more and more, people at all organizational levels and in all organizational functions are seeing opportunities to work in ways that affect the direction and momentum of the whole organization.

The best way for organizations to thrive in the face of this new reality is to become continual learning engines. In practical terms, that means that organizational strategy—the vision, the directions, and the tactics adopted to move toward success—ought to be held in an ongoing state of formulation, implementation, reassessment, and revision.

What kind of leadership is needed to transform organizations into continual learning engines that maximize performance potential? It is the kind that makes decisions and takes action not just to boost the organization's current performance but also to strengthen the organization's future effectiveness and competitiveness. It's not the kind of leadership that can be explained and practiced with a simple set of procedures, such as strategic planning, and managing change, for example (although those are critical activities). Instead, strategic leaders propel their organizations through successive iterations of a learning process with strategic thinking, strategic acting, and strategic influencing skills. These skills are needed in every element of the learning process, and leaders at every level in the organization can practice them. These skills create the fuel to drive the organization's learning process and link it to the organization's evolving strategic intent for creating and sustaining competitive advantage. Taken together, they constitute strategic leadership.

In this book, we show you how to develop and practice leadership skills with strategic intent. We show you how to form a nucleus of vision and action and how to spread that energy to others so that it multiplies and intensifies. In the process, you and others in your organization will gain the capacity to transform your organization into a learning engine that is adaptable, flexible, and resilient.

The Contents of This Book

Our book uses a comprehensive conceptual framework to help you understand this view of strategic leadership. It also presents practical suggestions about how to develop such leadership.

In chapter 1 we address the unique nature of strategic leadership and what makes it so difficult and challenging. We examine in some depth the idea of organizational strategy as a learning process and conclude by looking at the implications of adopting that view.

Strategic thinking, the subject of chapter 2, refers to the cognitive dimension of strategic leadership. This aspect might include, for example, discerning environmental trends that have strategic significance for your organization. It might also include the ability to sift through waves of information to identify the most strategically significant facts or issues. Other aspects include seeing things from an enterprise perspective, appreciating how all the different functions and departments in the organization contribute to an integrated whole and looking at things in new and different ways.

Chapter 3 takes up the mantle of strategic acting, the behavioral dimension of strategic leadership. The importance of acting with strategic intent can't be overstated. Great vision and detailed plans amount to nothing if they aren't carried out with purpose. Not even the sharpest insight has value unless it leads to decisions that commit resources toward certain activities rather than others.

Strategic influencing is the subject of chapter 4. It refers to the ways in which leaders influence others and the ways they open themselves up to influence from others. Influence is the channel through which thought and action flow throughout the organization. It's critical to maintaining positive traction along the organization's strategic path.

Because organizations depend not just on individual effort but on the effort of individuals working together—often on teams— we use chapter 5 to examine the nature and effectiveness of collaborative strategic leadership. We draw heavily on research that we have conducted on teams in the context of the Center for Creative Leadership's Leading Strategically program.

Individuals and teams enact strategic leadership when they create the direction, alignment, and commitment needed to achieve the enduring performance potential of the organization. But what kinds of conditions in organizations are most likely to encourage individuals and teams to develop and practice leadership in this way? Chapter 6 describes that kind of environment by looking more closely at leadership strategy. This chapter examines the aspects of organizational culture, structure, and systems most likely to produce and support the kind of leadership that will keep organizations moving forward along a path of continual learning.

In chapter 7 we conclude the book with practical suggestions about how readers can best develop their own strategic leader capabilities as well as how they can help advance the strategic capabilities of their entire organization.

Throughout the book our intent is to convey the changing nature of strategic leadership in a way that is both accessible and applicable while also doing justice to the increasingly complex and interdependent nature of work in our VUCA world. Every chapter provides examples to illustrate the interactive nature of strategic leadership at the individual, team, and organizational levels, *and* we provide useful exhibits and suggestions for individual, team, and organizational development in every chapter. And while that same spirit and intent characterized the first edition of this book, this new edition benefits from almost another decade's advances in our understanding and tools for developing strategic leadership in organizations. This is particularly true of advances in CCL's cutting-edge work in the areas of leadership culture and leadership strategy.

The Audience for This Book

Our premise is that strategic leadership is a process, not a position, and increasing numbers of individuals share in the responsibility of its development and practice in organizations. That shared responsibility extends to certain aspects of creating strategy and is not limited to just executing a strategy passed down from above. Furthermore, certain teams as well as individuals exert strategic leadership in their organizations, reflecting the increasingly collaborative nature of strategy as a learning process. More than any other organizational activity, strategy represents the confluence of ideas and action, and we often say that strategic leadership exists largely in the white spaces on organizational charts. No single functional area or group has the breadth of information and perspective necessary to effectively guide an organization through the learning process that brings sustained competitive advantage.

With that view in mind, we believe that this book offers somewhat distinctive benefits to three different groups: younger or junior managers, middle managers, and executives.

For younger or junior managers, the book is an introduction to the basic concepts of strategy and strategic leadership. It demystifies and makes relevant concepts that otherwise may sound confusing or irrelevant to one's role in the organization.

The book will also be helpful for middle managers. By definition they link levels above and below them, so they are critical to ensuring that strategy is both a top-down and a bottom-up process. Increasingly, we find, strategic leadership also has a "middle-out" dimension to it. The book suggests many ways of influencing the whole organization from positions other than the top.

Executives may have the best vantage point from which to affect the quality of strategic leadership throughout the whole organization. They have responsibility for bringing information into the organization and for making the furthest-reaching decisions, and they have the opportunity to create the necessary momentum among their peers, direct reports, and even their bosses. It's that energy that can transform an organization by bringing it full awareness of its circumstances and challenges, and that enables it to remain flexible, creative, adaptive, forward looking, and strategic in its intent. Those are the qualities of sustained competitive advantage, the goal of every strategic leader. The parts of the book dealing with how to create organizational conditions that encourage effective strategic leadership by individuals and teams will be especially useful to executives.

Chapter 1

What Is Strategic Leadership?

Imagine that you are standing on a beautiful beach, with the sand between your toes, looking out over the deep blue-green water. You feel a fresh and invigorating breeze on your face. You hear the roar of waves breaking in the distance. Every once in a while your warm feet feel the relief of cool water when a particularly strong wave makes its way up the beach.

Watching the ocean has a purpose, for you have a surfboard in hand. You've practiced at home: lying on your board in your living room and working to pop up to your feet in a quick and flowing motion. You've practiced with small waves: picking those big enough to pick you up, but not big enough to toss you over.

Now you want to try the bigger waves. You walk into the water, get on your surfboard, and paddle out to where the waves are breaking. The wind is strong today, and the waves are big. As you reach what appears to be the best spot, waves are crashing around you, and you are tossed about in the water. You try to catch a wave, turning the nose of your surfboard toward the beach and popping up to your feet on the board, but your timing is off and you find yourself back in the water with the wave and your surfboard crashing over you. You try again, and this time you make it to your feet, but as you stand up, you lose your balance and fall. You try again but are unable to catch the next wave as it rapidly passes by you. Attempt after attempt is met with sour results. You try to figure out what is going wrong, but waves are passing you by and your day of beautiful surfing is turning into a day of frustration.

Paddling back to shore, you are not sure what you did wrong, but you hope that the next time will produce a different result.

Now imagine yourself at work. You've worked hard for a number of years and have been rewarded with several promotions. But you've recently learned from your boss that while the organization values your operational leadership skills, people do not view you as a strategic leader. You asked your boss what that means, only to receive a long and confusing reply without any specifics. Just as it's difficult to learn to surf when you don't know what you're doing wrong, it's also difficult to become strategic when you don't understand how you are not that way now and no one can tell you what to do differently.

Increasingly organizations are calling on people at all levels to be strategic. Even if you have not heard that you need to be more strategic, we bet you can think of others with whom you work who need to develop their strategic capabilities. However, the path to that end is neither clear nor well defined. In some ways, it may feel a bit like learning to surf. You find yourself in the middle of chaos, business issues and initiatives swirling all around you like waves. You're not quite sure which one calls for your best energies (which waves to catch), and even if you pick one, you might not be able to find your balance and ride it to a satisfactory conclusion.

Our intent in this book is to help you become strategic. We also intend to help you help others throughout your organization become more strategic and help teams with strategic responsibilities to meet those demands more effectively. In this chapter, we lay a foundation and explore the nature of strategic leadership as we consider the following questions:

- What are the definition and focus of strategic leadership?
- How does strategic leadership differ from leadership?
- Who should be strategic?
- How is "being strategic" about making strategy?
- How is "being strategic" about making strategy come alive in the organization?

With this groundwork in place, we will turn our attention in successive chapters to the specific question of how individuals and teams exercise strategic leadership.

The Definition and Focus of Strategic Leadership

Individuals and teams enact strategic leadership when they create the direction, alignment, and commitment needed to achieve the enduring performance potential of the organization.

This statement is a real mouthful. But because it encompasses all of the critical elements of strategic leadership, we offer it as our definition. The focus of strategic leadership is the enduring performance potential of the organization—achieving the potential of the organization over time so that it will thrive in the long term. This is true whether the organization is for profit or nonprofit, governmental or nongovernmental. It depends only on whether your organization seeks and achieves enduring capabilities that provide distinctive value to stakeholders over the long term in whatever sector your organization operates or whatever bottom line you are measured by.

Later in this chapter, we discuss the strategy process in more detail and how to use it to help achieve enduring performance potential. We begin by considering two organizations that demonstrate the difference between an organization that achieves enduring performance potential and one that did not achieve that potential: IBM and Digital Equipment Corporation (DEC). Both companies faced challenges over the course of many years but navigated those differently and with different enduring results. IBM was founded in 1911 as the Computing Tabulating Recording Company, and in 2012 it was ranked the ninth most profitable company based in the United States ("Fortune's 20 Most Profitable Companies," 2012). DEC was founded in 1957 and ceased to exist after being acquired by Compaq in 1998. We focus on a particularly turbulent time in the industry: the 1990s.

IBM: *A Strategy Story*

In 1993, many experts in the technology industries had concluded that IBM was inching toward its last days as an organization. Although the company had its most profitable year in 1990, the early 1990s saw big changes in the world of computers. Smaller, more nimble companies were innovating their way into the hearts of consumers and businesses, and the traditional big computers that IBM produced were seen as outdated, old technology. IBM stock had dropped from its 1987 high of forty-three dollars a share to less than thirteen dollars a share at the end of the first quarter of 1993 (Gerstner, 2002). Lou Gerstner joined IBM as its CEO in April 1993. IBM was on the verge of being split into autonomous business units when Gerstner arrived, a move that would have dissolved the organization that had long been a computer industry icon.

Gerstner chose a different path for the company. He kept the company together and took critical and bold steps not only to keep the company alive but to revitalize it to the point where it again led the industry. Most notably, Gerstner adopted a new strategy that moved the company from a product-driven approach to a service-driven approach. This was no easy task. It required a complete retooling of the people, processes, and systems in the organization. But the work paid off, and IBM's stock rose every year except one until Gerstner retired early in 2002.

IBM continues on the path of constant retooling among segments and markets served. According to its website, in 2000, 35 percent of its pretax income came from hardware/financing, 38 percent from services, and 27 percent from software. By 2012, that distribution had shifted to 14 percent from hardware/financing, 41 percent from services, and 45 percent from software. Software alone is expected to bring in 50 percent of segment profit by 2015. Similar changes are being made regarding the geographic reach and scale. In the year 2000, 11 percent of revenue came from growth markets. In 2012, that figure was 24 percent, and it is expected to be 30 percent by 2015. Clearly IBM continues to identify and execute changes needed to perform as the industry shifts and grows.

Digital Equipment Corporation: A Strategy Story

Contrast IBM's story with the story of one of its key competitors, Digital Equipment Corporation (2004). Ken Olsen founded DEC in 1957 and ran the company until the 1990s, when Robert Palmer replaced him. DEC was known for several advances in the computer industry, including the first commercially viable minicomputer and the first laptop. It was also the first commercial business connected to the Internet.

With more than a hundred thousand employees, DEC was the second-largest computer company in the world at its peak in the late 1980s. But it does not exist as an organization today. With the successes of the 1980s, the company became more and more insular. Its products were well designed, but they would work only with other DEC products and so customers tended to overlook them. Olsen also believed that DEC's products, with their superior engineering, would stand alone and did not need advertising. When the new RA-90 disk drive came to market very late and several other products ran into trouble, competitors overtook the company with similar products at lower prices. DEC experienced its first layoffs in the early 1990s. The company was sold to Compaq in 1998, and then Hewlett-Packard acquired Compaq in 2002. Clearly DEC was led with great fervor during its early years, and the company was able to achieve great things. But that greatness was not sustained.

What Makes Strategic Leadership Different?

What led IBM to thrive and DEC to die? Why was IBM able to weather a very difficult storm, make necessary changes, embark on a new path, and reach success in a new way, while DEC was swallowed up by its competition? Was it just that IBM had smarter people? We know the DEC employees were smart enough to develop new technologies that pushed the technology industry forward. We also know the individuals who ran IBM before Gerstner arrived were also bright—in fact, he was taken aback by the potential and capabilities of the people he met when he arrived there: "How could such truly talented people allow themselves to get into such a morass?" (Gerstner, 2002, p. 42). Both organizations clearly had smart and capable people. So what differentiated IBM? The short answer is that effective strategic leadership—leadership focused on achieving enduring performance potential—was enacted at IBM.

When we discuss enduring performance potential as the focus of strategic leadership, some of the executives we work with ask us, "Isn't that just leadership? How are they different? If you're a good leader, aren't you, by definition, a good strategic leader?" Not necessarily. In general, leadership exists when a group of two or more people has created common direction, alignment, and commitment. However, this can happen in any context. For example, when a leader works with a direct report to structure assignments, provide resources for accomplishment, and checks on progress along the way, this is a form of leadership. The key to leadership that is strategic in nature is the context within which that leadership is occurring: it must have strategic implications for the organization. Specifically,

- Strategic leadership is broad in scope.
- The impact of strategic leadership is felt over long periods of time.
- Strategic leadership often involves significant organizational change.

Scope

The broad scope of strategic leadership means that it has impacts on areas outside the leader's own functional area and business unit—and even outside the organization. This broad scope requires seeing the organization as an interdependent and interconnected system of multiple parts, where decisions in one area provoke actions in other areas. The waves in our surfer's ocean provide an analogy: as each wave crashes to the surface, it disturbs the water, which moves in reaction to the falling wave. External forces such as the wind also affect the waves. In the same way, the scope of strategic leadership extends beyond the organization, acting on and reacting to trends and issues in the environment.

The scope of leadership does not necessarily extend this far. For example, a person who facilitates the decision-making process of a group demonstrates effective leadership even if the decision is small in scope, such as assigning group members to parts of a project.

Duration

Like its scope, the time horizon of strategic leadership is also far reaching. The strategic leader must keep long-term goals in mind while working to achieve short-term objectives. Nearly half a millennium ago, the Japanese military leader Miyamoto Musashi said, "In strategy, it is important to see distant things as if they were close and to take a distanced view of close things" (Advice on Strategy, n.d.). His apt observation describes the tension between short-term and long-term perspectives that strategic leaders must balance.

Many of our Leading Strategically program executives feel a tremendous pressure to make short-term numbers. In fact, it is the most frequently mentioned issue when we ask them to define the major personal challenge to their becoming strategic leaders. One executive characterized the challenge as "balancing current operational needs versus looking at the long-term perspective of growth and development of our staff and business practice." Another said, "I need to let go of the busy day-to-day activities and spend more time thinking about the future." In our experience, such executives have typically risen through the ranks by being rewarded for their strong operational leadership—their ability to fight the daily fires and come out ahead. In fact, one executive commented that he was so good at fighting fires that he sometimes created them just so that he could fight them! When a person has developed such strength in a particular area, it is very difficult for him or her to shift focus and do something different.

Lou Gerstner provides a potent example of someone who was able to make a decision for the long run, even though it clearly had negative short-term implications. When he took over IBM in 1993, the company was bleeding cash. Mainframe revenue had fallen from $13 billion in 1990 to around $7 billion in 1993, and competitors were slashing mainframe prices to levels significantly below the prices of IBM products. Customers were asking IBM to do the same, so keeping prices above the competition ran the long-term risk of losing key customers. However, cutting prices would threaten IBM's cash position even further in the short term. Gerstner (2002) chose to slash prices, and he believes this was one of the key decisions to saving IBM.

In contrast, not all leadership requires this forward view to be effective. Very good operational leaders manage day-to-day functions effectively and are skilled at working with people to ensure that short-term objectives are met. This is important work, but it does not always need to take the long term into account.

Organizational Change

In order to achieve enduring performance potential, organizations need to undergo periodic transformation, and therefore strategic leadership requires successfully navigating and leading these changes. To the extent that strategy involves interconnected patterns of choices throughout the business, strategic transformation requires a shift in these interconnected patterns, and this is complex and multifaceted.

The shift IBM made from a product company to a service company is one potent example. But there are others as well that may not involve the entire organization. Consider the strategic impact of a new compensation system that touches all parts of the organization, provides a structure for defining differences in roles and appropriate salary ranges, and ties performance plans and measures to the strategic objectives of the organization, giving people a clear understanding of what is required to advance along various career ladders. The human resources team that designed and implemented this system, replacing one that included no common understanding of appropriate salary ranges for roles, criteria for raises, and career progression, exercised genuine strategic leadership.

Effective leadership does not necessarily institute significant organizational change. For example, leading a team to complete a recurring task, such as closing out the organization's quarterly books, requires effective leadership but does not create significant change.

A final example of leadership that does not have strategic implications is leading a team to complete a task that is not strategic in nature. A team assigned to open up a new retail outlet store in a global company that has thousands of such stores worldwide is a case in point. The team may consist of several members whose collective goal is to open the new store in a timely and effective way. Such a setup team will move from one store opening to the next. Although this work is absolutely critical to the successful implementation of the organization's overall strategy, it is not in and of itself strategic in nature. The scope and time frame are not far-reaching, nor does this work involve significant organizational change. However, if members of this team work with others to review the distribution of stores across the world, understand trends among consumers, and create plans for new store openings and closures, then that work would have strategic implications.

Who Should Be Strategic?

Consider the case of Dennie Welsh. Does his name sound familiar? Probably not. In 1993, Dennie was running the Integrated Systems

Services Corporation of IBM, that is, the services and network operations in the United States. While the fact that he was running a unit within IBM may sound big, his role was relatively small given the size and structure of IBM at the time. As Lou Gerstner indicates in *Who Says Elephants Can't Dance?* "[This part of the organization was] a promising but minor part of IBM's portfolio. In fact, it wasn't even a stand-alone business in IBM. It was a sub-unit of the sales force" (2002, p. 129). So Dennie was not exactly a top manager within IBM.

Yet in many ways, Dennie can be credited with the major shift in IBM's strategy from a product company to a service company. Here is an excerpt from Gerstner's book in which he describes a meeting with Dennie:

> It was our first private meeting, but he didn't waste much time on small talk. He told me that his vision of a services company was not one that did just IBM product maintenance and strung together computer codes for customers. He envisioned a company that would literally take over and act on behalf of the customers in all aspects of information technology—from building systems to defining architectures to actually managing the computers and running them for the customers.
>
> My mind was afire. Not only was he describing something I'd wanted when I was a customer (for example, I had tried unsuccessfully to outsource the running of RJR Nabisco's data centers), but this idea meshed exactly with our strategy of integration. Here was a man who understood what customers were willing to spend money on, and he knew what that meant—not just the business potential for IBM, but the coming restructuring of the industry around solutions rather than piece parts. (pp. 129–130)

Gerstner might well have come on this idea himself given his desire to integrate the various parts of the company rather than sell them off; however, he did not need to do it himself. He had good people below him he could rely on, and he recognized the need to rely on those people. True, the CEO is ultimately responsible for choosing a path for the organization. True, the CEO often involves some team of senior management in that decision-making process. But that does not mean that these people are the only strategic leaders within an organization.

The competitive forces in today's environment require us to be as in tune with our environment as possible, and often those who are at middle and lower levels of the organization are best suited to know the customers, competitors, and industry trends. As they work to implement the strategic intent, they learn new information that informs and shapes the strategy. In this way, the lines between strategy making and strategy implementation, and the lines between planner and implementer have become blurred.

So the notion of organization as hierarchy with clear roles and responsibilities, and clear power distribution through levels, does not in fact adequately reflect the messiness of real organizations. Many people have referred to organizations as biological organisms—entities made up of interconnected and contiguous parts and self-sustaining processes. In these organisms, the power of change, influence, and leadership lies not at the top but throughout the organization and, in fact, in the connections between different parts of the organization that have the potential to be magnified and leveraged in new and different ways. In this way, we also think of achieving organization performance potential as nurturing the well-being of the organization and its inherent connections in the long run.

These are the reasons we've advocated for the notion that strategic leadership exists beyond the executive ranks. It also exists in individuals and teams throughout the organization who are close to the customer, consumer, and client and have access to data and information that are important for the long-term success of the organization. In this way, the best CEOs rely on and nurture input and insights throughout the organization to set the strategy, enact the strategy, and help in understanding how well the strategy is working. It is no wonder that more and more people throughout organizations are feeling the need to become more strategic.

The definition of strategic leadership, the ways in which is it distinguished from leadership in general, and a realization that the need for strategic leadership extends far into the organization are helpful in many ways. Yet they do not fully address the question that executives looking to develop in this area often have: What does it *really* mean to "be more strategic"?

There are at least two interpretations and approaches to this question, and both are important. First, leaders are more strategic when they are strong strategy makers, that is, when they develop effective organization strategies. Much progress has been made to help leaders understand what and how to do this, and we summarize essential components of the organization strategy process in the next section, including a discussion of areas that in our experience still need more attention and emphasis. We also illustrate the different components of the organization strategy process using the case of Netflix, a now global player in the movie and television show distribution industry.

We then address a second approach to the question: How do leaders, through their behaviors and interactions with each other, create the direction, alignment, and commitment needed to make the strategy come alive in the organization? In our experience, this is the question that receives less attention from scholars and consultants, yet it is critical: without an effective approach here, it almost does not matter how good the strategy is. This second question lies at the heart of this book.

What Do Effective Strategy Makers Do?

No question, much attention has been paid to the world of strategy over the past few decades. Leaders have been searching for answers regarding "how to be a better strategy maker" in their organization, especially as they balance the tensions inherent in a volatile, uncertain, complex, and ambiguous (VUCA) world. Investors, employees, partners, and all stakeholders are also keenly interested in the long-term viability and potential of the organization, so the need to do strategy well is something leaders feel strongly.

In an effort to meet this need, business schools have multiple courses on strategy, articles on strategy are plentiful in various business publications, and as of this writing, a search on Amazon .com for books using the word *strategy* returned over 142,000 results. These resources, as well as our experience with leaders striving to create strategy, have helped to highlight the "what" that must be accomplished in strategy making—that is, the elements of strategy.

While we use the term *elements*, we would not want to imply that strategy involves simply going through a list and checking off tasks that have been accomplished or questions that have been answered. In fact, strategy making involves fluid movement between and across these elements. It also involves successive iterations on them over time, such that the organization learns and enhances its capabilities in the VUCA world. In this way, the organization strategy process depicted in figure 1.1 is in fact a learning process, and leaders must enter into it with a learning orientation, including curiosity, inquiry, humility, and collaboration with others.

Strategy Is a Learning Process

We've never heard of a strategy to "keep doing everything the same." Strategy involves change, and achieving long-term performance potential in an ever-changing environment requires continuous change. The critical issue for strategic leaders is how to make changes that progressively build on each other and represent an evolving enhancement of the organization's well-being. That is, they must not just keep trying different things; although that is good, it is not enough. Rather, leaders must mine their trials for new information and knowledge that might in fact negate their strongly held opinions, and they must use this new information to guide the decisions and actions taken. In this way, they make changes that help the organization endure in the midst of a dynamic environment, not changes that sap energy and that cumulatively don't reflect developing capabilities and value.

Figure 1.1   The Organization Strategy Process

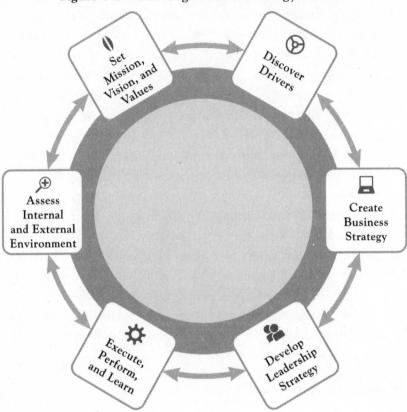

Imagine yourself again as the surfer we described at the beginning of this chapter. Remember how, when going for a big wave for the first time, you made changes to your approach by pointing your board in a slightly different direction, changing the timing of standing up on the board, making subtle changes to your weight distribution to keep your balance, and trying to catch waves at different points relative to their crest. But your changes had little impact because you did not understand the underlying issues that were keeping you from success. You just kept trying whatever came to mind without stopping to reflect on and learn from each of your attempts.

Leading an organization is clearly more difficult than surfing, but both require learning. Successfully achieving enduring performance potential through changes that progressively build on each other requires a learning engine that runs throughout the organization. Strategy-making and strategy-implementation processes provide the foundation for that learning engine, and strategic leadership is what drives it. Conceiving of strategy as a learning process requires a specific mind-set—a way of thinking about how to craft and implement strategy—that views successful strategy as operating in an ongoing state of formulation, implementation, reassessment, and revision. In figure 1.1, you can see those states represented in a circle with continuous arrows between them. And although the elements appear sequential, leaders and organizations in reality move around the circle in ways that are not step by step.

As we examine the different components of the organization strategy process shown in figure 1.1, we will illustrate some of the key concepts using Netflix. Netflix was founded in 1997 when Marc Randolph and Reed Hastings saw potential for a new way to approach the movie rental business. It has endured now for over fifteen years, adapting and changing as technology and the competitive landscape have changed. Netflix has moved through a major change in business model (and several smaller changes), and as of this writing, it is making yet another move to reshape itself.

Assess Internal and External Environment

The development of strategy clearly involves some level of analysis, and beginning with an assessment of internal and external factors impinging on the organization is a reasonable place to begin. Here, the work is to collect and make sense of information about the internal and external environments. The challenge in this element of strategy is to develop a collective and shared understanding of the situation (so that it is not just in one person's mind) and uncover and give focus to the tough facts in front of you. Most critical, you must understand how your organization might satisfy the critical wants and needs of your customers.

It is important to understand and gain agreement on the various external factors in play in the industry and the geographies in which the organization competes. For example, what are the economic, governmental, and social influences in a given region? What technological developments are at play? What demographic trends might be important to the industry? Who are the primary competitors? What are the factors on which they compete—for example, price, quality, service, selection, convenience?

Internally, what are the strengths and weaknesses of the organization that stack up against the customers' needs? How does capacity match demand? What are the current capabilities in the system? What are the strengths and attractiveness of the various products and services in the markets within which the organization competes? How satisfied are customers? How effective and sustainable is the current business model? Are the mind-sets of people in the organization ready for something new and different? What barriers need to be broken in order to move forward? What momentum is building?

The environment at the time of the founding of Netflix was marked by the advent of the DVD player. This new technology brought many possibilities for how digital media could be accessed inside and outside the home, and it clearly set the stage for a digital revolution. The DVD discs themselves were quite different from their predecessor, the VHS video; for example, they were easy to ship through the mail. Also at this time, the movie sales and rental industry had grown significantly, surpassing $24 billion in 2003 (Chatterjee, Carroll, & Spencer, 2010). Although the growth of DVD sales was outpacing the growth of rentals, DVD rentals were still growing. Generally, with the ticket and snack prices rising at the major movie theaters in the United States, people were turning more and more to watching movies at home on a frequent and regular basis. This type of family became the target market for Netflix.

On the competitive front, one key player was Blockbuster, which had established stores in major cities and operated under a fairly classic rental business model. People were used to going to the store, paying for their movie rental, and taking it home to watch. If by chance they returned it late, they paid a late fee. Other players were Hollywood Video and Walmart.

One final and critical environmental trend concerned the Internet. Internet retail sales were becoming more common and were growing as customers enjoyed the convenience of shopping in their homes and grew more trusting of online providers. In addition, there was the potential for future technology that could bypass physical storage devices such as the DVD, allowing direct download of films, movies, and music to various devices in one's home. This technology was still years away, but with the Internet interface for the retail aspects of the business, there was the possibility for a totally new way to distribute movies—one that Netflix intended to leverage.

Clarify Mission, Vision, and Values

Strategy is maximized when it also involves aspirational dimensions that touch the emotions of all the stakeholders involved: employees, current and future clients and customers, the general public, owners, and shareholders. Organizational mission, vision, and values are important aspirational components that create meaning and purpose for these stakeholders. These components serve to help people understand why the organization exists, how it intends to make a difference in the world, and what the important beliefs are that drive and connect the people in the organization.

These aspirational dimensions are an important part of strategy because they create a lens through which internal and external conditions are understood and evaluated; they are not derived from internal or external conditions. What is the identity of the organization? In what ways does that identity shape organization members' views of what is possible or not possible? For example, does the organization's mission suggest that certain strategies should not be considered?

Similar to the environmental assessment, a challenge in this area is developing shared understanding of these aspirational elements and the meaning they have for the organization and its stakeholders. In fact, in working to develop strategy, leaders often find that they do not have a shared vision of the future, and therefore are not even starting from the same place in strategy development. No wonder there is conflict about how to get from here to there.

The Netflix vision in its early days was fairly straightforward: to provide a premier film entertainment subscription service to a large and growing subscriber base (Chatterjee et al., 2010). Netflix was clear: it would cater to the high-volume consumer of movies who enjoyed a variety of films, especially those beyond the popular big screen titles. From the consumer's point of view, Netflix would help them get the movies they love (Keating, 2012). From the studio and producer's point of view, Netflix was a unique distributor that allowed them to bypass the larger, more expensive channels.

Discover and Prioritize Drivers

Whether or not there is a shared sense of the future, leaders frequently want to jump to defining a strategy for achieving it. In our opinion, they are missing one of the most critical components of the strategy process: an articulation and prioritization of the key strategic drivers.

Strategic drivers are those relatively few determinants of sustainable competitive advantage for a particular organization in a particular industry or competitive environment (they are also called *factors of competitive success*, *key success factors*, and *key value propositions*). These are the potential areas of investment that will have a significant impact on the organization's ability to achieve its performance potential—for example, its distribution system, global manufacturing capacity, or customer service. There are typically many possible drivers, so they must be prioritized to help to clarify where the organization's investments will be made. In this way, drivers are the levers the organization chooses to pull and the areas where they will excel. Drivers differ from outcomes, such as market share or revenue earned, but if they are done well, they should have an impact on those outcomes. Most organizations do not have more than three to five key (prioritized) strategic drivers at any one time, and these invariably represent a subset of factors on which different companies in the industry compete.

Organizations must make choices about which strategic drivers they want to invest in—and excel at—in order to differentiate themselves in their industry. The reason for identifying a relatively small number of strategic drivers for your organization is primarily to ensure that you become focused on what pattern of inherently limited investments will give you the greatest strategic leverage and competitive advantage. The challenge of identifying a relatively small number of drivers is that it forces choice: some things have to be more important than others, and consequently, they receive more organization attention and investment of time, energy, and financial resources. This challenge leads to inherent conflict and tension, and in fact may be why this part of the strategy process is frequently overlooked.

How do we know this part is frequently overlooked? Information collected from strategic leadership teams as part of CCL's Leading Strategically program indicates that it is rare for organizations to have a strategy that is discriminating (clear about what will be done and what will not be done). In addition, different surveys and polls (e.g., Beatty, 2003; Lazere, 1998) indicate that lack of a clear, well-defined strategy is a key issue. Collis and Rukstad (2008, p. 83) note, "It's a dirty little secret: Most executives cannot articulate the objective, scope, and advantage of their business in a simple statement. If they can't, neither can anyone else."

Avoiding difficult choices and refusing to focus and discriminate can lead to a "kitchen sink" strategy—one that includes a little bit of everything. The result is that people feel overcommitted and do not have a sense of what can come off their plates. In addition, a lack of common understanding about the strategy allows personal agendas to form and be pursued. Politics runs rampant as individuals try to look good against criteria that they have developed without having reached consensus across the organization that those criteria are indeed the right ones for measuring success.

Another challenge with strategic drivers is that leaders must be in a state of continuous discovery about those drivers. Several writers on strategy (e.g., Beer & Eisenstat, 2000) talk about the process of defining strategy as if a person or group of people can go into a room, talk about what their strategy should be, and as long as it is clearly defined, all should be fine. The word *define* implies that we can sit back and determine what drivers and strategy are best for us. Many writers (e.g., Treacy & Wiersema, 1995) have even gone so far as to define a limited number of categories of drivers and strategies—for example, product innovation, customer intimacy, and operational effectiveness—and declare that the work of leadership is to determine which one is right for the organization.

Instead, crafting strategy is more of a discovery process than it is a determination process or a process of choosing among a limited set of possibilities. It involves discovering the few key things—strategic drivers—the organization needs to do well and can do well to differentiate it in its industry. In *Good to Great*, Jim Collins (2001) describes this process as coming to understand the "hedgehog principle," a term based on the Isaiah Berlin essay "The Hedgehog and the Fox." Berlin divided the world into foxes, which "know many things" and see the complexity of situations and create different strategies to deal with that complexity, and hedgehogs, which "know one big thing." In this way "hedgehogs" in organizations simplify the complexity of the world into one unifying concept that fosters clear direction and alignment.

Collins also found that both good and great companies had strategies. However, while the good companies set theirs from bravado, the great companies set theirs from understanding. He summed up his findings with this statement: "A Hedgehog Concept is not a goal to be the best, a strategy to be the best, an intention to be the best, a plan to be the best. It is an *understanding* of what you *can* be the best at. The distinction is absolutely crucial" (p. 98). Collins (2001) notes that coming to an understanding of the hedgehog concept is an iterative process that takes four years on average. Bravado, however, can happen instantaneously. Perhaps that is why it is so appealing.

This discovery process is modeled week after week in our Leading Strategically program. We use a business simulation where executives run a company called Hawley-Garcia. In the simulation, participants have use of a computer model to simulate five years of operations at the company. Over the course of those years, their articulation of the drivers and strategy of Hawley-Garcia changes as they come to a deeper understanding of the industry dynamics and their company's position in that industry. For example, early on, one regional group articulated key points of its strategy as follows: "Maintain market share in the home market. Leverage alliances to become a leader in specialty tools." This statement suggests that *alliances* is the area of focused investment, and therefore the driver. *Market share* is the outcome or goal.

As their understanding deepened, they changed how they articulated their drivers and strategy: "Increase capacity and quality of manufacturing lines to support growth in high-end product lines while investing in research and development to support innovation." Here, *capacity*, *quality*, and *research and development* are drivers. More important, the two statements reflect profoundly different things. The first was essentially set through bravado—putting a stake in the ground with little understanding. The second evolved as they studied their industry, the key drivers in their region, and their region's role in the company overall. It represents a much more informed articulation of drivers and strategy.

In the early days of Netflix, video rental companies were competing in a number of ways. For example, in 2003 Blockbuster had clearly established itself with its nearly nine thousand stores that were conveniently located in large population areas (Keating, 2012). Since its inception, its leaders had chosen to focus on big-name movies that would be popular because of their marketing and recent release. Walmart continued to play in its niche: price leader.

Netflix chose a slightly different set of drivers: convenience through technology and selection. For this company, convenience was defined as the use of the Internet to order movies from home, with an interface that was intuitive and easy to use. Selection involved a focus on older, harder-to-find films. A sophisticated recommendation engine brought technology and selection together in a unique way that allowed customers to find movies they could not otherwise easily access.

In the early 2000s Blockbuster began to notice the impact Netflix was having on its business, and its executives decided to embark on an online offering. They surmised that the unique value they could bring is the combination of stores and online service: customers could easily access both. The challenge, however, is that they struggled to win people inside Blockbuster over to this strategy. In fact, two camps formed within the company (Keating, 2012): those who believed in the need to experiment with this new business model and those who believed it detracted from the work of maximizing the in-store experience. There were many such initiatives under way then, including experimenting with video games and trading programs. How could Blockbuster do all of these things?

This lack of prioritization and choice meant that the online work at Blockbuster was significantly underfunded for some time, and it also resulted in not really attacking the work of maximizing the integration between the stores and the online channel. In fact, leaders kept them separate so as not to cause more disruption. It wasn't until 2006 that Blockbuster introduced a promotion that leveraged the integration between the two, and at this point, it had a serious impact on Netflix's new subscriber rates (Keating, 2012).

Create Business Strategy

To the extent that drivers are agreed on and prioritized, business strategy will flow. *Business strategy* is the pattern of choices an organization makes to position itself for superior performance over time. It should clearly reflect the drivers and the organization's unique manifestation of those drivers.

Strategy involves a pattern of choices reflected in different parts of the business—that is, the choices are *coherent* throughout the organization. For example, if being a high-quality provider is a critical element of an organization's strategy (i.e., quality is a driver), then investments related to quality would be visible wherever you look: product design would include high-end features, manufacturing would ensure consistent production, customer service would be fully staffed with highly capable and knowledgeable people, the sales force would ensure a personal touch with customers, and so on.

In addition, strategy involves a series of choices. In order to dedicate more money to quality, the organization purposefully spends less money elsewhere. For example, it may realize that mass advertising does not play a role in its success, and so it limits expenditures there. These choices, of course, are related to the prioritization of drivers.

At Netflix, several strategies were enacted to address the drivers of selection and convenience. For example, Hastings and his team put significant energy into building relationships with various film studios and distributors. Whereas Blockbuster focused on recent big-name movies, Netflix found a niche in creating access to a wide range of films. It had unique relationships with independent film studios in particular—those that could not afford distribution through the typical channels (Chatterjee et al., 2010).

Netflix also leveraged the power of the Internet and the online shopping experience to create an entirely new way of providing selection and convenience. Specifically, it developed CineMatch, a powerful tool that assesses decisions each customer makes regarding films he or she chooses and watches for patterns across them. It also provides the opportunity for customers to rate films they watched and provide feedback. This information allows Netflix to learn from its customers which types of films they might enjoy, and it uses this information to make recommendations for new films to rent. People can find films to enjoy that they never could find in a store or in a large list of possible rentals that weren't attached to anything. This personalized film recommendation system is a core element of Netflix's strategy (Brochet, Srinivasan, & Norris, 2013; Chatterjee et al., 2010; Keating, 2012; Wesley, 2012).

Develop Leadership Strategy

Too often leaders assume that once they have the direction figured out, everyone should just align with it. While they may not say it exactly, the fact that human emotions, needs, beliefs, and desires are part of the change equation is often frustrating for those in leadership roles. Why can't they just follow? Why can't we all agree this is the best way to go? Why can't you get them to do what is needed? This frustration and the underlying assumption that human emotion is neither helpful nor needed are related to the statistic that 75 percent of change efforts fail to reach their potential. Organizations are full of human beings, and while we might wish that these humans wouldn't bring belief and emotion to the workplace, indeed they do.

In our experience, too little attention is paid to the human element of strategy: What must happen to ignite the new connections within the organization needed to enact the business strategy? Organizations must be as intentional about leadership strategy as they are about business strategy. *Leadership strategy* describes the organizational and human capabilities needed to enact the business strategy effectively. What type of culture should an organization engender to create success? What perspectives and abilities must individual leaders and teams have to be successful? What will they do to develop these skills and perspectives?

Leadership culture is the set of beliefs and practices that have an impact on how direction, alignment, and commitment are created (McGuire & Rhodes, 2009) and how things get done. When these beliefs and practices are not aligned with the needs of the

Figure 1.2   Culture Eats Strategy for Breakfast

business strategy, the strategy in fact has little chance of succeeding. That is, culture can overpower or "eat strategy for breakfast," as figure 1.2 shows. Because this is such an ignored element of the strategy process, we devote chapter 6 to the work of creating and engendering a leadership strategy.

Execute, Perform, and Learn

Once there is clarity about strategic intent for the business and the human component of the organization, leaders translate that intent into action by identifying and implementing tactics consistent with the strategies. It may sound easy, but even with a common understanding of the strategy, making choices that are consistent with that understanding can be hard to do. A study by Benchmarking Solutions (cited in Banham, 1999) found that only

27 percent of companies fully integrate their tactics and strategies. More companies (58 percent) have some form of integration at the highest level, but transferring that integration to lower levels does not often happen.

Tactics may be misaligned because people throughout the organization don't really understand what the strategy means for them on a day-to-day basis. Information collected from strategic leadership teams we have worked with supports the notion that individuals at all levels of their organization rarely understand how their roles support the organization's mission and strategy. In some cases, this is because the strategy does not create focus. But in other cases, formal and coordinated communication systems are ineffective or nonexistent, so people get mixed messages about the strategy. A Watson-Wyatt survey of 293 organizations in the United Kingdom (Stewart, 1999) found that 67 percent of employees in well-performing organizations have a good understanding of their overall organizational goals, whereas only 38 percent do in poorly performing organizations. Furthermore, the survey revealed that in all organizations, communication could be significantly improved.

The ability to make accurate predictions of Netflix customer preferences for movies was a critical factor in its early success. These predictions would drive customer satisfaction and loyalty. They would also help the company manage inventory, a significant contributor to costs. So the development and continued enhancement of the CineMatch technology was critical, and they adopted specific tactics to ensure its success (Keating, 2012). For example, after many starts and stops in its development, the CEO eventually invested to bring in mathematicians to assist. Cinematch was formally launched in 2000 using a "movies for two" promotion whereby Netflix advertised that it could assist couples in finding movies both would like.

By 2004, Blockbuster had launched its online service and was seeing successes at integrating that service with its store operations, posing a serious threat to Netflix. A large portion of Netflix's survival ability was in CineMatch. So in 2006 it launched a contest with a $1 million prize to the individual or group of scientists who could surpass its predictive ability by 10 percent. It took three years and fierce competition from teams of scientists and mathematicians around the globe before a winner was declared.

The "Execute, Perform, and Learn" component of the strategy process also involves assessing effectiveness against the organization's performance potential by measuring key indicators related to their drivers and their strategies. For example, Netflix pays attention to core metrics in the areas of sign-up rates, viewing, and subscriber retention (Netflix, 2013). It is also important for organizations to attend to their future capability. Are there measures to indicate success (or not) in building that future capability?

If the key indicators are as they expect, executives consider the organization to be on track. If the indicators reveal unexpected results, leaders will typically make changes. But all along the way, they need to keep the mind-set of learning: looking for patterns and trends that inform and deepen their understanding of the organization and the industry, as well as their sense of what the key strategic drivers are and what needs to happen within the organization to maximize those drivers. That is, the results as measured by the key indicators lead to a reassessment at the organization's new level of performance, starting the cycle all over again.

In this way, organizations go through life phases, which may be difficult to differentiate in the moment, and the transitions between phases are not perfect. But in hindsight, leaders can map the history of their organization to these phases and use them to describe the organization's evolution and growth. The evolutionary phases build on each other, progressively contributing to the organization's well-being. There is evolution, possibly even an occasional revolution, as the organization tries different approaches, learns from those attempts, and implements strategic change.

One key example of strategic change from Netflix began in 2005 (Wesley, 2012) when its competition was moving to replicate its model: both Blockbuster and Walmart went to online rentals in 2004. Netflix had invested heavily in distribution centers to decrease delivery time and increase perceived value and convenience. At this point, video on demand was emerging as a viable Internet-based technology, and it allowed customers to instantly download films directly to game consoles, computers, and mobile devices. This was an exciting development that had potential to significantly change the way consumers access their entertainment. Netflix began discussions about a possible partnership with TiVo, setting the stage for customers to have immediate access to movies versus waiting for them to arrive in the mail. In this way, this new technology directly supported their key driver of convenience. It also opened up the possibility of expanding globally. Netflix began to offer streaming in 2007 at a low flat fee of ten dollars per month for each kind of service. Their revenue continued to grow as it adapted its business to support this new model and began to expand internationally into Canada, Latin America, and the Caribbean.

By 2011, the streaming business had grown significantly (Brochet et al., 2013). There were some challenges, though, because the laws for distributing content using a streaming model were different from those for distributing the content through the rental of the physical DVD, and required direct negotiation of distribution rights with the studios. This added significantly to costs. At this point, revenues were over $2 billion, and there were more than 20 million subscribers.

As the business was growing more complex, a decision was made to split it into three parts: domestic streaming, international streaming, and domestic DVD rental (which still accounted for a portion of the business). Subscribers were informed of the change and the resulting impact: they would now need to subscribe separately to the streaming and DVD rental parts of the business. In addition, a price increase was announced not long after this change. Customers were extremely unhappy. Following these announcements, Netflix lost 805,000 subscribers, and its stock dropped 50 percent (Brochet et al., 2013). Eventually, having realized the impact of these decisions on the key driver of convenience, the decision to split the businesses was reversed. The leaders were learning and continuing to test their theories of the business, not always with positive results—but they were learning.

One lesson stood strong throughout this period: streaming technology was here to stay and was going to change the home entertainment landscape significantly. Netflix was placing a strong bet on consumers' desire to access any form of entertainment when they wanted it and where they wanted it: their television set, computer, mobile device, or something else. According to Netflix (2013), "Over the coming decades and across the world, Internet TV will replace linear TV. Apps will replace channels, remote controls will disappear, and screens will proliferate." It continued to invest in its streaming business, as well as the technology for members to rate movies and shows so that Netflix could make recommendations to each customer based on his or her prior choices and ratings. And sales continued to grow. In 2012, they passed the 30 million subscriber mark.

In 2013, Netflix made yet another move—still consistent with its drivers of convenience and selection. Specifically, it began producing original shows, building off its database of subscriber preferences to choose projects its executives thought would pay off in the long run. In fact, Netflix believes it is in a strong position to compete against television shows. Not only does it have the most extensive database available about consumer preferences, but its streaming technology means it does not have to attract audiences for a particular time slot on a given day. Rather, it just has to make the shows available for streaming, and consumers can download an entire series of multiple episodes at once. This level of flexibility is seen as a key strategic advantage (Netflix, 2013).

Throughout all of these phases, Netflix has stayed true to its key drivers of selection and convenience. Yet as technology and consumer behavior have evolved, so has the company even as it remains true to its mission, vision, and values:

> Netflix is the world's leading Internet television network with more than 36 million members in 40 countries enjoying more than one billion hours of TV shows and movies per month, including original series. For one low monthly price, Netflix members can watch as much as they want, anytime, anywhere, on nearly any Internet-connected screen. Members can play, pause, and resume watching, all without any commercials or commitments. (Netflix, 2013)

This mind-set of both learning and adapting along the way, yet being focused and disciplined enough to fully test out the theories of the business, is a tension that is inherent in the strategy process. In fact, it is a polarity that must be leveraged. It does not take having the knowledge of a process like that depicted in figure 1.1 to create learning and focus in an organization, but having knowledge of this process allows a common language to exist within the organization and might make navigating that process a bit easier. Successfully driving this process—whether it is explicit or not—does require effective leadership—the type of leadership we call strategic leadership.

Conceptualizing the strategy-making and implementation process as one of continuous learning is not new (Mintzberg, 1987, 1998; Senge, 1990). Yet, we find in our work with executives that strategy is not often thought of as a learning process. In fact, when we ask executives to describe how strategy is crafted in their organizations, we get long descriptions of off-site retreats with agendas filled with rigorous steps and analyses. The outcome of such a retreat is often a strategic plan that is so long and involved it fills binders and weighs down shelves. Once the retreat is over, the binders tend to sit on the shelf and gather dust.

Why don't executives explicitly talk about strategy as a learning process? One reason may be that learning implies that something is not currently known—and the cultures of many organizations emphasize *knowing*. Aren't those who know the most those who are promoted? Other executives are open to learning yet feel there isn't time for it. The reality is that organizations must learn, and those that have the best learning practices in place have a significant competitive advantage. As Senge notes, "It is no longer sufficient to have one person learning for the organization, a Ford or a Sloan or a Watson. It's just not possible any longer to 'figure it out' from the top and have everyone else following the orders of the 'grand strategist.' The organizations that will excel in the future will be the organizations that discover how to tap people's commitment and capacity to learn at *all* levels in an organization" (1990, p. 4). His words make us reflect that the concept of organizations as biological systems is not new either.

It is helpful for leaders to understand the elements and nature of the organization strategy process we have described, as it gives them a sense of what they must accomplish as they work to help their organization achieve its enduring performance potential. In many ways, articulating these elements and assisting with various tools and methods to complete them is the heart of the field of strategic management. Strategic management is defined as the "systematic analysis of the factors associated with customers and competitors (the external environment) and the organization itself (the internal environment) to provide the basis for maintaining optimum management practices. The objective of strategic management is to achieve better alignment of corporate policies and strategic priorities" ("Strategic Management," 2013). Strategic management is definitely the field on which leaders play.

Accomplishing the "what" does not ensure that strategy will necessarily come alive in organizations, however. The ultimate result of this work is heavily affected by how leaders engage in it: they need to engage the hearts, hands, and minds of people in the work to ensure shared direction, alignment, and commitment.

How Are Leaders "Strategic"?

Where should we take this business in the future? How do we capitalize on new developments in technology? What moves are our competitors making, and how can we outsmart them? How is our ecosystem evolving, and how do we shape that evolution? How do we continue to grow globally and scale the capabilities we have developed? How do we, as a nonprofit, continue to stay attractive to our funders? Questions like these are in the hearts and minds of leaders all over the globe. These are the types of questions that keep leaders awake at night and energize them to persist in the long days, weeks, months, and years of building and growing their organizations. In fact, they are so compelling, exciting, and exhilarating that they consume the energy of leaders at the expense of another critical question: How do I, as a leader of this organization and in this ecosystem, approach my leadership interactions with others to engage their hearts and minds in this work?

In our experience, the first set of questions can be answered with primarily a cognitive approach: "If I just figure it out and come up with a good solution, all will be fine." The second question is fundamentally different, however. It involves an exploration and examination of one's behavior, values, and identity as leader and therefore includes potential answers that challenge a person's sense of self. That is, these are not questions about what one does, but instead are questions about how and who one is.

Cynthia Montgomery (2012), past chair of the Strategy Unit at the Harvard School of Business, shares her experience with executives when they are asked to list three words they associate with strategy. In over two thousand responses, executives have provided 109 unique responses, including terms like *plan* and *competitive advantage*. Only two of these unique responses have anything to do with people as part of the equation, and they are *leadership* and *visionary*. If executives have such little inclination to associate strategy with people, imagine how rare it is for them to easily see their own behavior, values, and identity as critical to effective strategy.

This is one of the reasons we purposefully identify and include leadership strategy as part of the organization strategy process. Calling out the need to develop the human capabilities of the organization creates the opportunity for leaders to intentionally address the human element of the equation. Frequently, however, as leaders begin to address the questions associated with leadership strategy, they focus on "them," that is, others throughout the system. They still seem to fail to turn their perspective inward toward their own behaviors that support the leadership culture and practices they are trying to create in others.

In figure 1.3, we have added a core to the organization strategy process, and it is at the core of the model for a reason. Specifically, our research and experience have demonstrated that the core of strategy is indeed an examination of how strategic leaders do what they do and involves them first turning inward to look at themselves to examine and reflect on how they go about the strategy process. It involves questions in three areas:

- Have we achieved the leadership outcomes of shared direction, alignment, and commitment?
- How are we personally and collectively navigating the key leadership challenges in today's VUCA world? These are challenges of leveraging polarities, leading change, spanning boundaries, and leading culture.
- How am I personally demonstrating the core strategic leadership competencies of strategic thinking, strategic acting, and strategic influencing?

Direction, Alignment, and Commitment

Achieving the enduring performance potential of the organization requires the hearts, minds, and hands of all to be engaged. It is one thing to have that sense of engagement yourself. It is totally another thing to create, engender, and fuel that engagement with others. This distinction in fact is the heart of leadership. That is,

Figure 1.3   The Strategic Leadership Model

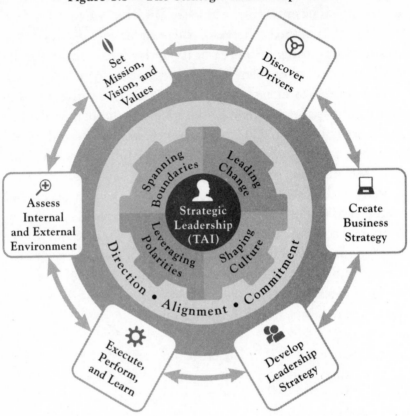

leadership is engaging others to create shared direction, alignment, and commitment (DAC).

Conceiving of leadership as its outcomes (DAC) allows the flexibility that the ways in which those outcomes are achieved are varied and context dependent (Van Velsor, McCauley, & Ruderman, 2010). In addition, defining leadership by its outcomes acknowledges that in today's VUCA world, leadership is demonstrated as much (if not more so) by collectives (groups, teams, the organization) versus one person. In the world of strategic leadership, it is clear that no single person can do what is needed to achieve the enduring performance potential of the organization. There is too much information to digest, the decisions are too complex, and success is too dependent on the blending of capa-bilities across the enterprise. Therefore, we often say that the most crucial work of a strategic leader is to engender strategic leadership in others by igniting the power and potential of the entire organi-zation in service of its performance potential.

DAC serves as signs or indicators that the leadership processes associated with strategy are working effectively. When there is shared direction, each person in the organization knows the goals, priorities, and plans to achieve those goals and also knows that other organizational members see these in the same way. So there is a common understanding about why various decisions are made and a sense of how they are connected to the overall goals of the orga-nization. Alignment exists when the decisions and tactics through-out the organization are coordinated, coherent, and consistent with the overall strategy. Commitment is the attitude that people hold toward the strategy. People are committed when they are willing to expand effort toward the needs of the organization over and above the effort needed to meet their own individual goals.

Key Leadership Challenges

How DAC is created is context dependent, and the VUCA envi-ronment of the world today helps to define some challenges of the context that are particularly relevant for strategic leaders. In this context, leaders must create the environment that fosters capabilities necessary to be honest and real with each other, make difficult choices even in the face of politics and conflict, attend to the human element of the system and not just the mechanical ele-ment, and foster learning along the way. Several such capabilities come to mind, including:

- Leveraging polarities
- Spanning boundaries
- Leading change
- Shaping culture

When done well, these capabilities result in new direction, alignment, and commitment in service of the strategic change needed for the organization to achieve its performance potential.

Leveraging Polarities La Quinta Inn and Suites is unique in the limited service hotel industry, as it both owns properties and franchises properties. While most of the competition relies heavily or exclusively on the franchise model, about half of the La Quinta properties are owned by the organization and about half are franchised properties. La Quinta must be successful at both to be successful overall. This is not easy, as there is a tension between the two. For example, it is relatively simple—and advantageous—to be entrepreneurial in the franchised part of the business, because this keeps the brand fresh and franchisees must stay up with the standards. However, the ownership side of the business must pay careful attention to costs and therefore is cautious about implementing new ideas. La Quinta must be doing something right. In a Canadian Imperial Bank of Commerce World Markets study (Katz, Rosa, & Slavin, 2007). La Quinta was the number one most profitable hotel for an investor of any hotels in their segment. In part, La Quinta is profitable because it is successfully leveraging the ownership-franchisee polarity inherent in its business model.

Polarity thinking—the art and science of leveraging two opposing poles, or interdependent pairs of forces that support a common purpose and one another—is a critical capability for organizations and individuals seeking to be more strategic (Johnson, 1996). Too often people see the world as either-or—for example, "We need to centralize our structure." "No, we need to decentralize." Or, "We need to focus on operations and efficiency." "No, we need to focus on innovation." Polarity thinking is both-and thinking. It recognizes that both poles of the polarity are needed to thrive, and if we emphasize one to the detriment of the other, we will experience the downsides of that pole and miss the upsides of the other pole. Polarities are at play all the time in organizations. With respect to strategic leadership in particular, several different types of polarities are common—for example:

- Both "I need to know what to do because I am the leader here" and "I need to be in a state of learning, which means I don't always know what to do"
- Both "We need to be successful in the long term" and "We need to make our quarterly numbers"
- Both "My function must meet its goals" and "The organization as a whole has to survive."
- Both "Strategy is a top-down process" and "Strategy is shaped from the bottom up"
- Both "We need a strategy for our business" and "We need a leadership strategy."
- Both "The organization must thrive" and "The organization's ecosystem must thrive"
- Both "We must focus on our key drivers" and "We must be competitive on other factors important to our customers"

Let's examine the short-term, long-term polarity. This is clearly a difficult one to leverage, particularly for publicly traded companies that are under their investors' microscope every day. For these organizations, balancing the pressure of investors is critical not only in the short run but also over the long run, because significant and sustained drops in stock price can have tremendous long-term impact. We are not saying that short-term success is not important. But when an organization consistently favors the short term over the long term by, for example, neglecting to make investments to keep resources and technology up to date, the organization will suffer in the end.

Another polarity—both success of the organization and success of the ecosystem—is being highlighted more and more often and is related to the notion of organization as biological system. Imagine if our surfer is in an ocean that is becoming so polluted the waters around him in fact are dangerous: toxic, full of rubbish, so much foam on the waves it is difficult to see or navigate his way. Also imagine if the surfer himself is contributing to the decay of the water through his choices that ultimately increase his ecological footprint. Surfing becomes more difficult for sure, and the surfer may not recognize his role in creating his own difficulties.

Michael Porter and Mark Kramer have (2011) emphasized the importance of this polarity for business and capitalism today. They note that a lack of attention to the social, economic, and environmental ecosystem on the part of organizations (for profit, governmental, nonprofit) today is shortsighted, and in fact, if organizations put the health of their ecosystems front and center as opposed to on the periphery, they can create shared value of the system as a whole.

Spanning Boundaries Syngenta, based in Basel, Switzerland, was formed in 2000 when Novartis and AstraZeneca merged their agribusinesses; as of this writing, the organization has more than twenty-seven thousand employees in over ninety countries. Syngenta's core mission is simple: bringing plant potential to life. The history of Syngenta and its predecessor companies shows a strong focus in two areas: seeds and crop protection. Until recently, these two areas of focus operated primarily independently. However, according to its website (Syngenta, 2013), Syngenta's integrated strategy is based on putting the grower at the center of everything it does, and in the grower's mind, seeds and crop protection are not separate. Therefore, it will be critical for Syngenta to span the boundaries between the two areas to fuel the innovation needed to meet the grower's needs.

Strategic opportunities exist in possible new patterns in the organization and its ecosystem. As such, strategic leadership happens in the white space on organization charts: between functions and groups, between levels of leadership, and between the organization and other external entities. Strategic leaders must encourage people to span boundaries and create direction, alignment, and commitment in service of strategic change. Boundaries can be vertical, horizontal across the organization, geographic, demographic, or with external stakeholders.

Leading Change Samsung Electronics was ranked twentieth on Fortune's 2012 Global 500 list, in large part due to its excellence in technology-based consumer products and a successful challenge to rival Sony. Samsung Electronics did not always excel in the consumer products sector, however. In fact, after entering it in the late 1980s, its products were of inadequate quality and were underperforming. So Samsung's leaders decided to step back and do something different: they changed course to focus on component manufacturing for other companies in the sector, with the intent of learning more about how to succeed in the sector in the future. This step required significant change—for example, exiting product lines and focusing instead on solving specific technology changes, such as dynamic random access memory—to create a real difference in the industry and impact for its products. As Samsung became successful here, it underwent a second era of focus on consumer products, and this one has carried it into the twenty-first century as a strong global player. Again, significant levels of change were required to reorient the company in a return to this sector (Michell, 2011).

Strategies inherently require change from the organization and the people within it. And strategic change by nature requires a shift in the connected, interdependent patterns of choices that the organization has made in the past. It is substantial, widespread, and transformational. Strategic leaders need to help people navigate the change process, assisting in learning new skills and capabilities, working with others in different ways, and acknowledging and authentically managing emotions through that change.

Shaping Culture The Broad-Based Black Economic Empowerment Act was put in place in South Africa in 2007 in an attempt to distribute wealth across a broad spectrum of South African society in the postapartheid era. This act requires organizations of various sizes to adopt management practices designed to promote equity among previously disadvantaged groups. Accordingly, the Foschini Group (TFG), a retailer with over two hundred stores in South Africa, is working to transform its workforce through various employment equity initiatives, with some success and some challenges. According to its website, "Whilst employment equity and diversity are embedded into succession planning, talent management and recruitment, black representation at senior management levels remains an ongoing challenge. TFG's strategy of choice is to develop from within and it thus takes time to achieve transformation at senior management levels."

There is no doubt that in order to be successful in this kind of transformation, a number of different processes and systems related to talent management will need to change. But that is not all. If employment equity is to become a way of life, the transformation will require a shift in core beliefs about people, their value, the importance of equity, and many other areas as well. The behaviors associated with those beliefs will need to change too.

Beliefs drive behavior in organizations, so in order to change behavior to a new way of doing things, beliefs need to change. This isn't easy to do: people can easily keep their beliefs to themselves, and they may not even be aware of them. Changing beliefs requires a level of open, honest dialogue that creates vulnerability in the organization.

Senior leadership in particular plays a strong role in shaping culture, and if the culture is to change, senior leadership has to hold out and examine their individual and collective beliefs as well. In fact, when senior leaders fail to examine their own role and identity, and acknowledge and demonstrate they need to learn, grow, and change as others are too, the culture will not shift as needed and the change effort is much more likely to fail. By allowing themselves to demonstrate some level of vulnerability with others, senior leaders invite people to engage with each other in different ways (McGuire & Rhodes, 2009). This is the core of the process to shift the beliefs and practices necessary to shape culture.

Individual Skill Sets

Strategic leaders navigate the challenges we have noted to create DAC. At the most concrete level, they do this by exercising the skills of strategic thinking, acting, and influencing. They use these skills throughout the cycle of learning to bring clarity and focus to the strategy, enact that strategy with purpose and direction, and engender the commitment of others to the future of the organization:

- Strategic thinking involves the cognitive and social processes that lead to a shared understanding of the complex relationship between the organization and its environment. It also involves using that understanding to set the direction for the organization's future.
- Strategic acting is taking decisive action consistent with the strategic direction despite the inherent ambiguity, chaos, and complexity inherent in organizational life. At its core, it involves translating thinking into priorities for collective action.
- Strategic influence is engendering commitment to the organization's strategic direction by inviting others into the strategic process, forging relationships inside and outside the organization, and using organizational culture and systems of influence.

Each skill set has a specific role and purpose, but it would be a mistake to view them as totally separate. It's not the case that a strategic leader first thinks to determine what to do, acts to make the necessary decisions and choices associated with that thinking, and then influences others to get them onboard. In reality, thinking, acting, and influencing are interdependent. For example, if learning is at the core of strategy, a strategic leader will take action that then informs future thinking about the strategy. She will also invite others into the strategy-making process—not just to facilitate their buy-in to it but also to produce a better strategy than could have been developed in isolation. Finally, the more that people are engaged in crafting the strategy, the more they understand its nuances that are important to creating coordinated actions.

Figure 1.4   Integration of Thinking, Acting, and Influencing
in Service of DAC

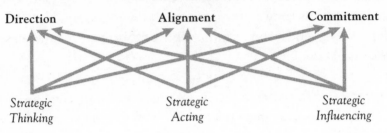

Not only are thinking, acting, and influencing interdependent, they also work in tandem to produce the leadership outcome of direction, alignment, and commitment. It's not as if thinking is all that is needed to lead to direction, acting is all that is needed to lead to alignment, and influencing is all that is needed to lead to commitment. Each is needed to produce each outcome, as shown in figure 1.4. In the chapters ahead, we focus on each area, but the best strategic leaders weave them together to leverage the power of the people throughout the organization toward the ultimate performance potential.

What Lies Ahead

The chapters that follow focus on the leadership necessary to enact the organization strategy process successfully. We take the organization strategy process in figure 1.1 as context, but primarily focus on who you are in this task. How do you define your leadership identity in the midst of the strategy process? What are your strengths and weaknesses with respect to the work of engaging with people to develop and implement strategy to achieve the enduring performance potential of the organization? How do you lead teams and the organization as a whole to learn over time such that the organization can endure? In short, this book focuses on the human element of strategy.

We begin with the individual, core skill sets of strategic think-ing, acting, and influence. Each chapter covers specific competen-cies and perspectives related to each of these skills and each skill's place in driving the learning required for the organization strategy process. These chapters are full of concrete exercises for you to apply the lessons and competencies explored in the chapter. As you read the next three chapters, keep in mind the various ways that thinking, acting, and influencing work together. Each chapter concludes with a discussion of that interdependency to help you make that connection.

Chapters 5 through 7 focus on areas related to the climate for strategic leadership around you. Chapter 5 addresses teams as the vehicle for strategic change and provides an overview of how you can help key teams in your organization lead with collective pur-pose in mind. Chapter 6 addresses the important role that leader-ship strategy plays in engendering the human capabilities needed to enact the business strategy. Finally because strategic leadership is a lifelong process of developing and molding yourself and those around, we conclude the book with chapter 7 focused on that development process.

As we close out this chapter, we invite you to read this book with yourself and at least one other person in mind—someone you are working with who needs to be more strategic. Think about ways you can apply the assessments and exercises throughout this book to guide this person's development. You might even consider working alongside that person as you both develop so that you can provide support to each other.

Chapter 2

Strategic Thinking

What do Bill Gates and Peter Jackson have in common? Surely one characteristic common to both of them is vision. From an early age, Gates had a vision of the possibilities of personal computing, and that vision helped shape an industry. Now, enabled by that success, his vision is transforming the world in other ways through the scope of his philanthropic efforts. When Peter Jackson read *The Lord of the Rings* trilogy at the age of eighteen, he couldn't wait until the books were made into movies. Twenty years later, he made them himself, and then in 2013, his production company released the first part of another trilogy, this one too based on a Tolkien work: *The Hobbit*.

Another characteristic these two leaders share is the ability to take stock of the conditions bearing on their situations—to scan their environment. They are gifted at questioning implicit beliefs and assumptions. Both have to deal with the complexity that's part of a visionary enterprise, and both are skilled at ensuring shared understanding within their organizations and teams and at thinking systemically to uncover the answers to complex problems. In this chapter, we look closely at the thinking competencies that are essential to effective strategic leadership. Before doing that, however, we first need to examine something we call the *mind-set of strategic thinking*. It represents a point of view about strategic thinking that is foundational to the strategic thinking competencies we address later in the chapter. In a similar manner, the mind-sets of strategic acting and strategic influencing will precede the competency sections of those chapters too.

The Mindset of Strategic Thinking

An analogy might help clarify what we mean by strategic mind-set and illustrate what we mean by its foundational importance. Almost all counselors in training must learn to deal constructively with silence. That usually requires disciplining themselves to tolerate silence and not jump in quickly to talk again if a counselee chooses to sit passively in response to a question. That's because many people in a group find silence uncomfortable (counselors in training included) and have unconsciously learned that discomfort can be reduced by saying *anything*—by just talking—to fill the silence. But reducing discomfort is not the same thing as making progress in counseling; a counselee's mild discomfort in fact can be a constructive stimulus to that person's taking greater personal responsibility in his or her own development.

Furthermore, counselors in training may naively construe the nature of "good counseling" in terms of the amount of talking counselors do—the more, the better, as though talking is what counselors are being paid for. With time and practice, however, they come to view counseling effectiveness in terms of the responsibility and active work the counselee assumes rather than the amount of talking the counselor does. Effectiveness, in other words, depends on developing a point of view that it is counterproductive to reinforce counselee passivity even though it may be a neophyte counselor's inclination to take the more active role in the relationship herself.

In a similar manner, effective strategic leadership is not just a set of skills and competencies analogous to "tolerating silences." The very valuation of those skills makes sense only in the context of a particular point of view concerning strategic leadership. Therefore, we will set the stage for examining the competencies of strategic thinking, acting, and influencing by looking first in these chapters at the distinctive strategic mind-set undergirding each respective set of competencies. The mind-set of strategic thinking comprises three elements:

- Strategic thinking is a collective process.
- Strategic thinking is about the present, not just the future.
- Strategic thinking has an artful side as well as a rigorous and analytical side.

Strategic Thinking Is a Collective Process

There is a common but unhelpful stereotype of great strategic thinkers as gurus—individuals possessing extraordinary knowledge, expertise, and foresight. Not surprisingly, therefore, some people in organizations carry around unrealistic and counterproductive expectations that to be seen as "strategic" requires coming across as a self-sufficient expert having all the answers. But not only does this mistaken understanding of strategic thinking create unhelpful pressure of feeling one should try to live up to that unrealistic expectation; it also inevitably diminishes one's inclination to look to others as strategic contributors themselves, having relevant and important insights.

This misguided notion that the best strategic thinking comes from a single individual having singularly great insight and expertise is especially problematic in today's volatile, uncertain, complex, and ambiguous (VUCA) world. Here's why: the kind of strategic environment contemporary organizations face is different from what organizations have confronted before, at least in degree. Furthermore, the strategic challenges arising in such an environment tend to be different in nature from those an organization has faced before, and consequently the organization's portfolio of existing capabilities may be ill suited to successfully addressing the new kinds of problems. There may be widely differing views within the organization of the nature of the new strategic challenges, since the relatively unprecedented nature of the challenges resists easy classification. This is complicated by the fact that organizations today must deal with a broader range of stakeholders than ever before, each having different interests and different priorities. Problems having parameters or conditions like these have even been given a name: *wicked problems.* By their very nature, wicked problems can't be solved merely by collecting additional data or defining issues more clearly; they don't even have "right answers" in any normal sense of the word. What does all this imply, then, about the kind of strategic thinking that should be brought to bear in such an environment?

To put it simply, strategic thinking should be understood as a collective, or social, process that includes diverse perspectives from both inside and outside the organization. The danger of not adopting such a mind-set is potential blindness to critical contextual dynamics affecting organizational viability and success. This means most organizations need to find ways to involve more people in their strategic discussions. Strategic thinking should no longer be considered the sole purview of senior executives or, even more narrowly, only those on the top leadership team. Many people both inside and outside an organization can contribute valuably to dialogue about ways to best ensure its continuing vitality and sustainability. Organizations need to create more and better ways to make strategic thinking a collective process that engages diverse perspectives and viewpoints.

Take Kone, an industrial engineering company, as an example. Kone employs about thirty-four thousand people and has sales of about 5 billion euros worldwide. It specializes in people-moving systems—elevators and escalators—and has a presence in fifty countries. Vincent Tang, former president and CEO of Kone Americas, candidly described his own experience as his organization embraced more collective leadership (Tang & Moore, 2009):

> Every time that we got together, I still had that anxiety because I didn't have a clear path that I could share back with my colleagues and my peers of how we were going to achieve this. And we all had to learn, whether it was me or the senior leadership team, how to deal with that ambiguity. And that was a huge step for us because we were very operationally focused. We know how to get things done. This was different. We had to discover, collectively, together, interdependently. That was a challenge. That was a real challenge.

As another example, part of Apple's sustained success was that Steve Jobs recognized the importance of involving multiple people in the company's strategic thinking. Jobs would meet once a year with "The Top 100," Apple employees selected on the basis of a simple criterion: the one hundred people you would take with you "on a lifeboat" to start a new company. At this annual retreat, Jobs led the group through a process of identifying "the top ten things we should be doing next" (Isaacson, 2011, p. 378).

Western Union is another company that has provided great opportunities for strategic leadership to its own top-rated employees. We'll take a close look at how it tapped the collective strategic thinking of some of that group in a major initiative critical to the company's future.

Western Union has a rich history of innovation throughout its 160 years in the financial services industry. It completed the first transcontinental telegraph line across North America, it introduced the service of money transfer, and it introduced the first customer charge card. It now has 500,000 agent locations worldwide, handling nearly 150 million consumer-to-consumer money transfers. Only very recently, however, did Western Union decide to aggressively enter the digital age of financial services.

Historically Western Union has done "cash-to-cash" business between different agent locations (sites). That's why expanding the number of agent locations worldwide to today's impressive number has been such a strategic emphasis since around 2000. Increasingly over that period, however, there has also been recognition of an opportunity for online business for Western Union; that would amount, in a sense, to selectively dispensing with the middleman of agents in specific company locations, plentiful as they may be.

For a decade or so, Western Union has provided a modest level of online capability for money transfer, but until recently, the total amount nonetheless represented little more than dabbling. That began to change around 2009. Since then, the number of online transactional websites has increased from a presence in two countries to twenty-three. Even with that increase, however, online revenue still has represented only about 3 percent of corporate revenue. The strategic challenge became one of creating a credible business case for investing significantly in the marketing, talent, and technology needed to create positive customer experience and ultimately change the customer mind-set so that Western Union would be seen as having globally available, easy-to-use, high-quality online capability in addition to its traditional cash-to-cash operation.

One significant step in that direction was hiring Khalid Fellahi in 2011 as senior vice president and general manager of Western Union Digital Ventures. As befits a role intended to serve in part the 140 million small businesses around the world, Fellahi is a forty-seven-year-old Moroccan and African Arab educated in France who previously ran Western Union operations in Africa.

Shortly after his appointment, Fellahi asked his board to approve creation of a cross-functional team that he could sequester for two months to develop a business case for developing a robust digital capability for Western Union. It took two more months for the board to approve the proposal, but it ultimately did, further chartering the team to focus its proposal on effectively selling the concept to the board itself and the executive team. In that regard, it's worth noting that over the years, several other business plans for an expanded online capability in Western Union had been presented and reviewed, but none was persuasive. In 2012 the team was sent to work in San Francisco (in part to create a presence there to attract talent) and directed to provide regular check-ins to the board and top team.

Twelve people were selected to be on the team, and only slightly more than half had worked at all in the online business. The team was cross-functional in composition and diverse in members' level of responsibility, including people with titles ranging from manager to senior vice president (Fellahi himself). Julie Cannava, for example, was one of the younger members at thirty-four years old and one of those whose prior experience had been entirely in the online business. There also were five team members from an independent consulting firm who provided process and facilitation advice and assistance. The team lived and worked in a rented complex and, as Julie describes it, "truly was sequestered, working from around 7:00 a.m. to 11:00 p.m. each day."

The work itself was accomplished by a number of subteams of two to three members each, and each of these subteams addressed a different element of the business plan (e.g., marketing, distribution, web design, customer experience). Each of the twelve members served on several subteams.

Julie remembers well the team's final check-in with members of the executive team who had traveled to San Francisco for that purpose. She recalls the chief financial officer saying afterward that it was the first time he'd seen the story of the potential online business come together so compellingly. It must have been so, because he approved the team's recommendation of a tenfold increase in the marketing budget alone over the next four years. The team convincingly had demonstrated that online business was an important part of Western Union's future and that it required correspondingly substantial investment to make viable.

Western Union continues to endorse its major investment in its online business. Its goal is to quintuple annual revenues from online and mobile money transfers by 2015. Toward that end, it invested $35 million in new digital products, technology, and talent in 2012 alone.

So just who had been selected to be on this now-validated strategic team, beyond its "designed diversity" already noted? Julie found out at one of the check-in dinners when she asked the CEO how these particular members of the team had been selected. He said, "Oh, didn't you know? You're all on my list of our top employees, my highest performers. It's the folks I particularly need to focus on to assure our continuing success."

The twelve on the online team were demonstrably high performers in their own rights beforehand, but what proved critical to making a persuasive case for online business at Western Union was how they demonstrated effectiveness in their collective strategic thinking. It seems clear that the chief financial officer's characterization of the team's business case as "coming together so compellingly," when several earlier efforts had failed, was due to the diverse nature of the team itself. The case came together so well because the team itself represented the diverse kinds of stakeholders the case itself would need to ensure senior leadership commitment. Strategic thinking is a collective process.

Strategic Thinking Is About the Present, Not Just the Future

A mind-set of strategic thinking also requires understanding how strategic thinking is different from strategic planning—especially an approach to strategic planning based on a now anachronistic model of intricate five-year plans of successive sets of future actions. Until relatively recently, such plans often sat largely untouched on shelves in three-ring binders. When that occurred, it typically was because those plans were unhelpful in informing decisions when conditions changed, that is, when planning assumptions no longer proved valid and thereby undercut the very premise of proposed future actions. The potential disconnect between specific future plans and actual conditions many years in the future becomes even more problematic in our current VUCA world in which unanticipated developments may create emergent strategic challenges and opportunities that must be addressed now. Even so, the concepts of strategic thinking and strategic planning deal with the future. Strategic thinking, however, deals with the present, not just the future.

There are two ways that strategic thinking involves the present as well as the future. The first is in how it contributes to an understanding of the capabilities an organization needs to invest in now in order to be prepared for the future. Western Union's investment in its online business is an example. The second is understanding what current capabilities are the strategically most important for an organization to be putting the highest priority on now in order to ensure sustainable competitive advantage. Our experience with client organizations as well as with the Center for Creative Leadership's strategic leadership simulation provides almost constant validation that few organizations do a good job of identifying their strategic priorities and then aligning their tactics to match those priorities.

To be sure, organizations are routinely clear about what their strategic goals are—whether quarterly goals, one-year goals, or even five-year goals. Goals, however, are not the same as strategic priorities. *Goals* refer to what an organization wants to achieve; *priorities* refer to those organizational capabilities that are most distinctively critical to a particular organization's continuing success and vitality. Strategic priorities are the capabilities an organization must invest in most significantly to achieve its goals; goals are what the organization intends to accomplish if it has invested wisely.

We use the phrase *strategic drivers* to identify those relatively few capabilities that truly drive organizational success. Not uncommonly, though, an organization may invest disproportionately in things that are not key drivers of success for that organization in that competitive environment. For example, investing extensively in marketing may not be a wise tactic if the organization's most important strategic driver is customer service. One might ask, of course, why an organization would do that. In our experience, it's because executives at all levels tend to place much greater emphasis on, and are much clearer about, what their goals are than what their actual strategy is. And in that regard, it's important to understand that identifying an organization's key strategic drivers is more akin to a process of discovery than executive edict. That's why we call strategy a learning process.

Strategic Thinking Has an Artful Side as Well as a Rigorous and Analytical Side

The last element of having a strategic thinking mind-set pertains to the cognitive processes required to collect, generate, interpret, and evaluate information and ideas that drive an organization's sustainable competitive advantage. Unfortunately, the cognitive tools that strategic leaders have relied on to accomplish these tasks too often have been unnecessarily constrained. A whole class of tools has been left out of their tool kits, and it's virtually impossible to make strategy a learning process in an organization without them.

Think of it this way: there is a soft side as well as a hard side to strategic leadership and strategic thinking. In general, the hard side of strategic thinking calls on the kind of rigorous analytical tools and techniques taught in business schools. But strategic thinking has a softer side that is also a vital part of understanding and developing strategy, vision and values, culture and climate. The word *softer* does not imply weakness but rather includes those qualitative thinking skills that are held in opposition to hard-minded, quantitative rigor.

It's partly what Carly Fiorina, the former Hewlett-Packard CEO, told MIT's graduating class in 2000: "At any one moment in time you often can't see where your path is heading and logic and intellect alone won't lead you to make the right choices, won't in fact take you down the right path. You have to master not only the art of listening to your head, you must also master listening to your heart and listening to your gut" (Fiorina, 2000). Fiorina was speaking to graduates embarking on their lives as well as embarking on work, and her advice reflected wisdom of the unforeseeable twists and turns life takes. But her words also reflect today's business reality. Planning and implementing strategic change is becoming harder than ever before, given the increasing pace of change, the increasing uncertainty about the future, and the increasing complexity of challenges organizations face in both the corporate and nonprofit sectors. Virtually every organization today faces complex challenges that defy existing solutions, mental models, resources, and approaches. Leaders must learn to apply their full range of strategic thinking competencies to the complex challenges their organizations are facing and to supplement analytical skills with a multifaceted understanding that includes the following insights:

- Strategic thinking requires synthesis as well as analysis.
- Strategic thinking is nonlinear as well as linear.
- Strategic thinking is visual as well as verbal.
- Strategic thinking is implicit as well as explicit.
- Strategic thinking engages the heart as well as the head.

Synthesis and Analysis Analysis involves breaking down something into its constituent elements. It's a very useful skill and one at which most managers are quite proficient. Synthesis refers to the combination of separate elements into a more complex whole. Many managers today are considerably less practiced and competent in synthesis than in analysis. But creating strategy depends on synthesis as much as on analysis.

An analogy here might be useful. A musical composition can be broken down into the separate parts that each individual instrument plays. In fact, the composition needs to be broken down in order for the musicians to practice their separate parts effectively. But that's not enough. The concert itself—at least a good one—depends on skilled craftsmanship combining the separate elements into a pleasing and coherent whole. In a good concert, the whole is more than the sum of its parts. The same is true for strategy.

Strategy reflects choices between what an organization will do (or will be) and won't do (or won't be). Only certain patterns of choices, or combinations of alternative investments, contribute to a coherent whole, that is, a viable strategy. For example, the pattern of choices a company might invest in to enact a strategy of product innovation would be quite different from the pattern of choices it would invest in to be the low-cost producer in the industry.

Nonlinear and Linear Linear thinking involves looking for (or assuming) cause-and-effect or sequential relationships between things, as in the form, "A follows B." This is a valid and useful approach to many strategic problems. For example, projecting future sales by incremental adjustments to past sales often works quite effectively—but not always. What if your competitor launches a new product that makes yours woefully unattractive to customers? Such events represent discontinuities for which linear thinking—basing future plans and actions on past experience—is inadequate. Linear thinking cannot solve challenges in a nonlinear world. One powerful indication of the extent to which the future will hold exponentially more surprises can be seen in figure 2.1, which depicts the rate-accelerating impact of technological change over time. While the data in the figure represent technological change on the Internet, it is typical of the impact of new technologies more generally.

The world of business is increasingly defined by surprise and uncertainty. Until relatively recently, most organizations had grown accustomed to the idea of fairly continuous change; now

Figure 2.1   The J Curve and Rapid Exponential Change

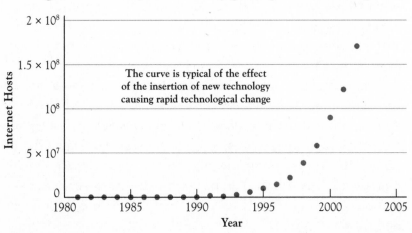

Source: Blue Horizons (2009).

the challenge is to learn to deal not only with continuous change but with disruptive change. Succeeding in such environments requires nonlinear as well as linear thinking.

Visual and Verbal As noted earlier, many people associate the word *vision* with strategic leadership. Less frequently do they fully appreciate the essential meaning of the word itself: having a vision is about *seeing* something. The greatest visionaries are those who are able to paint a picture of a more desirable future. Vivid words and phrases rich in imagery help them convey that picture.

Two of our colleagues at CCL, Chuck Palus and David Horth, have developed a simple and powerful tool for tapping this visual dimension of thought in rich and constructive ways (see a full account of their work in Palus & Horth, 2002). The tool, Visual Explorer, is a set of several hundred diverse photographs and art reproductions selected for their visual richness and potential metaphorical association with varied business and personal challenges.

We frequently use Visual Explorer to facilitate conversations among executives about different business issues. We might begin, for example, by asking each of them to think about a strategic challenge facing his or her organization and then to select a picture that depicts an aspect of that challenge in some way. Almost always those conversations take on a richness and depth that is missing in the primarily verbal and often abstract conversations typical in most business meetings. For example, one participant who was responsible for transforming his organization's information technology function selected a picture of bumper-to-bumper traffic on a congested highway. The group's discussion brought up issues like the relative disconnectedness among passengers in all the cars, confusion about where they've been and where they're going, and suspicions about whether they like the trip they're taking—all relevant to the business issues this leader was facing.

Implicit and Explicit We all know more than we are able to put into words. Whether they call it intuition, instinct, or trusting your gut, effective leaders have learned to trust their judgment even when they are not able to make their rationale completely explicit. This ability becomes particularly important as leaders move into roles and positions of strategic responsibility in their organizations.

CCL has collected and analyzed data on the thinking styles of thousands of executives who have attended our programs, and it is interesting to examine how they vary in personal preference for dealing with information in relatively more explicit or implicit ways. Some prefer to make decisions in the context of well-defined problems using information that is objective, factual, concrete, and unambiguous. They especially trust their practicality and past experience. Others prefer to make decisions in the context of ill-defined problems by focusing more on patterns and relationships in data rather than on specific pieces of data. They especially trust their insight and imagination.

Our data indicate a somewhat greater representation at the top levels of management of individuals whose natural preference is toward trusting their insight and imagination. Slightly over half of middle and upper-middle managers have this preference, and 60 percent at the senior executive level do. By comparison, more than two-thirds of the general population prefer to rely on a sense of practicality and experience.

These differences are consistent with our understanding of the nature of strategic thinking. The strategic challenges that executives confront are often novel, complex, and ambiguous. For that reason, strategic decisions are often not entirely data driven; they demand executive judgment that attends to the best information available but rarely can be determined solely by it. In other words, strategic thinking is implicit as well as explicit.

Heart and Head The concept of employee engagement has received a lot of attention in the past decade. It refers to the difference between people in an organization just doing their jobs versus being personally committed to the organization's success. The extent to which people throw themselves into their work is a function of many things, but partly depends on whether the organization has clear and compelling aspirations. Articulating organizational aspirations that inspire members to higher levels and quality of effort is one of the key tasks of strategic leadership.

Organizational aspirations involve understanding who we are and where we want to go. We have emphasized the value of developing and communicating a vision that people can see, and one big reason it's important is that a vivid vision can touch hearts as well as heads. An organization's aspirations can give meaning to the work and energize people to do more than they thought they could or would.

That's why vision or mission statements that are merely quantitative in nature so frequently leave people uninspired (to be number one in the industry, for example, or to improve earnings). Imagine that you work for a pharmaceutical company. A goal might be to double sales—not a bad goal in itself. But quantitative goals like that rarely engage the whole person. Compare it with the examples in exhibit 2.1—aspirational statements that touch the heart as well as the head.

One of the challenges to developing your strategic thinking is that organizations historically have tended not to encourage and equally reinforce the two complementary sides of strategic thinking. Thus you might not have had much opportunity to practice or observe certain kinds of strategic thinking at work. You can get an idea about that by just scanning the two groups of words in exhibit 2.2 to see whether one set captures the typical kind of strategic thinking in your organization more than the other.

If you're like most other managers, the set on the left is more characteristic of the kinds of thinking words people in your organization are accustomed to using. Nonetheless, both kinds of thinking competencies are required of strategic leaders today. The rest of this chapter is about developing these less developed competencies.

Before you begin the next section, we suggest you assess your strategic thinking skills with the brief survey in exhibit 2.3.

EXHIBIT 2.1
Examples of Organizational Aspirations

Xerox: Helping people find better ways to do great work.

Celestial Seasonings: To create and sell healthful, naturally oriented products that nurture people's bodies and uplift their souls.

Bristol-Myers Squibb: To extend and enhance human life.

Starbucks: To become the most recognizable brand in the world.

University of Texas MD Anderson Cancer Center: Making cancer history.

Nike: To bring inspiration and innovation to every athlete* in the world.

*If you have a body, you are an athlete.

Toys 'R' Us: Our vision is to put joy in kids' hearts and a smile on parents' faces.

The Walt Disney Corporation: To make people happy.

Developing Your Strategic Thinking

We now turn to several strategic thinking competencies that we have identified through our work with managers and executives. In that work, we usually ask them to describe their own greatest challenges to becoming a better strategic leader. Here are a few representative responses:

- To develop a vision for where my organization needs to be in five years
- To have a broader perspective on the competitive landscape
- To step back and see the big picture
- To be more comfortable thinking out of the box

We also pay attention during our work to what aspects of strategy as a learning process are most challenging and most helpful for

EXHIBIT 2.2
Words for Thought Processes

Traditional Strategic Thinking Words	Complementary Mode Strategic Thinking Words
Observe	Reflect
Compare	Connect
Test	Create
Data	Pattern
Discuss	Visualize
Plan	Illustrate
Identify	Brainstorm
Assess	Represent
Define	Imagine
Outline	Demonstrate
Analyze	Synthesize
Classify	Associate
Manage	Integrate
Evaluate	Simulate

managers and executives to understand and learn to apply. Based on this experience, we have identified five strategic thinking competencies that we believe are embedded in the broader challenge of strategic leadership and also typically the least developed: scanning, visioning, reframing, making common sense, and systems thinking. The relationship between these competencies and the mind-set of strategic thinking is depicted in figure 2.2.

EXHIBIT 2.3
Evaluate Your Strategic Thinking Skills

For each of the behaviors listed below, use the 1–5 scale to assess your need to improve in that area. Circle the number that corresponds to your assessment.

1	2	3	4	5
Considerable Improvement Needed		Moderate Improvement Needed		No improvement needed

Scan the environment for forces and trends that could have an impact on the organization's competitiveness.

1   2   3   4   5

Ensure that all necessary information is considered.

1   2   3   4   5

See things in new and different ways.

1   2   3   4   5

Identify the truly key facts or trends amid the large amount of data available to be considered.

1   2   3   4   5

Understand your own biases, and do not let them play too strong a role in your thinking.

1   2   3   4   5

Identify key points or issues, and discern the truly significant information among the explosion of data confronting you.

| 1 | 2 | 3 | 4 | 5 |

See patterns and relationships between seemingly disparate data, and ask probing questions about the interactive effects among various parts of the business.

| 1 | 2 | 3 | 4 | 5 |

Offer original, creative ideas.

| 1 | 2 | 3 | 4 | 5 |

Collectively, these strategic thinking competencies also tap the aspects of strategic thinking that we've noted are vital yet underdeveloped in most managers (Linkow, 1999). Scanning and systems thinking both involve nonlinear thinking. Visioning strives to touch the heart as well as the head. Reframing often depends on implicit thinking and also can involve visual thinking. And making common sense requires synthesis more than analysis. Now we will look more closely at the nature of each of these five strategic thinking competencies as well as at how to develop them.

Scanning

The danger of inadequate scanning is captured in the now comical perspective of Thomas Watson, who as chairman of IBM in 1943 said, "I think there is a world market for maybe five computers." Though the strategic learning process can actually begin anywhere, it typically begins with assessing where the organization is.

Figure 2.2 The Mind-Set and Competencies of Strategic Thinking

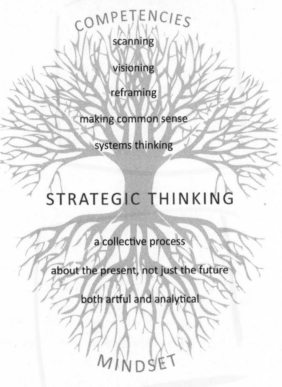

COMPETENCIES

scanning

visioning

reframing

making common sense

systems thinking

STRATEGIC THINKING

a collective process

about the present, not just the future

both artful and analytical

MINDSET

This means examining the organization's current strategic situation, and it includes an analysis of the opportunities and threats in the industry and broader competitive environment as well as the strengths and weaknesses inside the organization.

This is commonly called a SWOT analysis; the acronym stands for strengths, weaknesses, opportunities, and threats. A more detailed description of a SWOT analysis is presented in exhibit 2.4. To see how this works, go through an exercise like the one described in exhibit 2.5.

This organizational examination and analysis is sometimes called *environmental scanning*. It's not unlike what sailors did in the age of wooden ships—having a man in the crow's nest with a

---

EXHIBIT 2.4
SWOT Analysis

SWOT analysis is a common method for *assessing where we are.*
Following is a closer look at the SWOT analysis elements:

Strengths. What internal capabilities or assets give the organization a
competitive advantage? In what ways does the organization serve
its key internal and external stakeholders well?

Weaknesses. What internal capabilities or assets is the organization
relatively ineffective or inefficient at performing or possessing, or
so limited in capacity as to put it at a competitive disadvantage? In
what ways does the organization fall short in serving key internal
and external stakeholders?

Opportunities. What conditions or possible future conditions in the
external environment might give the organization a competitive
advantage and help achieve its vision if taken advantage of?

Threats. What conditions or possible future conditions in the external
environment might put the organization at a competitive disadvantage and inhibit achievement of its vision if steps are not taken to
minimize their impact?

---

telescope to scan the horizon for sight of land or another ship, a ship
that could be friend or foe. It's a vital organizational competency
to master, lest the organization fail to recognize and take advantage
of strategic opportunities—or fail to recognize and thus fall prey to
strategic threats. Extending the metaphor further, think of scanning even more broadly than just what happens from the crow's
nest. Think of it, too, as all that went into preparations before the
ship even left harbor: What might the seas be like? What storms
or other conditions might we encounter? What equipment, stores,

---

EXHIBIT 2.5
SWOT Conversations

Do a SWOT analysis on your own organization by examining its internal strengths and weaknesses and the opportunities and threats from the external environment. Then have conversations with four other individuals from your organization:

- Someone two levels senior to you
- Someone from a different functional area
- Someone with a reputation for creative business thinking
- A manager with a reputation for being solid and level-headed

Ask each of them independently what they consider to be your company's three or four most strategically important strengths, weaknesses, opportunities, and threats, and also what overall strategic implications they draw from their respective analyses. Compare their responses with each other as well as with your own analysis. What were the points of agreement? What were the points of disagreement? What did you learn about your own insight and appreciation for your organization's strategic situation?

---

and provisions do we need to take to be prepared for unexpected challenges? What other ports are available to us in case we need to change route? In the most general sense, then, scanning involves vigilantly monitoring environmental conditions that could affect mission success or cause mission failure. Such conditions could be competitor behavior, technological change, political and economic conditions, human capital, and so on.

For the individual manager, scanning as a strategic thinking competency involves attending to the informational horizon beyond one's own job, team, division, function, company, or even industry. Unlike an organizational SWOT analysis, which tends to be relatively systematic, individual scanning is likely to be quite nonlinear. The point is to be looking all around, to be vigilant for potentially useful information anywhere, whether from news reports about competitors, conversations with customers and suppliers, or elsewhere.

Good strategic thinkers scan their environments for data, trends, or ideas that could potentially have significance for their organization's future competitiveness.

To put it differently, scanning involves freeing yourself from the silos you may have erected in your mind and looking beyond self-imposed constraints that focus attention on information within a limited domain. Good strategic thinkers often scan diverse sources of information, such as magazines and journals outside their business or industry literature. They seek out perspectives from others involved in diverse kinds of work. They can sift through information quickly, not necessarily deeply but with an eye for the anomalous or otherwise interesting bit of data.

A telling example of the danger of self-imposed mental constraints is the failure of Kodak executives in the 1990s to take advantage of the transformation from film to digital photography. At a personal level, everyone now of a certain age remembers when cameras and film went together, in the words of an apt song, like a horse and carriage. In the 1990s, though those days were clearly and rapidly passing away, Kodak executives could not change their view of their company as essentially a *film* company. Ironically, this was despite the fact that at the time, Kodak had its own very high-quality digital technology. Kodak is still recovering from this strategic myopia and filed in early 2012 for bankruptcy protection.

Visioning

A vision represents a view of what the organization (or a department, group, or other unit) can and should become. There can be formal expressions of organizational aspiration, as in official vision statements or core values. At the same time, however, many individuals also hold personal but unspoken versions of organizational aspirations. Unfortunately, they seldom share these personal visions.

Knowing the different implicit aspirations individuals have for their organization can be informative and even inspiring. As an example, consider our work with the leadership team at Harlequin, a publisher of women's fiction (most notably in the romance genre) and subsidiary of the Canadian communications company Torstar. During an off-site strategic planning session, we asked each of the dozen executives on the team to compose his or her own individual version of Harlequin's future. Our specific instructions were as follows:

> Your assignment is to write a one-page newspaper article portraying your vision and aspirations for Harlequin. The article should represent what would make you proud to be able to say or write about Harlequin three or four years from now. Therefore, each of you should write your own version of that article (that might be published in, for example, the *Toronto Star* or the *Wall Street Journal* in 2007), describing Harlequin's achievements.
>
> Write this article so that it tells the story of Harlequin's success and is not merely a list of "bullet points" or specific facts and achievements. Write the story so that it evokes feelings of pride when you read it, and conveys a sense of what kind of company Harlequin is, as well as what it has accomplished. As any good journalist would, of course, you will want to cite a variety of supporting material including quotes, business results, anecdotes about corporate culture and morale, etc.

As we expected, the team initially balked a bit at these instructions and lobbied to merely outline their respective organizational visions with a few bullet points. They acceded to our approach, however, and were amazed and pleased at the quality and richness of input across the board. Here is an excerpt from one of their articles, set in the personalized form of a communiqué about Harlequin from Oprah Winfrey on her Web site:

> When I walked into the Harlequin office in Toronto, I came face to-face with a floor-to-ceiling sign that read World Domination of

Women's Fiction. And I thought *I* had big goals! But as I walked around the office, I felt not a sense of domination, but of appreciation.

Appreciation for the passion of reading, for all of the people that bring passion to life for millions of readers, and for the skill and talent that it takes to accomplish that. All the while Harlequin is demonstrating this appreciation, it continues to sell more books every year—over 200 million at last count. On Friday I'll share with you some of my encounters with the people who help Harlequin put the entertainment back into reading.

Harlequin is my kind of company—one that cares about its family of readers, and its employees, and can still be successful. And on top of that, it provides me all of the entertaining fiction I could ever dream of wanting. I can't believe it took me this long to discover Harlequin—and now I can't imagine my world without it.

Take a moment to introduce yourself to a new friend—you'll have this one for life.

O.

It's sometimes said that vision must come from the top. Perhaps, but it's also true that activities like those described in exhibit 2.6 can enrich the vision-setting process. It affords broader opportunity for people to share personal versions of aspirations for the organization. It also can inform people throughout the organization of the many different possibilities and visions that can exist simultaneously (not necessarily inconsistently) within one organization. Perhaps most important, an activity like this can generate collective inspiration for an organization's future, even amid differing individual versions of it.

And while the focus here is on visioning as a general strategic thinking skill, it is still worthwhile to be aware of several guidelines for crafting an organizational vision statement (Criswell & Cartwright, 2010). CCL recommends that organizational visions:

- Express ideals and values (not just short-term goals or mere tactics)
- Affirm the human dimension (not just financials)

- Put the organization's story in a meaningful context that connects members to its core identity
- Clarify expectations about the kind and amount of desired growth
- Describe key drivers of change

EXHIBIT 2.6
Suggestion for Development: Craft Your Own Organization's Story

Compare your own aspirations for your organization with others using the newspaper article technique described in this chapter. Have a group at work craft their own individual versions of your organization's story following instructions similar to those used in the Harlequin illustration.

After the stories are completed, share and discuss them, and use them as a springboard for developing a shared vision.

Individuals in the group can exchange their respective articles and note points of correspondence as well as differences. They can use questions such as these to guide their reading:

- How high are your aspirations for the organization?
- What are the biggest differences between the current organizational reality and your (and others') aspirations?
- Were there ways that others saw the organization changing that did not occur to you?
- What could make you more conscious of changes like those whether or not you see them as desirable?

Reframing

Reframing is the ability to see things differently, including new ways of thinking about an organization's strategic challenges and basic capabilities. It involves questioning or restating the implicit beliefs and assumptions that are often taken for granted by organization members. It plays a critical role in the formative phases of the strategic learning process. There are many techniques for reframing. The process can be aided by using metaphors like those in exhibit 2.7.

Kodak's failure to sense the true scope of the revolution taking place in photography is also a case study of its executives' inability to reframe their view of the company. Steve Jobs's development of the iPod, on the other hand, demonstrates what can happen positively through reframing. In Walter Isaacson's words, the iPod was

---

EXHIBIT 2.7
Suggestion for Development: Using Metaphors

Complex phenomena like leadership are often grasped more easily through the use of metaphor. Many different kinds of metaphors are used to describe leadership. Here are a few:

- Leadership as combat
- Leadership as sport
- Leadership as art
- Leadership as a machine
- Leadership as gardening

Use metaphors to describe strategic leadership in your organization. Explore how these or other metaphors might describe some aspect of your own organization's approach to leadership.

"the device that would begin the transformation of Apple from being a computer maker into being the world's most valuable company" (Isaacson, 2011, p. 384).

Reframing the Nature of the Business at Starbucks Reframing can be an essential part of resolving an organizational dilemma, but it also can be experienced as unhelpful and disruptive to those who may not perceive any dilemma.

Starbucks began in 1971 as a very different company from the one we know today. Originally it was a store that sold coffee beans and coffee-making equipment, not the places for *drinking* brewed Starbucks so omnipresent now. The difference resulted in large part because of the way its chairman, Howard Schultz, reframed the kind of business Starbucks should be in. Schultz joined Starbucks in 1982 to head its marketing and retail store operations. While on a trip to Italy in 1983, he was amazed by the number and variety of espresso bars there—fifteen hundred in the city of Turin alone. He concluded that the Starbucks stores in Seattle had missed the point: Starbucks should not be just a store but an experience—a gathering place.

Everything looks clearer in hindsight, of course, but the Starbucks owners resisted Schultz's vision; Starbucks was a retailer, they insisted, not a restaurant or bar. His strategic reframing of the Starbucks opportunity was ultimately vindicated when, having left Starbucks to pursue the same idea with another company, he returned to purchase the whole Starbucks operation in Seattle, including its name.

Reframing Decisions Advantageously Research on decision making indicates that how decisions are framed makes a significant difference in the decisions actually made. Even just labeling of external conditions as opportunities or threats can change the ways people respond to them. For example, the perception of external conditions as opportunities tends to broaden organizational participation in the response and evoke decisions representing relatively small changes that are directed at the external environment. When conditions are perceived as threats, however, organizational response tends to occur in a top-down manner evoking much larger-scale responses, often involving more significant internal changes (Floyd & Wooldridge, 1996). Exhibit 2.8 provides an exercise in strategic reframing.

EXHIBIT 2.8
Suggestion for Development: Strategic Reframing

Prompt your own reframing of strategic leadership in your organization by asking yourself questions like these:

- What would we do differently if we really listened to our customers?
- What are some different ways we can think about what *quality* means in our work?
- What could we be the best in the world at doing? How might doing that change the nature of our organization?
- Instead of thinking about ourselves as an organization that [fill in how you currently characterize your work], what if we thought about ourselves as an organization that [fill in a different way of thinking about what your organization does].
- Have certain processes and activities in our organization merely become ends in themselves rather than means to an end?
- Is our structure serving our strategy, or is our strategy serving our structure?
- Use the idea of the inverted pyramid organization as a metaphor: that is, instead of thinking of the senior leaders at the top of the pyramid and being "served by" everyone else in the organization, think about senior leaders as the bottom of the pyramid and serving everyone else. What else might it be helpful to "turn upside down" here?

Research has shown that one of the most powerful factors affecting decisions is whether the stakes are framed as potential gains or potential losses. Daniel Kahneman and Amos Tversky developed a paradigm for decision research that has stimulated numerous studies of this dynamic. Here's the kind of problem used in this research (see Hammond, Keeney, & Raiffa, 1998). Say that you are responsible for the installation of a new information technology system in your organization at three separate operating locations. Unfortunately you have discovered that a computer virus has infected the system. The virus seems resistant to all existing countermeasures, and the entire system will be lost if the virus is not successfully countered in the next twenty-four hours. The value of the system at each location is $1 million. A new virus detection company may be able to save all your equipment, but the result is not certain. The company gives you two options:

Option 1: This will save the equipment at one of the sites, worth $1 million. The equipment at the other two sites will be lost.

Option 2: This has a one-third chance of saving the computer equipment at all three locations, worth $3 million. But it has a two-thirds chance of losing the computers everywhere.

Given these alternatives, more than 70 percent of people choose the "less risky" first option. But what if the choices had been different? What would you do if instead you'd been given these choices?

Option 3: This will lose all of the computers at two of the locations, worth $2 million. The equipment at one of the two locations will be saved.

Option 4: This has a two-thirds chance of losing the computers at all three locations, worth $3 million, but a one-third chance of saving everything.

Faced with these choices, 80 percent of people choose option 4.

That is intriguing, especially when you realize—as you probably did here—that the two pairs of alternatives are identical but worded in different ways. The different patterns of responses reflect a strong aversion to taking risk when a choice is framed in terms of gains (computers saved) but a willingness to take risk when avoiding losses (computers ruined). People tend to avoid risks when they are seeking gains, but they choose risks to avoid sure losses. This finding implies that you shouldn't automatically accept the way an issue is initially framed. Explore alternative ways of framing the problem to see whether that makes a difference in the relative attractiveness or apparent desirability of the options.

The Value of Reframing The value of reframing depends on the situation and context. In becoming a strategic leader, you must adapt your personal inclination to reframe an issue with the needs of the situation. (Is reframing actually required?) People differ in terms of their preferences about how to approach change. Some prefer change that is fairly methodical and cautious, whereas others prefer change that is more expansive and immediate. Those who prefer methodical and cautious change also tend to be most comfortable working within a particular paradigm or framework, whereas those who prefer more expansive and immediate change tend to see things differently and want to reframe things. Greater awareness about your own preferred approach to change leads to insights about when and how your penchant for seeing things differently may be most helpful. In some lines of work, for example, constantly generating new ways of seeing things may be particularly unhelpful. We recall an operations manager at a nuclear reactor who said, "In our work there is a fine line between vision and hallucination." As part of our Leading Strategically program, we give participants feedback about their preferred approaches to change. We always highlight how different managers vary considerably in their preferences and underscore how all preferences make distinctly valuable contributions to the change process—it's not a matter of good preference or bad preference.

Invariably these insights about change preferences give leaders a new way of understanding the source of tension they've experienced with others when trying to agree on or implement change. When people who prefer expansive and immediate change suggest a fairly dramatic reframing of a situation, it may create tension with those with a different change style. And when people who prefer more methodical and cautious change resist reframing, that can create tension with their counterparts too.

Making Common Sense

One of the most important things leaders do—especially strategic leaders—is to help others in their organizations make sense of the world around them, the challenges they collectively face, and how they will face them together. They help create shared understanding.

Increasingly, groups and organizations face problems and challenges that belie easy definition and resist routine solutions. When leaders are facing ambiguous situations or ill-defined problems, the temptation for many might be to create structure and certainty by imposing a personal view of the situation: in a sense, to make everyone else adopt their own sense of it. In truly ambiguous situations, however, that's often a dangerous path. In the long run, it is often more constructive to make common sense of the situation—that is, create a shared understanding of the situation, not to assume that one person's interpretation of it is correct.

In our work with executives, we sometimes use an outdoor activity called orienteering—finding a route across unfamiliar back country without an established trail—which gives them many opportunities to create shared meaning. For example, those unfamiliar with terrain maps do not always discern the significance of contour lines on the topographical maps provided to participants (contour lines that are close together, for example, indicate steep terrain). Similarly, reaching consensus as to where they are as an orienteering team often involves all the members of the team sharing how they interpret different sorts of clues in their physical environment and then indicating where they believe that puts them on the map.

Strategic leadership requires making common sense amid complex and ambiguous conditions. The dynamic challenges facing organizations today contribute to a common experience of lack of clarity about direction and alignment and a sense of disorganization and confusion. Strategic leadership involves making common sense amid just such chaotic conditions. It involves giving some coherence to what could otherwise feel like confusing and contradictory communications and signals at work. Like reframing, making common sense is particularly useful during the earlier stages of strategy as a learning process.

Developing shared understanding is important because people often rely on implicit knowledge rather than on explicit knowledge when it comes to communicating or sharing ideas. Unarticulated knowledge can cause people to feel unclear or confused about the apparent disconnectedness between the priorities, policies, and processes of different teams, departments, or divisions in their organization.

This is less likely to happen when people share a common understanding of their vision and strategy.

At work, people need to make common sense about a whole range of things:

- Their vision of the future
- Their understanding of challenges facing the organization
- Guidance from higher authority
- How the team will work with other individuals and groups
- Obstacles to group or team success and ways to overcome them

Making common sense is challenging in any situation, but it is especially difficult when building shared understanding among groups separated across boundaries of rank or power, functions or expertise, organizational affiliation and commitment, demographics or geography (Ernst & Chrobot-Mason, 2011).

An Illustration: Making Common Sense in a Hospital A large independent health care facility had an excellent reputation in its community but was trying to position itself favorably amid new competition, regulations, technologies, and a changing demographic characterized by immigration and aging. The hospital's senior management articulated a new vision of becoming a customer-focused hospital. The technical elements of such a vision were benchmarked, but the implications for social and cultural change at this conservative organization seemed daunting.

The senior team was thinking about a leadership strategy to support its new vision. Mindful of a need to broaden participation in this initiative, it invited a number of directors to a retreat. Some of those who attended were surprised by the format of the retreat. They had thought they would be briefed by the CEO on a management direction for the hospital and then given guidance about how the change would be managed. But the retreat, although deeply concerned with direction and leadership, was focused on sense making and using dialogue as the means to achieve it.

The group started by looking at the results of an internal climate survey and hearing about the key challenges facing the hospital as viewed by the different people in the room. They listed sacred cows—the maddening quirks of work at the hospital that are typically not to be questioned in public. They asked: Why have we come together? What are we seeing? What's missing? Why change?

As the dialogue moved to more difficult topics, an improvised change in the room setup proved especially helpful. The group moved from behind the long tables into a circle of chairs. Body language became more obvious. Several members of the group said they felt more exposed. One person said, "Now it feels more like a meeting of hearts and minds and less like a standard business conversation."

The group then used the Visual Explorer activity (described earlier in this chapter). Each person examined dozens of pictures clipped from magazines and the Internet, which were spread out around the room so people could browse through them. The instruction was for each of them to pick a picture or two that somehow captured what stood out in the survey data. Each person in turn presented a picture and what it represented. Others in the dialogue could then respond in a constructive manner: "What I see in your picture is . . . and the way I might connect it to the challenges we face is . . ."

One picture was of a boy lying awake in bed. The person who chose this image saw comfort and recovery from illness. But others in the group saw fear in the boy's expression. An image of a farmer walking behind a plow also raised the topic of fear, as people said, for example, "We are so traditional. It can be frightening to break new ground."

The group had thus uncovered a troubling theme: fear was not uncommon at the hospital. But why fear? Where did it come from?

The hospital was managed to high standards. The middle managers especially had come to see themselves as primary owners of these standards, feeding a hyperresponsibility for success. Yet out of this management culture also came a strong sense of fear about even the possibility of censure and reprisal for any mistake. The CEO's invitation to take risks in the name of leadership seemed at odds with tight management.

One manager illustrated this cultural norm in a story of a nurse who was reprimanded for being five minutes late to a patient consultation meeting because she was ushering another patient and family to their room. The nurse was caught between the traditional hospital norm of "everything on time" and the new norm of "customer focus." She was afraid to do the wrong thing. A number of such stories led the group to ask themselves, "How do we handle these inevitable collisions between inventing new forms of customer-focused leadership and the strict professional management disciplines of running a hospital?"

Such feelings of fear were difficult to talk about in public. But others listened and sought to understand. The CEO in particular had to work through his reaction ("People are afraid of me . . . *me?*") and see his unique place in a hierarchical management culture that was perceived as paternal and threatening to innovation. Several examples of how this fear played out were discussed— quite tentatively at first. A new level of openness in the dialogue began to take shape.

An important step to making shared sense across the organization was the senior team's sharing the results of the dialogue with the organization. Instead of saying, "Here's our plan," it chose to invite the rest of the organization into a similar process. Some of the pictures from the dialogue were circulated, including a description of the issues they evoked. Often the reaction was, "That's good work, and I want to be a part of it."

The process of using dialogue as a tool for shared sense making laid the groundwork for the bold actions required to become a customer-focused hospital. Hospital employees now say that they feel more "on the same page." The changing direction of the hospital makes more sense to them. Now they better understand and can deal with some of the strong emotions that had previously blocked progress. The effort has also deepened appreciation for the many positive things happening in the organization. ("You are doing great work! Don't be afraid!") The hospital's leadership initiatives are increasingly based in freshly explored shared values rather than short-term pressures.

The hospital continued using these forums for making shared sense of the challenges it was facing as an organization, involving more people in them, including managers at every level from around the hospital. The general aim of all these forums was to ensure shared learning on questions of fundamental importance across the hospital. Where are the patients (customers) in the hospital's new sense of itself? Where are the doctors? Where are the local community leaders? How can these groups and others be included in the process of building shared understanding? The process outlined in exhibit 2.9 will let you try a similar experiment.

EXHIBIT 2.9
Suggestion for Development: Making Common Sense

- Explore with others the strategic implications of alternative images or pictures of your future.

- Collaborate with others in a collective effort to represent your mission or vision using words or images.

- Have a dialogue with others about your strategy using stories or metaphors.

- Communicate your strategy using pictures, visual images, or other data displays.

- Ask questions of others' perspectives during conversations so as to deepen your understanding of their views.

- Express doubts or criticism in a constructive way.

- Collaborate with others in building new strategic perspectives.

- Hold a complex issue open to debate and deliberation without rushing to an answer.

- Create ways to discuss what has been undiscussable.

- Seek strategic insight with a sense of learning and curiosity by holding all possibilities loosely rather than as positions to be defended and debated.

It's not just hospitals, of course, that can benefit from this kind of work. In 2010, for example, CCL was invited to help senior leaders from the US Army and the State Department make common sense across their two quite different organizational cultures. This was deemed essential to ensure effective collaboration between the agencies in carrying out their complex and interrelated responsibilities in Iraq. In a workshop lasting just a few days, leaders developed a shared vision and common language, built trust and mutual understanding, and improved their ability to work interdependently (Hughes, Palus, Ernst, Houston, & McGuire, 2011). This work will be explored in greater detail in chapter 4 where we'll look at strategic influencing.

Four Ways of Communicating to Make Common Sense We hope it is clear now that making common sense is an essential part of working in chaotic environments with others having different agendas and different interests. But how do you do it? Are there specific ways to practice collective strategic thinking and make common sense with others? Yes there are, and some of the most powerful are developing a broader and more skillful repertoire of the ways we speak to each other.

A colleague of ours, Bill Torbert, refers to this as interweaving four parts of speech. If that sounds painfully reminiscent of studying grammar in school, we should consider Torbert's reminder that "speaking is the primary and most influential medium of action in the human universe" (Torbert & Associates, 2004). In Torbert's scheme there are four basic parts of speech: framing, advocating, illustrating, and inquiring.

Framing means explicitly identifying the purpose for any particular occasion (e.g., a conversation or a meeting). It requires putting both one's own and others' perspective on the table for examination, an element that Torbert says is the one most often absent in conversations and meetings. Too often a "person in charge" (say, the meeting moderator) simply assumes everyone knows and agrees with the overall objective and proceeds without explicitly identifying such assumptions. She might say, for example, something like, "Since our team recommendations are due next week, I think it's vital that by the end of our meeting today, we reach consensus on a draft version." At the same time, someone else in the meeting may be questioning whether the team has yet even agreed on a shared understanding of the problem it's supposed to be solving (i.e., making recommendations about). Framing serves the purpose of creating an explicit understanding of the work or idea a group of two or more is addressing.

Advocating means explicitly asserting an opinion, point of view, or desired course of action. It occurs when a person says, in effect, "Here's what I think," or, "Here's what I think we should do." Unfortunately, advocacy has become the dominant and sometimes even sole part of speech for many managers and executives. Perhaps this is because it superficially appears consistent with other seemingly desirable qualities like openness and self-confidence. It also may seem one's most direct way of influencing events. But as with most other skills, it can be underused as well as overused. It tends to be most significantly underused when it involves advocacy about how people feel about what is happening in a personal or work-related interaction. This can be because people have learned to avoid expressing feelings in public settings, or perhaps even recognizing their own feelings. A predictable consequence therefore is the unskillful advocacy or expression of feelings that can erupt when they become too strong to restrain (e.g., "I'm tired of you trying to dominate every meeting!").

Illustrating involves telling concrete stories that add vividness and detail to an otherwise abstract or general idea or proposal. The increased clarity and specificity of illustrations help orient and motivate others to behaviors most likely to achieve desired results. Consider this "mere" advocacy: "We've got to get shipments out faster." On its own, responses to this call for action might understandably lead to extensive and expensive systemwide process changes. So consider this alternative: "Pacific Systems is our oldest and largest client, and they just received a sizable rush order that will require getting our component to them faster than normal. We need to support them on this." Adding the details of this illustration to the same advocacy will probably lead to a more calibrated and effective orientation and response.

Inquiring is asking others questions in order to learn something from them. Simple as it may sound, effective inquiry is both fairly difficult and uncommon, for several reasons. For one thing, when we question others in a too-direct manner without context or background (seemingly out of the blue), it can feel like an attack or accusation to the other person or that we have some ulterior purpose in asking it. In either case, we're not likely to get our questions answered entirely honestly. For another, we sometimes phrase things in the form of a question when we don't always genuinely want to hear the other's answer (e.g., "How are you?" or "You agree, don't you?"). Inquiry is almost always most effective when it is preceded by framing, advocacy, and illustration. This helps clarify expectations and assumptions and reduce the likelihood of misunderstanding. Effective inquiry, when used along with the other parts of speech, is a powerful way of discerning what perspectives and ideas others are bringing to the table, how they might differ from your own, and thus an essential part of making common sense. Be aware, however, of inquiry's disadvantages. See Exhibit 2.10 for more on that.

Learning to use all four of these parts of speech in your communications with others and balancing your use of them depending on the needs of the situation are perhaps the two most important ways you can practice collective strategic thinking and make common sense with others.

Systems Thinking

Effective strategic thinkers are able to discern the interrelationships among different variables in a complex situation. For example, they might wonder what would happen to sales of a product if the price to consumers was reduced. Or what would happen to sales if marketing was increased? If these variables operated in a simple linear fashion, then either choice would increase sales. But if they represented variables in a complex and dynamic system, as is more often the case, the results would be less predictable. For example, if product quality was an important component of product attractiveness for consumers, then a decrease in price might be perceived as an indicator of poor product quality and consequently slow sales, no matter what was spent on marketing.

Systems thinking can help you better understand complex problems like these, so it's an important tool for your strategic

EXHIBIT 2.10
Suggestion for Development: Appreciative Inquiry

A form of dialogue called appreciative inquiry has become increasingly popular over the past two decades because it tends to generate constructive collaboration among people. It is based on the simple idea that we move in the direction of what we ask about. When our focus is on solving problems, we may inadvertently constrain the range of future possibilities by focusing on deficiencies and deficits rather than on strengths and possibilities. While individuals, teams, and organizations clearly need the ability to solve problems, a downside of what we might call the problem-oriented approach to inquiry is that it can reinforce an impression that something is broken and needs to be fixed. Here are a few examples of the problem-oriented approach and appreciative inquiry to make the distinctive nature of appreciative inquiry a bit clearer.

Problem-Oriented Examples	Appreciative Inquiry Examples
What are some of the biggest problems you see in your organization?	What are three things your organization could do to become even stronger and healthier?
Tell me what seems to be happening when your team fails to reach its potential.	Tell me what is going on when your team is performing at its very best.
What aspect of your organization would you change if you could?	What about your organization makes you proud to be a part of it?
What are some of the biggest challenges you face when trying to work across boundaries in this organization?	What does it look like when people from different parts of the organization are all pulling in the same direction?

thinking tool kit. The basic premises of systems thinking may seem a bit odd at first because they run counter to customary ways of thinking about things. If you try to practice the discipline of systems thinking, however, you might understand complex problems in new and helpful ways.

In the following sections, we provide an overview of five tactics for better systems thinking. Each of them is emphasized in CCL's Leading Strategically program (the framework presented here has been adapted from an excellent treatment of systems thinking by Barry Richmond, 2000):

- Look for patterns over time.
- Look at the big picture.
- Look for complex interactions.
- Hypothesize key causal relationships.
- Validate your understanding of what causes what.

Look for Patterns over Time The first tactic we'll look at for better systems thinking is looking for long-term patterns in phenomena over time. This is an antidote to people's more common approach, which we call *static thinking*.

With static thinking, attention and energy are focused on whatever the current crisis seems to be (a rising number of traffic accidents, for example, or decreasing profits or high employee turnover). Success tends to be defined in terms of solving that crisis—by decreasing the number of accidents, increasing profits, or reducing turnover, for example.

This approach seems reasonable (or at least familiar), but there are two problems with it. One has to do with the path by which the current state was reached, and the other has to do with knowing the best path for getting from the current state to a more desirable one in the future. With static thinking, little attention tends to be given to "how we got here," and equally little attention tends to be given to "how we'll get from here to there." *Dynamic thinking*, by contrast, examines how key variables brought a system to its existing state (and may be keeping it there) and uses understanding of the past to guide future initiatives.

This emphasis on understanding pathways is important, since undue focus on current conditions tends to be associated with assumptions of linear trajectories from the past to the present and from the present to the future (e.g., the number of traffic accidents went up because penalties for poor driving were too low; therefore, increasing penalties should immediately decrease accidents).

In contrast, dynamic thinking assumes the path forward is often nonlinear rather than linear. This certainly is the case for many organizations. For example, solving tough organizational challenges often requires investments that take time to have an impact. There is often a short-term cost of some kind before a desired effect takes hold. It's not a straight line from investment to results. It is often true that things get worse before they get better—and sometimes, as in the example in exhibit 2.11, they can be getting worse despite an appearance that things are improving.

EXHIBIT 2.11
Suggestion for Development: Charting Changes over Time

It is often useful to focus on relative indicators of performance rather than absolute indicators of performance. For example, a financial institution that monitored several aspects of credit card use noted that the number of cardholders was increasing, total revenue was increasing, and the number of transactions was increasing. Everything was trending up, and that seemed good. But a group at this company then examined relative revenue measures. It discovered that dividing annual revenues by the number of cardholders produced a trend line that first curved upward but then curved downward. This suggested that the company was increasingly attracting marginal customers.

Source: Richmond (2000).

Look at the Big Picture The second tactic we'll look at for better systems thinking involves looking at the big picture. Catholic Healthcare Partners (CHP) is a large faith-based health care system. Its senior vice president for human resources and organizational effectiveness was Jon Abeles, whose responsibilities included developing executives throughout that complex system. Jon himself is a big-picture thinker, but more to the point, he wanted leaders throughout the system to be good big-picture thinkers themselves.

Within the population of upper management at CHP are executives who have strategic responsibilities at the facility level (within individual hospitals employing as many as a thousand people), some who have responsibility at the regional level (for many hospitals and encompassing up to eight thousand people), and some who have responsibility at the system level (ten regions encompassing forty thousand people). Abeles wanted leaders who understood the big picture from their own vantage points in the system, as well as from higher perspectives, and who could be strategic leaders of the whole system at whatever level they were assigned.

Such big-picture thinking involves seeing at each level how the different parts of a system operate as a whole (in CHP at the facility, regional, and enterprise levels). And big-picture thinking at each level is not possible using the detailed quantitative analysis of parts (functions, departments, divisions, silos, and so on) that is ubiquitous in organizations today. Barry Richmond (2000) puts it cogently: "Breaking things down into more detail and increasing numerical accuracy rarely provides the leverage needed to break a logjam in our thinking, identify a high-leverage strategy, or defuse resistance to an organizational change effort. Instead, what we need is exactly the opposite: more synthesis, more knitting pieces together so as to see new connections" (p. 15). Exhibits 2.12 and 2.13 will get you started with big-picture thinking.

Look for Complex Interactions The third tactic we look at for better systems thinking involves understanding that an observed condition is often the result of complex interactions among

---

EXHIBIT 2.12
Suggestion for Development: Raise Your Sights

Elevate your perspective so you can rise above your immediate circumstances. A good way to do this is by finding where boundaries exist in your organization's environment. Boundaries may take the form of assumptions people make about a problem, about the work, or about the walls separating different teams, functions, or departments. (Connected Leadership, a major new research-and-practice thrust within CCL, pursues the idea that many leadership challenges within organizations today involve the disconnectedness of different parts.) The task here is to practice taking a high enough perspective that boundaries recede (and perhaps new sorts of boundaries will emerge). Second, look for similarities rather than differences in the companies, people, problems, and so forth that you come across. Looking for similarities is harder than it sounds because humans are hardwired to notice differences (e.g., contrasts and contours). But cultivating an ability to discern similarities amid superficial differences will help you see through to the essence of issues.

Source: Richmond (2000).

---

variables. Systems thinking looks at how multiple components of a system interact in complex ways to produce a combined effect that is not intuitively obvious. An example that is quite salient to one of us (R.H.) comes from a different sector of publishing industry that he's become aware of in the course of coauthoring a textbook through eight editions.

The second edition of that textbook was published just three years after the first one, and the primary emotions the coauthors felt in news that a next edition would be forthcoming was pride in the book's success. Then two years later, the authors were informed that a third edition would be due in one more year. Since the textbook's initial publication in 1993, a next edition

---

EXHIBIT 2.13
Suggestion for Development: The Elevator Speech

Craft an elevator speech about your organization's strategy (or what your division's, department's, or team's role in that strategy is). An elevator speech is so brief it can be delivered in just a minute or two, the duration of a short elevator ride. Its very brevity makes it a challenge. It isn't easy to identify what is central to say, and to say it clearly and succinctly. (As Mark Twain once said, "I would have written you a shorter letter, but I didn't have the time.") Many good leaders have found it a helpful practice to have several different elevator speeches always at their disposal, as need or occasion arises.

---

is published exactly three years later. What, the authors quickly began to wonder, drove this predictable cycle of next editions?

It seemed possible, for example, that the three-year period might produce sufficient "new knowledge" to warrant a new edition. But that hypothesis didn't seem persuasive to us since a cycle based on such reasoning would be driven by the authors (who are in the best place to know a field's state of "new knowledge"); instead, the cycle seemed driven entirely by the publisher. What, we wondered, drove the three-year cycle for next editions?

The answer to that question is apparent in figure 2.3. It depicts two curves, one representing new textbook sales over time and the other representing used book sales of the same edition on college campuses over the same period. In the first year any new edition is published (year 1 in the graph), there obviously would be no used books available. In each successive year, however, there would be increasingly large numbers of that edition available on the used books market. As college students and their parents well know, textbooks are quite expensive, and so used textbooks are an attractive purchase. In a relatively few number of years, therefore, the purchase of used textbooks starts cannibalizing the market for new textbooks significantly. That happens, it turns out, in about three

Figure 2.3   Notional Representation of the Relationship Between New and Used Textbook Sales

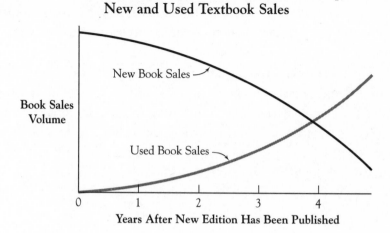

years, and so that's why new editions are published: to avoid the predictable cannibalization of new textbooks by used versions of their same edition.

Another example of complex interactions comes from work we in CCL did with a company called DriveTime. The primary customers of DriveTime, the largest chain of used-automobile dealerships in the United States, are people with poor credit records. Since 2002 its vision has emphasized innovation, quality, and outstanding service. Needless to say, those are qualities few people associate with the legacies and traditions of the low-end used car industry (McCauley et al., 2008).

In fact, the company had been rather typical of its industry until 2002 when its newly appointed CEO (an industry outsider) began a corporate transformation based on a new vision, a new culture, and a new strategy for DriveTime. As just one example of the broad-based transformation, DriveTime committed itself to making a positive difference in people's lives and, most important, in the lives of its customers. Among other initiatives serving that objective, it initiated the School Time Program with local elementary schools that served predominantly at-risk students, children of DriveTime's customer base. In a variety of ways, the program contributed resources to the schools and supported both teachers and parents. Furthermore, it developed relationships that allowed employees to better understand and empathize with a community that is normally treated like vulnerable prey by DriveTime's competitors in the used-car industry.

This exemplifies the nature of complex interactions since the School Time Program makes sense only in the broader context of DriveTime's commitment to a culture of interdependence within the company itself and with its broader stakeholders, including its customers. It's not just that the program isn't a natural fit in the business model of the typical low-end used-car company; it's that the very values on which the program is based are incompatible with the values and other practices of most used-car companies.

Hypothesize Key Causal Relationships The fourth tactic we look at for systems thinking is hypothesizing key causal relationships that drive desired outcomes. Strategy is about trade-offs: choosing to do this rather than that, choosing to be this rather than that, choosing to develop one capability over another. By its nature, a good strategy is not all things to all people. A good strategy is clearly centered on a few key priorities.

Determining what the key priorities are for your organization in your particular competitive environment is the challenge. Ironically, one aspect that makes it challenging is our ability to identify many different factors that all seem relevant to organizational performance.

For example, assume that your task is to identify corporate success factors in a manufacturing organization. You might identify a variety of factors: supply costs, manufacturing efficiency, product quality, marketing, product development, manufacturing capacity, product pricing, sales force effectiveness, brand strength, organizational structure, and culture. Although each one might well play some part in overall success, it's unlikely that investing in them equally would be a wise strategy. The strategic challenge for any organization is to integrate understanding of its aspirations, strengths, and weaknesses with understanding of its competitive environment in order to identify the two or three critical leverage points that bring success. These are the key strategic drivers.

Validating Your Understanding of What Causes What The final systems thinking tactic we examine involves confirming (or disconfirming) your hypotheses about causal relationships among variables. In some ways this is the very essence of good strategic thinking. It's important for leaders in organizations to confirm their theory of the business. Of course, few people merely assume their organization is performing well; most look for signs or results to indicate they're leading the organization in the right direction. But there is a hidden danger in how leaders sometimes validate their search for signs, as the following story suggests.

In 2004, a tragic accident occurred on a Colorado highway: three people were killed when a forty-ton girder fell on their car from an overpass under construction (Associated Press, 2004). What made the accident even more tragic was that a passing motorist had spotted the girder's precarious position on the overpass earlier and reported it to the state patrol. The motorist, experienced in bridge construction himself, indicated that the girder "just didn't look right." A transportation crew was dispatched to investigate the situation, and it coincidentally discovered a downed sign in the middle of the highway in the general vicinity of where the problem had been reported. The crew told authorities that the problem could be repaired later and then left, believing it had discovered the problem that the motorist had reported and did not require immediate attention. The crew looked no further, so it never saw the precarious beam that had prompted the motorist's call.

This kind of thinking is such a common source of error that it's been given a name: *confirmation bias*. People, including leaders, have a tendency to look for information that will confirm what they believe (or "know to be true") rather than to look more intentionally for information that could disconfirm their preconceptions. The danger in organizations is that if people look only for signs that they are on the right path (that their theory of the business is valid), they can often find them. But if they do not also look for signs that they are wrong, they will miss critical information.

This kind of thinking error was studied by P. C. Wason (1960), a psychologist who asked college students to guess the rule he had used to develop a particular three-number sequence: 2–4–6. To check their understanding of the rule, he had them generate their own sets of three numbers; Wason would then tell them whether their sets conformed to his rule. They could test as many different number sets as they wished, and when they felt confident they knew the rule, they were to announce it.

By the time the students announced their answers they were never in doubt, but they were seldom right. Typically they formed some erroneous hypothesis (e.g., counting by twos) and then searched for information that would confirm it. Since Wason's actual rule was "any three ascending numbers," their own three-number sequences always conformed even though they misunderstood the rule itself. Similar research also suggests that people are more likely to seek evidence that will verify their thinking than evidence that might refute it.

Exhibit 2.14 is an exercise in theory development and testing. And just like Wason's students, people in organizations can feel extremely confident about what drives organizational success ("what causes what") even when factually they are in complete error. Good strategic thinking depends on validating causal relationships among variables.

EXHIBIT 2.14
Putting Theory to the Test

First, identify some specific and testable implication of your current theory of business. Then determine what kind of result or data would be consistent with that implication. Also try to identify what data or result could disconfirm it.

How Strategic Thinking Relates to
Acting and Influencing

This chapter has focused on strategic thinking, one of the engines that drive strategy as a learning process in organizations. The next two chapters focus on the other two engines: strategic acting and strategic influencing.

Before going on to chapter 3, however, we should note again, as we did in chapter 1, that strategic thinking is not an entirely separate process from strategic acting or strategic influencing. Consider the strategic thinking skill of making common sense. It certainly involves thinking, but the modifier *common* implies a communal nature. It means making sense together, not just within your own head. The essence of the skill is to create in a collaborative way a common and shared understanding among different individuals with different perspectives, not to issue an edict. In other words it's an influencing process as well as a thinking process.

Making common sense involves the interaction of strategic thinking and strategic influencing as well as the interaction of different individuals. Larry Bossidy and Ram Charan (Bossidy & Charan, 2002) made a similar point in emphasizing the importance of constructing and sharing a common picture of what's happening inside and outside an organization. Doing so, they said, requires a "social software" in which debate and negotiation take place, but in ways that are more collaborative and creative than adversarial. When this happens it represents the interaction of thinking and influencing—and ultimately of strategic acting too—that lies at the heart of effective strategic leadership. We believe that execution, the discipline at the core of Bossidy's book, is basically about this interaction of strategic thinking, acting, and influencing.

Chapter 3

Strategic Acting

Strategic thinking and strategic acting have a close connection to one another and to strategic influencing. In most organizations, translating strategic thinking into priorities for action is one of the most challenging aspects of strategic leadership. This chapter looks first at the mind-set for strategic acting and then at several essential strategic acting competencies.

The Mind-Set for Strategic Acting

There are four elements of the mind-set of strategic acting:

- Only some actions are strategic.
- Strategic acting is both short term and long term.
- Strategic acting is an opportunity for learning.
- Strategic decisions always involve uncertainty.

Only Some Actions Are Strategic

It's one thing to have a strategically compelling idea. It's quite another to take action based on that idea. In part, that's what former Chrysler CEO Lee Iacocca meant when he said, "If I had to sum up in one word what makes a good manager, I'd say decisiveness. You can use the fanciest computers to gather the numbers, but in the end you have to set a timetable and act" (Iacocca, 1984, p. 50). But Iacocca told only half the story there. He captured one kind of tension between thinking and acting: the kind when prolonged thinking delays action. Another kind can occur when perpetual action precludes critical thinking.

Here's what we mean. Most managers probably feel as though they spend most of their working day in an acting mode. We don't mean playacting or pretending, but rather that they are constantly doing something: making decisions, taking a call, hurrying to one meeting after another, finishing almost overdue reports, and so on.

If you're like most of the other managers and executives we work with, the demands on you for action of one kind or another may seem so incessant that you find precious little time for thinking. In this sense, you are acting all the time. Managers and executives, often by both their roles and dispositions, are busy people. But our focus in this chapter is not on all forms of acting; it's on the more specific idea of strategic acting: *committing resources to build sustainable competitive advantage.* This kind of decisive action sets strategic direction of the organization even amid the ambiguity, complexity, and chaos inherent in organizational life. Examples abound:

- Which of several new product possibilities should receive the greatest share of development resources?
- Where should you place your marketing emphasis: on developing existing markets or new ones?
- Which new project will offer the greatest long-term advantage?
- Whom do you appoint to lead the new corporate innovation team?
- What stand should your company take with regard to questions being raised about its environmental impact?

So long as questions like these are merely under consideration, strategic thinking is involved. But when resources are committed—money, time and energy, personal or corporate reputations—strategic acting comes into play.

Does this mean that every action is a strategic action? No. Just as not all leadership is strategic, not every action is strategic. The critical issue is whether it's reasonable to expect an action to have an impact on the organization's future performance potential.

Selecting the next manager of the company mailroom would not likely have a strategic impact on the organization, nor would choosing one catering vendor over another. But selecting a new chief learning officer would probably be *intended* to have strategic impact.

Strategic Acting Is Both Short Term and Long Term

People sometimes assume that "being strategic" means focusing on the long term, but that's only half right. Strategic acting requires attending to both short-term and long-term objectives. It's not just about making long-range plans; it's also about how actions now (tactics) align with strategic priorities.

Data that we've collected from more than five thousand members of teams in organizations indicate that this can be a challenging tension to manage effectively. About 20 percent of the respondents on a Center for Creative Leadership survey who assessed the effectiveness of organizational teams disagreed with the assertion that an appropriate balance had been struck between dealing with short-term and long-term needs (see chapter 5 for a closer look at strategic leadership teams). While these data pertain specifically to perceptions of team effectiveness in balancing short-term and long-term needs, it's consistent with what we hear from managers in general about how difficult this balancing act can be. Jack Welch put it this way: "I always thought any fool could do one or the other. Squeezing costs out at the expense of the future could deliver a quarter, a year, maybe even two years, and it's not hard to do. Dreaming about the future and not delivering in the short term is the easiest of all. The test of a leader is balancing the two" (2003, p. 124).

Acting strategically requires the discipline to invest in both the present and the future, and that requires having a strategy that is clear to people from the start. In our survey, we also asked about the extent to which respondents' organizational strategies were discriminating, so that people have a clear sense of what they will do and also what they will not do. Fully a quarter of the respondents disagreed with the assertion that their strategies were clear.

Without strategic clarity and focus, leaders cannot make wise decisions about tactics. The exercise described in exhibit 3.1 invites you to think about what it will take for your own organization to succeed in the long term.

By its nature, investing in future capability often means investment unlikely to demonstrate immediate payoff. Many organizations launch key initiatives that never seem to gain a foothold or lead to lasting and meaningful change—in part because their leaders do not stay committed to strategic purposes and ends. With regard to the total quality movement, for example, research indicates that investments in total quality can pay off significantly only when the investment is significant and enduring over years, not months.

While perhaps the most obvious example of acting decisively is making a decision, it can also be reflected in consistent and determined support of key strategic priorities over time. Welch's own actions epitomize that. He talked about the need for focus and passionate commitment around those long-lasting initiatives by which leadership tries to change the fundamental nature of an organization. "I followed up on [those initiatives]," he said, "with a passion and a mania that often veered toward the lunatic fringe" (2003, p. 298). Welch was clear about the few most important priorities for GE's success. He stayed the course—and made sure everyone else did too.

EXHIBIT 3.1
Suggestion for Development: Envisioning Capability

Imagine your organization (department, division, or whatever) one or two years from now. What new or stronger capabilities would significantly contribute to your organization's effectiveness? What investments (financial, technical, human) should you be making now to strengthen your capabilities in the future?

How can you identify the most important priorities for your organization's long-term success? And perhaps even more important, how can you facilitate a collectively developed and embraced set of such priorities? Exhibit 3.2 offers you specific guidance for one way of doing just that.

EXHIBIT 3.2
Suggestion for Development: Prioritizing Needed Future Capabilities

How do you measure capabilities necessary for future success? Not surprisingly, the first and most critical step is to identify what they are. But that's not a simple matter. Here's one approach that involves having a structured conversation among key stakeholders to identify your organization's key strategic drivers. This exercise works best when between six and twelve people participate, each with a deep and distinctive perspective on the organization's operations and competitive situation. It usually takes half a day to work through this five-step process:

1. Spend several minutes individually brainstorming specific things you believe are critical to drive the organization's long-term competitive success. They can include current capabilities—whether effective (and needing to be maintained) or ineffective (and needing to be improved)—or currently nonexistent (and needing to be developed for future success). Strategic drivers can be a skill or talent, a competitive capability, or a set of conditions a company must achieve. They can relate to technology, marketing, manufacturing, distribution, and organizational resources.

2. Identify which four or five of those in your judgment are the most critical to future success whatever their current state of effectiveness. Write each of these on a separate sticky note.

3. Post everyone's notes (each person's top four or five) in a large common area (e.g., on a large whiteboard or on a presentation

(continued)

easel), and as a team begin sorting individual notes into affinity groupings. For example, those dealing with product development might be sorted into one group. This process typically leads to between eight and twelve distinct groupings.

3a. Sorting the notes into affinity groups is more of an art than a science. It's important for your team to have a shared understanding of what each grouping means, and it's important for each grouping to represent as specific a driver as possible. For example, a cluster of notes categorized as "leadership in product development" is usually more helpful than a broader and more heterogeneous grouping dealing with the general area of "innovation"; a cluster of notes categorized as "attract and retain top talent" will be more helpful than one dealing with "strong people programs."

3b. Involving everyone present in this sorting process is critical. Determining these categories is one example of the strategic thinking skill of making common sense. It requires creating shared understanding about what each of the various groupings means (and what they do not), not superficially designating some shorthand label for each grouping that might be interpreted differently by each person present.

3c. Moving some notes from one cluster to another, creating new clusters, and renaming clusters are all natural as the discussion proceeds and the team refines its understanding.

3d. Often there will be a few notes that never align well with any groupings. Keep them alive nonetheless, and don't assume they're less important just because the issue was identified on only one or two notes. Sometimes just one person initially identifies what ultimately proves to be a key strategic driver.

3e. One of the most common errors during this process is to confuse strategic drivers with desired outcomes. A strategic driver is best thought of as something you can invest in; an outcome is not. For example, increased market share might be a desirable outcome, but what would you invest in to achieve it?

4. When you've agreed on a final set of potential drivers, the next step is to discuss and assess the relative importance of each one with every other in turn.

4a. It helps if the discussion is framed in a fairly precise way. Ask this question for each pair of alternatives: If you could invest in only one of these two, which one is more critical to ensuring sustainable competitive advantage for the organization? (For the time being, don't worry about relative costs between the alternatives.)

4b. Each person present should make a forced-choice vote for one alternative or the other in every pairing. In almost every pair of alternative drivers, there will be some people who see one alternative as more important and some who see the other alternative as more important.

4c. When everyone is ready to vote, count and record the number of votes each alternative receives. This will be easier if you prepare a matrix with each alternative appearing in both the rows and columns of the matrix. In each appropriate cell, put the number of votes received by the item in the respective row when it is paired with each different item in every column (see, for example, appendix A).

5. These votes will ultimately lead to a rank-ordered list of key strategic drivers. But that's not yet the basis for measuring the capabilities needed for future success. Ultimately you'll want to focus on the two or three drivers representing patterns combining the highest relative importance and lowest current effectiveness. These will be the drivers for which you will develop metrics to

(continued)

assess for future capability. One way of identifying those drivers is as follows:

5a. As a whole team, go down the rank-ordered list of key strategic drivers. Rate each driver on a scale of 1 to 5, indicating your judgment of the organization's current effectiveness in using it to drive sustainable competitive advantage (1 = nonexistent or not effective at all; 5 = extremely effective).

5b. When you have completed these effectiveness ratings, identify the two or three drivers that are most important to your future strategic success and that the organization is least effectively (or not at all) implementing now.

5c. These are the drivers that will need substantial investment before their potential contribution to long-term success can be realized. By definition, they're unlikely to demonstrate attractive returns in the short term. During this period of driver investment, therefore, use metrics that reflect your buildup of that capability.

Strategy requires clarity of focus. It involves knowing what not to do as well as what to do; strategic clarity facilitates decisions about when to get into and when to get out of things. At a tactical level, it facilitates decisions about what projects or programs to launch and what projects or programs to stop.

During Welch's early years as CEO of GE, his seemingly draconian personnel cuts—a quarter of the company's staff left the payroll within five years of the time he took on the position—earned him the nickname "Neutron Jack." (A neutron bomb kills people but leaves buildings standing.) Welch said the nickname hurt, but he also hated the bureaucracy and waste in GE at the time.

Despite his nickname and despite once being named the Toughest Boss in America, Welch now feels that he actually did too little too late: "The ironic thing was that I didn't go far enough or move fast enough. When MBAs at the Harvard Business School in the mid-1980s asked me what I regretted most in my first years as CEO, I said 'I took too long to act'" (2003, p. 132).

Finally, strategic leaders should remember that acting with the short term and the long term in mind involves not just deciding what future investments need to be made but also what existing assets need to be preserved. Isabel Swift, a vice president at Harlequin, commented on the paradoxical difficulty posed by the strength of all her company's lines of business. "One of our challenges," she said, "involves redirecting and growing an organization that is actually quite successful." An important part of that success is readers' familiarity with the brand, so one of Harlequin's strategic challenges is to maintain the promise of the brand while still changing it. "The power of that brand is very precious," she said, "and we don't want to walk away from it." There are many approaches to ensuring strategic alignment within an organization, and most include measures or metrics by which the organization assesses its performance. Checking progress with credible and useful metrics is important, of course, but it's important to understand that metrics should be used as more just than an after-the-fact performance scorecard. By their nature, key metrics also direct organizational efforts toward some ends rather than others. That means leaders should assess both current performance and future capability, or what we've referred to as operational results and strategic results. This helps ensure that all units are pulling in the same direction—and that it's the right direction for the organization's long-term sustainability.

Selecting the right metrics to assess current performance and future capability is one of the most important things you can do as a strategic leader. Here are a few things to remember as you do so. First, in keeping with the idea that strategy is about making choices, it's important to have a relatively small number of key metrics. That's because your key metrics should be based on your strategic drivers, of which there should be no more than a handful; you might have one or two metrics for each driver. Second, these measures ought to hang together as a logically integrated expression of organizational strategy. Often organizations develop metrics that merely represent a diverse array of measures, mistakenly believing this qualifies as a balanced scorecard (Kaplan & Norton, 1996). This often leads them to use too many strategic measures. The problem is that the very act of identifying many strategic measures usually reflects a lack of clarity about those relatively few things (strategic drivers) that are most critical to enduring organizational success.

The other problem occurs when a variety of measures are selected without due consideration of their logical relationship to an overall integrating strategy. If a scorecard merely represents an assortment of different sorts of measures independent of their logical relationship to each other and an overall strategy (they just seem like good things to measure), then the net effect on the organization could be to pull it in different directions. It would decrease effort and dilute rather than leverage success.

Strategic leaders should select key metrics with the objective in mind of putting the chain of reasoning underlying business and leadership strategies to an empirical test. Therefore, since these strategies are ultimately intended to help ensure sustainable competitive advantage, it is vital to examine how you are doing now (e.g., this quarter's sales, for example), as well as how effectively and wisely you are investing in the future capabilities most critical to your enduring success (e.g., investment in research and development or evidence that you're attracting and retaining top talent). One approach to identifying these critical future capabilities was described in exhibit 3.2. But a caution is in order: metrics can be used constructively but they also can be misused, a point we explore further in the following section.

Strategic Acting Is an Opportunity for Learning

Strategic acting requires a mind-set in which acting is understood as an opportunity for learning. That involves conceiving of business strategy as an organization's theory of what it takes to be successful. Over time, organizations accumulate data relevant to the usefulness of that theory and on the validity of particular expectations and experiments (e.g., tactical business decisions).

This underscores the interdependence of strategic acting and strategic thinking. Strategic thinking generates hypotheses that are subsequently tested through strategic action. But as we have seen, simple causal relationships are not always what they appear to be or the whole story. In this case, learning also can occur if strategic acting precedes strategic thinking. In fact, the iterative nature of thinking and acting makes identifying the starting point somewhat arbitrary. The crux of the issue is how to test strategic thinking with acting and how to learn from action that has been taken.

In case it's not obvious, we're trying to draw an analogy between how science progresses and how some organizations are able to learn from their mistakes as well as their successes. When business tactics are thought of as hypotheses by which business strategy is tested, tactics have two related purposes: the obvious one is execution, but another is learning. Perhaps not surprisingly, organizations tend to deemphasize the role of tactics in the service of learning because that purpose is less appreciated.

That's one reason it's useful to see strategy as a top-down *and* a bottom-up process. Strategy needs to be set at the top, but it also needs to be informed by the insights of others throughout the organization. If it is not, it is likely to be seriously flawed. Campbell and Alexander (1997) observed that it's unwise to separate strategy formulation from its implementation since it's operating managers themselves who are the source of most of the insights important for strategy formulation. Henry Mintzberg (1987) coined the term *crafting strategy* to reflect the dynamic ways managers in the field act strategically in adapting to new opportunities and threats as they arise.

As Campbell and Alexander (1997) note, however, the importance of tactics is not only to implement today's strategy but also to help discover tomorrow's strategy. Their view is consistent with understanding strategy as a learning process in the way the results of implementing tactics provide feedback loops that inform current performance as well as future capability. Of course, for such feedback loops to work optimally, part of the task of determining tactics should involve addressing the question of how they can be designed to collect data relevant to informing future strategy.

This brings us back to the issue of metrics raised in the preceding section. Leaders should not approach their use of metrics merely as a new or different set of procedures. Rather, they should understand metrics in the broader context of relationships and organizational norms in which they will be used. When used well, metrics can serve the shared purpose in an organization of people collectively discerning its internal and external conditions. But metrics can be misused too. An organization's long-term vitality and success can be sustained only when shared commitments to truth seeking and truth telling undergird assessments of organizational effectiveness. Sometimes, however, truth telling in organizations can be subverted and metrics can be used to misrepresent actual conditions. That can happen, for example, when senior leaders create an impression they want to hear only good news, or when metrics are used to portray things in inflated and artificially positive ways to keep anyone from looking bad. The constructive use of metrics, in other words, is not so much a set of procedures as it is a fundamental dimension of organizational culture and values, a kind of covenant among its members. And it is only then that individuals and the larger organization can realistically be expected to learn from their mistakes because it is only then that they are likely even to publicly admit their mistakes and missteps.

We should also note that strategic acting creates opportunities for individual learning just as it does for organizational learning. Some of the richest opportunities for developing as individual strategic leaders can come from effectively mining the lessons of one's experience. In one of CCL's seminal research projects, successful executives were shown as tenacious in extracting lessons from their experiences. And they did so from the same kinds of experiences that less successful executives also had; they simply learned more from them (McCall, Lombardo, & Morrison, 1988).

Their achievement is all the more remarkable when one considers the inherent difficulty of learning personally valid lessons about leadership from one's own experience. By their very nature, leadership experiences are often ambiguous, they typically involve multiple stakeholders having multiple perspectives and interests, and emotional stakes can be high. Such ambiguity, complexity, and emotionality can make it difficult for a leader to determine causal relationships between his or her behavior and specific outcomes, or whether different behavior would have led to different outcomes. Learning about leadership from one's raw experience is not easy, not even for those with "extraordinary tenacity" to do so. But of course it can and does occur, and a recent study sheds light on how it can be fostered.

It turns out that while unaided learning from experience is difficult for all the reasons just noted, it can be enhanced through disciplined practice (DeRue, Nahrgang, Hollenbeck, & Workman, 2012). This involved after-the-fact reflection and facilitated discussion on personal leadership experiences; for example, the potential impact that alternative leadership behaviors might have and how individuals believe they might behave differently in the future. The study found that individuals who participated in this reflective practice improved the effectiveness of their leadership over time, whereas little or no development occurred from the same experiences among those who did not participate in that reflective practice. It's also worth considering if the discipline and learning focus inherent in the practice might also contribute to heightened consciousness of opportunities for organizational learning as well.

Strategic Decisions Always Involve Uncertainty

The most sensational event in President Obama's first term was arguably the Navy SEAL raid that led to the death of Osama bin Laden. It seemed to have gone so perfectly, and with such a positive result, however, that it's tempting to assume that launching the raid was an easy decision to make. After all, planning had been extensive and meticulous, and the intelligence was good. Mitt Romney, Obama's opponent in the presidential race, said that he would have done the same thing. In retrospect, of course, successful decisions often look easy from a distance, especially those that have momentous impact and popular appeal. It's worth remembering, though, that even some of Obama's principal advisors believed the raid was a mistake at the moment of decision and so counseled the president. In fact, Obama ordered the raid against the advice of his secretary of defense, his own vice president, and the general who was then his number two military advisor. The fallout of a failed mission would have had international and national repercussions, including the potential of a destroyed presidency. Obama nevertheless chose to act (Bergen, 2012).

What gives certain leaders the confidence to take bold strategic action when the outcome is uncertain (which, by the way, it always is)? Marilyn O'Connell, vice president of marketing for Verizon's retail markets, gave some insight into that sort of executive judgment—not a judgment involving life-and-death stakes, but one typical nonetheless of the strategic decisions made in business every day.

Verizon was facing a strategic decision concerning the deployment of fiber-optic cable. One side of the decision equation was well known: the cost to deploy the cable. What was not knowable was what capabilities the deployment of the fiber would enable over the next ten to twenty years. Thus, the strategic decision became a matter of judgment.

Would Verizon be able to solve problems in the future and develop the capabilities it would need in the future to make the investment feasible? O'Connell said it boiled down to this: "Do I believe we'll figure this out later?" But you can't wait until later to make the decision. She said, "If you always look at what you know and what you've always done in the past, you will never do anything."

A more recent example of how Verizon acted strategically in the face of uncertainty was its 2008 purchase of rights to a key portion of the wireless spectrum for $3.6 billion. It was the first step in Verizon's plan to blanket the United States with the wireless broadband technology known as 4G LTE. It was a high-risk strategic move because at the time, the technology had not been deployed or tested anywhere. Quite simply, Verizon invested billions in buying rights to a broadband spectrum before it (or anyone) had the technology to use it. The investment paid off: Verizon is now the largest commercial 4G LTE network in the world.

Thus far, we've been referring to uncertainty in a fairly general way. Perhaps it would be helpful here to become more specific about just how much uncertainty is acceptable when making strategic decisions. Ultimately, of course, that question can't be answered in any precise way.

There are too many other variables to suggest a simple formula, but in his autobiography, Colin Powell describes his own approach to decision making: "The key is not to make quick decisions, but to make timely decisions. I have a timing formula, $P = 40$ to 70, in which P stands for probability of success and the numbers indicate the percentage of information acquired. I don't act if I have only enough information to give me less than a 40 percent chance of being right. And I don't wait until I have enough facts to be 100 percent sure of being right, because by then it is almost always too late. I go with my gut feeling when I have acquired information somewhere in the range of 40 to 70 percent" (1995, pp. 380–381). The exercise described in exhibit 3.3 will help you clarify your own decision-making tendencies.

EXHIBIT 3.3
Suggestion for Development: Analyzing
Your Strategic Decisions

Review specific strategic decisions that you made in the past. For each one:

- Briefly identify the decision.
- Recall as best you can the different sorts of factors you weighed in making the decision.
- Try to estimate the subjective probability you had at the time that your actions were right (i.e., would produce a successful outcome).
- Recall the process you went through (e.g., data collection, discussions with others, and so on) by which you were ultimately ready to act or decide.

How frequently did your action or decision fall within the 40 to 70 percent range that Colin Powell recommends?

Now look at any strategic decisions that you are facing now. For each one:

- What is your subjective probability now that an action or decision in this case will be correct or successful?
- If you are above the 40 to 70 percent range, have you delayed the decision unnecessarily?

Before we close this section on the mind-set for strategic acting and turn our attention to strategic acting competencies, it might be helpful for you to complete a brief self-assessment of your own strategic acting skills (see exhibit 3.4).

EXHIBIT 3.4
Evaluate Your Strategic Acting Skills

For each of these behaviors, use the following scale to assess your need to improve in that area.

1	2	3	4	5
Considerable Improvement Needed		Moderate Improvement Needed		No Improvement Needed

Set clear strategic priorities.

1   2   3   4   5

Manage the tension between success in daily tasks and success in the long term.

1   2   3   4   5

Implement tactics consistent with strategy.

1   2   3   4   5

Make decisions that are strategically consistent with each other.

1   2   3   4   5

Facilitate others' actions by providing them a helpful balance of direction and autonomy.

1   2   3   4   5

(continued)

Find ways to reward appropriate risk taking.

1   2   3   4   5

Recognize the need to adapt existing plans to changing conditions.

1   2   3   4   5

Learn from actions by deliberately reflecting on their consequences, and use such learning to inform future decisions and actions.

1   2   3   4   5

Examine mistakes for their learning value (as opposed to apportioning blame).

1   2   3   4   5

Act decisively in the face of uncertainty.

1   2   3   4   5

Take quick and effective action when it's needed.

1   2   3   4   5

Learn appropriate lessons from your personal and organizational actions.

1   2   3   4   5

Strategic Acting Competencies

Three key strategic acting competencies complement the mind-set for strategic acting. They include acting decisively in the face of diversity; fostering agility; and creating alignment by setting clear strategic priorities. Those competencies and their relationship to the mind-set for strategic acting are shown in figure 3.1. The strategic acting competencies will be addressed in following sections.

Act Decisively in the Face of Uncertainty

Acting decisively in the face of uncertainty, especially when the stakes are high, can be mentally, emotionally, and physically challenging. There are many reasons this is so—for example:

Figure 3.1   The Mind-Set and Competencies of Strategic Acting

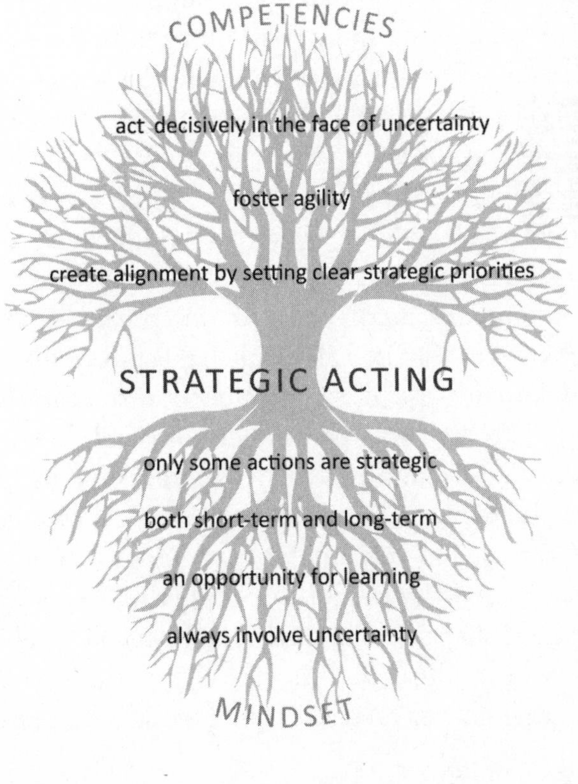

- Changing conditions make it difficult to accurately assess the risk-reward ratio of an action.
- Failure of an initiative carries potential risk to one's own career, department, or entire organization.
- Organizational cultures or formal and informal reward systems sometimes discourage risk taking.
- It is tempting to reduce uncertainty by investing in safer bets, even if the payoff may also be commensurately less.
- Action imposes opportunity costs of not pursuing other options.

Strategic decisions typically pose high levels of complexity and the potential for information overload as well as uncertainty. This can lead to the often-noted "analysis by paralysis" sometimes associated with an obsessive determination to consider every bit of data possibly attainable before making a decision.

It will be helpful here to clarify further what we mean by the word *uncertainty*. In some situations, a future event may be uncertain but still one of finite and specific probability. For example, the odds of randomly drawing a card in the suit of spades from a deck are one out of four. The odds of drawing the ace of spades from the same deck are one out of fifty-two. Situations like these allow one to make decisions on the basis of uncertain outcomes but known probabilities. In general, however, this kind of uncertainty is not the sort organizations commonly face.

A more familiar kind of uncertainty in organizations involves so many unknowns that they defy calculable probability estimates. To take an extreme case, it is impossible now to definitively identify what will be the two greatest technological threats to world peace twenty years from now. That's impossible in the face of exponentially increasing rates of technological change in fields like cyber, directed energy, chemistry, biology, nanotechnology, and others (Blue Horizons, 2007). While there is no way to predict the specific shape of long-term technological capabilities and key actors, though, there are still constructive things that can and should be done now to prepare for a range of future possibilities.

As we said, though, that's an extreme case; not all are so complex. Acting strategically requires knowing the level and kind of complexity inherent in the circumstances one is facing and then adapting leadership behavior to it.

The effectiveness of strategic actions will vary depending on the nature and degree of complexity in the environment. Snowden and Boone (2007) described four sorts of circumstances, or contexts, in which leaders might find themselves: simple, complicated, complex, and chaotic.

Simple contexts are the domain of best practice. Such contexts are relatively stable, and virtually all participants have a shared understanding of the situation. Leadership and management in simple contexts are straightforward, with procedure and practices fairly routinized. The "right answers" in simple contexts are essentially undisputed by anyone once the facts of a given situation are identified and the problem is diagnosed.

Complicated contexts are the domain of experts. The answers to problems in complicated contexts are not obvious and known to everyone, and multiple answers or approaches may be valid. Leaders in this domain naturally rely considerably on the analysis and advice of experts, but that's where things also can go awry. Experts can become captive to their own entrenched and inherently limiting ways of thinking and analysis, and thereby constrain potential organizational responses when novel circumstances present themselves. Leaders therefore must be able to recognize when circumstances have changed and the situation requires something other than an expert's solution. Sometimes, for example, a constructive way ahead may best come from nonexperts precisely because they are able to see a situation in novel ways. In addition, experts not infrequently disagree among themselves. That's why it's often a good practice to get a second physician's opinion about a complicated medical condition. But sometimes the situation cannot adequately be resolved merely by finding the expert with the most comprehensive and respected credentials. Sometimes the situation is truly complex and not merely complicated. When that's so, the leadership challenge becomes something different from just finding the right expert to listen to.

Complex contexts are the domain of emergence, and in this domain, "right answers" can't be known—at least at first. Snowden and Boone illustrated the difference between complicated and complex contexts by contrasting a Ferrari with a rain forest. A Ferrari is a highly complicated machine, but that's all it is. It is finite; although it is complicated, the whole is still static and can be defined in its entirety. A rain forest, however, is in constant flux. Like complex contexts more generally, a rain forest is a realm of "unknown unknowns." In complex contexts, the environment operates in such dynamic, unknown, and unpredictable ways that it is impossible in any normal sense of the word to analyze it (the appropriate approach in complicated contexts). Instead, the first priority in complex contexts must be to discover the emerging patterns of order on which organizational decisions and actions should be based. And this is the context, in fact, toward which much contemporary business and other sectors are shifting. That's why small-scale experimentation is such a key element of acting strategically today. Small-scale experiments are a way of discovering the new patterns of order on which larger-scale organizational commitments should be based.

Chaotic contexts are the domain of rapid response. The leader's first responsibility in these conditions is to act quickly to limit damage and establish order even before unknown and complex causal factors become identified and understood.

To be effective, strategic leaders must be able to identify the nature of complexity in the circumstances they're facing and adapt both their own and their organization's behavior to the distinctive requirements of that context. Even in the face of uncertainty, strategic leaders must be ready to take decisive action. This does not, however, mean making impulsive, big, and risky decisions. This is a point we examine further in the next section when we see how decisiveness in the face of uncertainty can be enhanced by fostering organizational agility.

Foster Agility

In a 2010 study, most executives surveyed said they were working in continuously shifting and changing conditions. In the same survey, executives in high-performing organizations were almost twice as likely as those in lower-performing organizations to say that they anticipated and planned for change before it happens (Institute for Corporate Productivity, 2010). That's just one indicator as to why agility is an essential competency for strategic acting. By *agility*, we mean an organization's ability to sense and respond to turbulence in the competitive environment quickly and effectively. Meg Wheatley (1992) cast that ability in the form of a metaphor, contrasting the staid and inflexible behavior of many organizations with streams, whose forms and paths are constantly changing:

> What is it that streams can teach me about organizations? I am attracted to the diversity I see, to these swirling combinations of mud, silt, grass, water, rocks. This stream has an impressive ability to adapt, to change the configurations, to let the power shift, to create new structures. . . . The forms change, but the mission remains clear. Structures emerge, but only as temporary solutions that facilitate rather than interfere. There is none of the rigid reliance that I have learned in organizations on single forms, on true answers, on past practices. Streams have more than one response to rocks; otherwise, there'd be no Grand Canyon. Or Grand Canyons everywhere. (p. 2)

Streams, of course, follow dynamic and changing paths solely because of the physical properties of forces they meet. Organizations change only in response to changing conditions if someone first notices the changing conditions. That underscores the importance of scanning, a strategic thinking competency discussed in chapter 2. But what else does organizational agility require besides noticing changes in the competitive environment?

Agility also requires acting quickly and effectively in response to a dynamic and perhaps even turbulent situation.

Agility Requires Fast and Effective Action Today's competitive environment involves ever-increasing uncertainty, complexity, ambiguity, and pace of change. That's why agility has become such a prized organizational capability: it takes agility to compete in this kind of environment. Agility is also prized because it's a difficult organizational capability to master. It runs counter in many ways to long-standing notions about how organizations need to operate to be successful. Hierarchical command-and-control authority structures and detailed formalization and standardization of policies and procedures used to be the norm in organizations. Most organizations did operate effectively with those structures and procedures in relatively stable and predictable environments, but few organizations face those conditions today. The agility needed in organizations today requires the capability to act both quickly and effectively when needed. That depends in turn on an integrated blending of organizational values and practices suited for today's dynamic competitive environment.

In other words, agility involves more than reducing an organization's time to act. It's more complex than reducing product development cycle time, something to be measured solely by the calendar or clock. That's why we say that agility involves quick and effective action.

Barriers to Agility One of the major barriers to decisive action in the face of uncertainty is the tendency in some organizations (or by particular senior leaders) to value "mistake-free behavior" more than actual achievement. This was a particularly strong factor in the case of one large manufacturing company we worked with. Time and again, its executives described this sort of dynamic as part of their culture. They all agreed that it was far more beneficial for any manager's career in this organization to set relatively low strategic targets and then exceed them than to set significant stretch targets but barely miss them. Managers got bad marks even if they barely missed an ambitious stretch target and good marks if they met a safe target despite the actual performance level being higher in the "just missed" case (measured, for example, by sales revenue). The executives we talked to all recognized how this cultural norm distorted target forecasting and possibly even sup-pressed actual performance (it was politically unwise to develop a reputation for chronically poor forecasting), but they seemed help-less to change so powerful a norm in so large a company.

Even if you can't change the culture of the whole organization, you can take steps to change the culture and behavior of people in your part of it. It is important to do what you can where and when you can do it. As a strategic leader, you can create protected space for prudent initiative and risk taking by those who report to you, even if you may not enjoy that freedom yourself. It may be helpful in that regard to review a broad set of indicators of what we might call the latitude of risk within in your own group or team. Exhibit 3.5 provides some useful factors to review.

Helpful as it might be to review the latitude for risk in your team or organization, let's not forget it is just one potential con-tributor to agility. An agile organization is one in which quick *and* effective actions are taken when necessary. Reducing structural and cultural barriers that slow the pace of work may be neces-sary for agility but are rarely enough. Agility is grounded on an aligned constellation of characteristics and capabilities, including an organization's way of handling internal conflict; implicit and explicit criteria about how success is measured; the availability and transparency of information throughout the organization; its capacity for rapid response when needed; the degree and quality of collaboration in the organization; and the existence of clear, widely shared, and practiced values. You can assess own organiza-tion's capacity for quick and effective action with exhibit 3.6.

Agility Is Enhanced by Making Strategy a Learning Process Strategic acting is an opportunity for strategic learning, and

EXHIBIT 3.5
Suggestion for Development: Measuring Latitude for Risk

Use these questions to explore the broader climate and context of risk taking within your group or team.

- Are we encouraging an appropriate level of risk taking for us to be successful?

- What are some examples of appropriate risks that we've taken in the past?

- What are some examples of seemingly appropriate risks that we didn't take?

- Are there any patterns in those two sets of examples?

- Are there certain kinds of risk that we need to be more prepared to take?

- Are the criteria clear about when taking a particular kind of risk is appropriate?

- How do we handle mistakes? Does the response to failure stifle even moderate levels of risk taking?

- How much risk taking takes place under the radar? Would it be better if we had a better understanding of the actual level? What would that take?

- When we know an action was successful, do we also know the degree of risk taken to achieve that success?

- How well do we use examples of risk taking with both positive and negative outcomes as teaching opportunities for shared learning and development?

- How safe do people feel that they won't be punished for taking what appeared to be a reasonable risk if it eventually goes south?

- What barriers have we imposed on ourselves that constitute obstacles to appropriate risk taking?

- What can the leader do more of (or less of) to encourage appropriate risk taking?

EXHIBIT 3.6
Assessing Organizational Capacity for Action

Read each pair of statements, identifying whether the statement on the left or right in each pair best describes your organization.

Disagreements are avoided in order to keep the peace and not disrupt things.	Disagreements among people and between groups are used to help solve complex challenges.
A person's success is judged by how well the person's boss thinks he or she is doing.	A person's success is judged by how well he or she helps the whole organization work together.
Information is territorially guarded within this organization.	Information is shared widely in this organization.
This organization never acts quickly.	This organization can act quickly when it needs to.
Ineffective collaboration across organizational boundaries is ineffective.	Collaboration across organizational boundaries is effective.
People in the organization feel a major disconnect between its publicly espoused values and the actual behavior of people within the organization (especially at the top).	The organization's espoused values are widely embraced and practiced among all members.

If four or more of the statements you identified were from the column on the left, then perhaps better agility should be a strategic priority for your organization.

something essential in the today's volatile, uncertain, complex, and ambiguous (VUCA) world. In chapter 2, we discussed how "wicked" problems, which characterize the kinds of strategic challenges many organizations face, require a collective problem-solving process; by their nature, they're beyond any individual's ability to solve alone. Another way of saying this is that wicked problems can only be addressed constructively, through a learning process.

In complex contexts especially, learn from small bets first before you bet the farm. That means learning to conduct business experiments using tactical actions to develop information that can inform and refine strategy.

Here is an example of appreciating the value of using tactical decisions to enhance potential learning. An executive in a media company had been given responsibility for a qualitatively significant, if financially modest, corporate diversification. Part of his challenge in making the case for diversification was to demonstrate understanding of the strategic drivers in this unfamiliar business. He was by nature quite innovative and entrepreneurial, and he looked forward to implementing a great variety of tactical decisions. A colleague, however, advised him to be more scientific by curbing his natural impulse to try everything in his choice of tactics. The colleague suggested that the executive would not be able to reach a clear conclusion if he changed every variable with every different test and advised that he choose something specific and vary it systematically.

The insightful colleague in this case may not have realized it, but her advice was consistent with research into management practices associated with successful, discontinuous innovation: breakthrough, revolutionary innovation rather than that based on incremental improvement. Researchers have found, for example, that although conventional forms of market research are useful in guiding incremental change, they have limited impact on more radical kinds of innovation. Of far greater value is what the researchers termed a *probe-and-learn* process. This process amounts to a series of market experiments and the introduction of prototypes into a variety of market segments (Lynn, Morone, & Paulson, 1996). Early versions of products are introduced (probing), and insights gained from market reactions to that probing (learning) guide continuing product development. For example, Motorola introduced its first handheld cellular telephone in several cities in 1973, ten years before fully commercial systems were sold. While the early prototypes generated relatively little interest, they did provide Motorola with valuable market insight. For example, it learned that those versions were bulky and heavy, and size and weight became critical design factors for several decades.

The probe-and-learn process suggests that the way to assess the strategic viability of an idea or opportunity is literally to pursue it—to introduce an early version of a product or service, learn about the market and technology, and then modify the offering based on that learning. Although the process has much to recommend it, however, it nonetheless should be used selectively. It reduces strategic uncertainty—but at considerable cost. No company could pursue this approach—or sustain the process over many years—with more than a small fraction of potential opportunities. It is best suited to opportunities for discontinuous innovation that are strategically central to the enterprise.

Jim Collins uses an interesting image to convey this same idea (Collins & Hansen, 2011). Based on research with companies demonstrating sustained success in turbulent environments, Collins advises "firing bullets first and then cannonballs." By that he means to invest in low-cost and low-risk tactical experiments ("bullets") until you learn enough to confidently concentrate significant resources in a new strategic venture ("cannonballs"). The exercise described in exhibit 3.7 invites you to conduct your own business experiment.

EXHIBIT 3.7
Suggestion for Development: Find a Strategic Initiative

Identify a new initiative you could launch to take advantage of changing competitive conditions while helping to sharpen your own senior leadership's strategic vision and insight. Now think about it as a business experiment. What strategically useful lessons could you learn from the initiative's success? What could you learn from its failure? What kind of data would you need to collect that would be relevant to validating your experiment?

One way to systematize learning from your actions is with an after-action review (AAR), a systematic method of learning from your actions. The US Army developed the procedure, which civilian organizations have adopted and adapted. The focus is on performing better in the future by capturing key insights quickly and then translating them back into action. It's about becoming more action oriented, not more analytical. And it is not about fixing blame on individuals or teams. It won't work in an environment of fear. An AAR has six key steps (Baird, Holland, & Deacon, 1999):

1. *What was the intent?* What was the action's intended outcome or purpose? What was to be accomplished, and how was it to be accomplished?
2. *What happened?* What were the results, and what events contributed to them? Who were the critical parties, what were the critical communications, and what other critical junctures or connections were revealed? One way of getting at this information is by asking key participants or stakeholders to reconstruct events chronologically. Another is to ask stakeholders what the key events were and then probe for clarifying information.
3. *What was learned?* What's known now that wasn't known before? What lessons learned will help someone else do better next time?
4. *What actions should be taken?* Based on the lessons learned, what should be done? What can be done to produce immediate benefits? What can be done to affect systems, policies, and practices? What can be done in the long term to affect strategies, goals, and values?
5. *Take action.* The whole idea of an AAR is doing something with what has been learned.
6. *Disseminate the findings.* Make sure others who might benefit from this learning are made aware of it.

Create Alignment by Setting Clear Strategic Priorities

In the preceding section, we mentioned the importance of strategically aligning organizational resources and capabilities. Without alignment, the organization's investments of resources and energy won't have the strategic effect intended and could even work at cross-purposes.

Setting clear priorities is one of the most important things strategic leaders can do to ensure alignment. Setting priorities facilitates coordinated action across the enterprise, and it also provides a basis for acting decisively with the short term and the long term in mind. Of course, priorities can change, and sometimes circumstances necessitate exceptions to the general rule. Nonetheless, decision making about allocating resources is easier when you know the relative importance of the different possibilities. It confuses people when leaders publicize key organizational priorities but then put more resources into other things. It also frustrates people when leaders send unclear signals by communicating, in essence, that everything is important.

Another common example of unclear priorities occurs when costs must be cut. Does the organization's leadership implement, for example, across-the-board 15 percent cuts in each functional area, or does it differentiate among those that represent greater and lesser strategic priority for the organization and allocate resources accordingly? The latter alternative is less common but more strategic. It requires differentiating between alternative ways of allocating scarce resources in terms of their relative contributions to the organization's future vitality. All managers and executives deal with supply-and-demand challenges: they face more demands for resources than they have available, whether the resources are dollars, bodies, or time. The organization needs to invest more in marketing, for example, but it also needs more sales staff. It needs to invest more in product development, and it also needs new IT systems. It needs to improve quality control in its manufacturing processes, and it also needs to create more competitive compensation packages to attract talented people to its technical staff. The trade-offs go on and on.

Setting clear priorities will be easiest and have the most enduring impact when people throughout an organization share a common understanding of the three or four factors that are contributing most to its long-term success. In chapter 1 we introduced the idea of strategic drivers: the relatively few factors that any given company considers most important to building and maintaining sustainable competitive advantage. Most organizations have no more than a handful of these drivers, and these represent a select few among the larger population of factors on which companies in an entire industry compete. Thus, one of the key decisions for any organization is the selection of strategic drivers on which it will competitively differentiate itself from others in its industry.

Doing so helps set priorities with regard to resource allocation. Which two or three aspects of your business merit the most resource allocation if the goal is to maximize the company's sustainable competitive advantage? The list of candidates for greater investment is long in any organization and often includes alternatives such as these:

- Changes in product pricing
- Changes in customer service staffing
- Enhancement of product development efforts
- Reduction of product development cycle time
- Changes in manufacturing capacity
- Changes in manufacturing efficiency
- Enhancement of quality
- Changes in sales force size
- Changes in sales force compensation
- Changes in marketing

Getting clarity about these priorities, or key strategic drivers, is only the beginning. It's still necessary to determine a specific strategy based on these priorities. And still more priorities must be set to guide decisions about the organizational culture, structure, and systems needed to implement the strategy effectively, especially if it represents a major change.

Clarity about its own strategic drivers is a big reason Cirque du Soleil has succeeded so spectacularly in what had been thought to be a dead part of the entertainment industry: the circus. Three of Cirque du Soleil's key strategic drivers are performance talent, lavish production, and constant innovation (Tischler, 2005). Its scouts canvass the world for talent, putting a priority (perhaps surprisingly) on near-great athletes and performers who have nearly the same skills as, say, Olympic medalists but still have something to prove and are often better team players. Cirque also selects talent based not just on athletic skill alone but also on a person's showmanship and ability to "ham it up." Another driver of Cirque success is its investment in lavish (and expensive!) production standards, including specially designed and permanent venues for each new show. And the phrase "each new show" underscores the importance of innovation, a third strategic driver of Cirque success. Cirque has demonstrated an ability to regularly top each new show with another one even more spectacular and amazing than those before. Quite simply, Cirque du Soleil is clear about its priorities, and it invests commensurately in them.

But let's explore that last phrase a little more deeply. Who is the "it" that does the investing? The answer, of course, is Cirque's leaders and managers across the organization. The reason, in other words, as to why clarity about strategic priorities enhances alignment and strategy execution is that it shapes the criteria for decision making across the organization. This is consistent with research showing that the most important contributor to effective strategy execution is the extent to which everyone in an organization has a clear sense of the decisions and actions for which he or she is responsible (Neilson, Martin, & Powers, 2008).

Finally, we should remember that leaders sometimes confuse priorities and undercut their own effectiveness by sending mixed signals. This can happen in a number of different ways. You have probably observed some of these common instances:

- A leader thinks out loud (without noting it as such), and some people take such words as a call to action but others do not.
- A leader doesn't walk the talk. The leader's actions and words are inconsistent, for example, emphasizing the importance of cost-consciousness to everyone else yet not applying the same frugality to personal expenses.
- A significant gap opens between espoused strategy and strategy in practice (or between deliberate and emergent strategy).
- A leader highlights "key organizational priorities" and yet goes on to put more resources into other things.

Some leaders don't differentiate among competing priorities at all, implying that everything is a priority. In such cases, others will be left to their own devices to know what's important, and poorly aligned actions are nearly inevitable. Exhibit 3.8 suggests a way to see whether you've sent mixed signals about the priorities in your own organization.

Ensuring Strategic Alignment at Xerox For several years, CCL worked with Xerox Corporation in developing what we believe is a best practice in ensuring strategic alignment among executives

---

EXHIBIT 3.8
Suggestion for Development: Getting Feedback

Ask for candid feedback from one or two of your more trusted and astute colleagues (ideally your direct reports). Find out whether they recall specific times when you have sent mixed messages to them or others, and if so, precisely what it was that you did that confused others as to your intent.

---

across all corporate functions and lines of business. This successful initiative depended on the interplay of strategic thinking, acting, and influencing.

In 2002, Xerox held five Executive Strategy Alignment Workshops for its top executives worldwide, drawing as many as seventy-five participants to each of the sessions. The purpose of the workshops was to achieve common vision and endorsement for Xerox's new corporate strategy among its top three hundred executives. That goal was to be achieved by the following actions:

- Ensuring consistent understanding of the new corporate strategy, business imperatives, and financial picture
- Translating the new strategy into its implications for organizational leadership
- Agreeing on what changes in current organizational practices were required to make the new strategy successful
- Providing a forum for two-way communication and feedback about the strategy and its implementation between the executive team and the top executives worldwide

In addition, the workshops were intended to prepare those top leaders to cascade the strategy to their employees. Each of the workshops followed a similar format. For half a day, the executives, who came from all functions and lines of business, listened to presentations by various members of the Xerox management committee about the new strategy. For the rest of the day, they were divided into diverse seminar-size groups of about fifteen. Each group addressed a common set of questions about the strategy and reached consensus about the most critical responses to each. The questions were as follows:

- What excites you about the strategy?
- What concerns you about it?
- What barriers to successful implementation need to be addressed?
- What questions or comments do you have for the CEO or other members of the top team?

Following these group discussions, members of the management committee, including CEO Anne Mulcahy, visited each of these groups to listen to each group's summary and to answer questions.

This format was very popular with the executives in that it allowed relatively personal and open dialogue about evolving corporate strategy and its implementation with the corporation's top leaders. It was followed two years later by a similar workshop, slightly different in format in that it involved all three hundred top executives meeting in one session, with similar success.

Jim Firestone, Xerox's chief strategist and president of the company's corporate operations group, described the process this way:

> The purpose of these workshops was to create proactive, hands-on sessions where our leadership community could engage, ask questions, push back, and raise issues that impeded their ability to execute.
>
> Open discussions around the implications, issues, and requirements for implementation enable leaders to deal with conflict and ambiguity and to make the right decisions toward a common goal. Our sessions in 2002 gave us feedback on areas we needed to work on and provided our executives with what they needed in order to cascade and implement the strategy in each of their organizations.
>
> Alignment is one of the most important steps in successful strategic change. Nothing is more powerful for creating alignment and commitment than openness and responsiveness. At Xerox, we were successful in engaging the right people to help influence and implement a solid strategy that is delivering impressive business results.

Managing Strategic Priorities at Starbucks Facilitating coordinated action across the enterprise requires knowing what initiatives represent the most important strategic priorities for the organization at any given time. Unfortunately, what seem like priorities to one person may not seem like priorities to another.

Some short-term requirements are important to attend to, but without strategic clarity, it's difficult to determine which are more important than others. Starbucks is an excellent example of how an organization can identify priorities for strategic action.

Starbucks is one of the most recognizable brand names in the United States and is becoming increasingly so around the world. It has grown from its inception in 1971 as a single retail store in Seattle to the dominant retailer of specialty coffee in North America, with more than eight thousand stores worldwide.

Being a dynamic and high-growth organization has obvious advantages, but it also presents distinctive challenges. One of them is having numerous competing priorities, which can inhibit a company's ability to execute things well and focus its resources and energy on the right things at the right time.

Helping Starbucks set those priorities was Margaret Wheeler's responsibility when she was manager of prioritization alignment and calendaring for the company's retail operations in North America. Wheeler served as an "air traffic controller" for any type of activity that occurred in the North American business unit. More specifically, she played a key part in translating the company's strategic objectives into prioritized action. After strategic objectives were set and key programs identified to drive those strategic objectives, her team took over to provide a road map for translating that high-level strategy into action.

One important element of the process was realistically assessing how much capacity the organization had for new initiatives. How many new projects could it take on during the course of any given year and execute effectively from the perspective of the operating field stores? For example, how many new beverages could Starbucks successfully introduce in a year? How many learning initiatives could be introduced—and done well?

Wheeler's North American leadership group met twice a month to review all the organization's initiatives at the start of their development. The group provided a final answer to the question: Will we roll this out? Complicating this decision-making process were the inevitable unplanned opportunities that arise and require resetting priorities. The organization's reaction to Wheeler's group was positive because this decision-making process allowed people throughout Starbucks to focus on actions that would make the most difference at any time.

Margaret Wheeler's story at Starbucks is an excellent example of how strategic thinking and strategic acting go hand in hand, and it's also a good example of strategic initiative coming from the middle of an organization. It was Wheeler's insight that the task she'd been given—getting the calendar of initiatives in order—was in some ways the wrong one; she recognized that the challenge was really about strategic priorities. As she explains, "We started with a very small, specific mission, which was to fix the calendar. Now . . . we've come up with a decision making and prioritization process linked to strategic planning. No one told us to do that. We uncovered an organizational need, and there were a lot of people who were really supportive of it and who wanted to make things better aligned, and we were able to do that." Wheeler clearly deserves credit for the initiative she took, but so does Starbucks for having created a climate that encourages that kind of initiative.

What Happens Without Clear Priorities: A Story of Failure One telling example of the importance of setting clear priorities concerns a project to develop a handheld meter in a company that manufactured large industrial equipment like boilers, pumps, and valves. Unfortunately for the company, the project was a flop—but for us it can be an instructive one. For one thing, the project took three years to complete rather than the six months originally programmed. Furthermore, in the words of the project manager,

> The cutting-edge performance criteria we were shooting for became yesterday's news. When it finally came to market, the device was slow, clunky and outdated. It barely worked. . . . We'd projected that the product would sell in the tens of thousands. I think we sold five. . . . In trying to create a new device, my team

and I set out to make the wrong product for the wrong customer in a way that ensured the deck would be stacked against us. When I think about what I would do differently if I had to do the project over, the answer is simple. I wouldn't make the product at all. (Petnaik, 2009)

The moral of the story here is that to be strategically useful, priorities need to be specific enough to inform constructive action. It is not helpful to have an "innovation strategy" that is not clear about specifics like what kind of innovation this company needs now, to serve what or whose need.

How Strategic Acting Relates to Thinking and Influencing

The competencies covered in this chapter highlight the close connection between strategic thinking and strategic acting. For example, the value of clear priorities is greatest when they are derived from good strategic thinking. In the first two chapters, we emphasized the importance of identifying key strategic drivers—those relatively few leverage points most critical to enduring organizational success. Identifying those drivers depends, among other things, on systems thinking. But identifying them isn't enough. It's just as important to use knowledge of those strategic drivers to set priorities for allocating resources. Strategic thinking and strategic acting go hand in hand.

In a similar vein, the advisability of decisive action in the face of uncertainty depends largely on the quality of strategic thinking brought to bear on the situation. That would require having scanned the environment to accurately understand the organization's current strategic situation, including the opportunities and threats in the external environment. It also typically requires bringing others into the process for making common sense of the situation. And decisive action in the face of uncertainty is likely to serve constructive ends only if it is grounded in a deep understanding of the complex variables involved—systems thinking.

The value of systems thinking also applies to acting with the long term as well as the short term in mind. It presumes a deep understanding of those relatively few factors critical to an organization's enduring success, not just to its current performance. Again, strategic thinking and strategic acting go hand in hand.

It should be equally clear that strategic acting is also closely connected to strategic influencing. For example, creating conditions for others' effectiveness is all about influencing others. So is acting to make strategy a learning process. The whole point of both competencies is to influence people throughout an organization to act individually and collectively in ways most likely to build sustainable competitive advantage.

It's appropriate, therefore, to turn our attention now to a more detailed look at the third key element of strategic leadership: strategic influencing.

Chapter 4

Strategic Influence

When Kevin Hart joined Kaiser Permanente as vice president and business information officer, the organization had set some ambitious goals. Kaiser Permanente is an integrated managed care organization based in California. It blends care delivery (facilities and medical groups) with an insurance plan to bring an integrated experience to its patients. Hart was hired at a time of rapid expansion to other areas of the United States and significant investment in technology to support electronic medical records. In fact, investment in facilities for the year he was hired was three times the investment of the prior year. One of Hart's first big responsibilities at Kaiser was to partner with the leadership of eight different regions, as well as the facilities function, to rapidly build and retrofit multiple hospitals with technology to support the strategic direction of the organization. Growth of this magnitude had not happened previously, and it had to be completed efficiently and effectively. Hart had the hard work of strategic influence in front of him.

Strategic influence is how leaders engender commitment to the organization's strategic direction and learning and is essential to sustaining competitive advantage in contemporary organizations. But the complex, chaotic environment in which organizations operate makes it difficult for their leaders to set a plan, get others onboard, and implement a strategy in some lockstep fashion. Organizations and the people in them must adapt and learn on the fly. Leading them through strategic influence is a never-ending quest.

Like any other quest worthy of the name, it is rife with challenges. Strategic leaders often know the path to pursue (through their strategic thinking) and might be decisive and confident enough to walk that path despite the uncertainty (through the courage of strategic acting), but enlisting others in the effort can be much more difficult. It is often the most critical element of building sustainability.

When asked, "What challenge do you personally face to being a better strategic leader?" many executives attending CCL's Leading Strategically program specifically discuss gaining endorsement of and commitment to their ideas. In addition, CCL client requests for development in the area of strategic influence have been on the rise over the past several years. Executives describe the challenges of influencing others in today's world. For example, matrix structures result in a lack of clear authority; virtual work results in the need to influence where there are not strong personal relationships; and cross-cultural work results in the need to influence people who hold different worldviews. Yet faced with these different challenges, the leaders we work with share one realization: strategic leaders can't achieve success by themselves. Success requires the committed efforts of many, and good ideas alone are not enough to get that commitment.

Kevin Hart faced many challenges around influence. The health care industry itself is chaotic, with advances in technology to facilitate care as well as technology to share information more readily between caregivers. The competitive landscape is fierce, with mergers and acquisitions rampant so that health care systems can maximize their breadth and reach. Within Kaiser Permanente, the structure is matrixed, such that Hart reports directly to the chief information officer, yet has dotted line reporting to the National Facilities Services. He also serves many disparate stakeholder groups including the leadership teams of the eight regions and the various medical groups that comprise the caregivers. It was not going to be easy to generate commitment across these groups to how this expansion would proceed.

For anyone working to become a strategic leader, developing and using strategic influence requires forging relationships inside and outside the organization, inviting others into the process, building and sustaining momentum, and purposefully using organizational systems and culture. It demands that leaders be clear about what drives them so that they can authentically navigate the political landscape, be able to see and understand other perspectives, and be patient and persistent to continue influencing as strategic initiatives unfold. Paradoxically, strategic leaders must also be open to influence from others.

Influence That Is Strategic in Nature

Just as not all leadership has strategic implications, not all influence is strategic in nature. Consider, for example, a team in a major health care system that is responsible for opening one new facility in a high-quality fashion. Mutual influencing among the members of the team invariably takes place; for example, one person may try to persuade another that some adjustment to the schedule might be appropriate in light of a change request from senior management. That might well be an important change to make for the work to be successful. However, we would not say this kind of influence is of strategic importance to the organization. But suppose those same individuals happen to be on a team like Hart's: significantly changing the way they approach facility planning and execution to accommodate rapid growth and significant changes in technology to execute the strategy. The nature and quality of their mutual influence in a situation like this clearly have strategic implications for the organization, and so we would consider it strategic influence. On a more general note, influence is strategic when it is part of the strategy-making and implementation efforts that are in service of the long-term performance potential of the organization. It often involves influencing other parts of the organization and even those outside the organization. For example, the strategic leader may exert influence to achieve the following types of outcomes:

- Get people on the same page regarding a long-term strategic direction.
- Engender buy-in from people for a strategic venture so that there will be true commitment to it, not mere compliance (or, worse, active or passive resistance).
- Significantly shift the way resources are being deployed or invested in line with strategic intent.
- Share insights and observations with more senior executives relevant to the strategy's viability, effective implementation, or capacity to match competitors' moves.

The Mind-Set of Strategic Influence

As you work to develop your strategic influence abilities, it's helpful to begin by thinking about the following elements, or "roots," that such development requires. These roots are depicted in figure 4.1, along with the skills necessary for strategic influence that will be discussed in the remainder of this chapter:

- Strategic influence requires more than persuasion.
- Strategic influence is far reaching.
- It's as important to be open to influence as it is to influence others.
- Strategic influence starts with a hard look at yourself.

Strategic Influence Requires More Than Persuasion

People often think of influencing in terms of persuasion: you have an idea or point to make, and it takes some particular interaction or series of interactions with people to persuade them to see it your way. Your thoughts frequently focus on others:

- What are they thinking?
- Will they agree with my ideas?

Figure 4.1   The Competencies and Mind-Set of Strategic Influencing

COMPETENCIES

building trust

managing the political landscape

boundary spanning

involving others

connecting at an emotional level

building and sustaining momentum

STRATEGIC INFLUENCING

requires more than persuasion

is far reaching

requires being open to influence

starts with a hard look at yourself

MINDSET

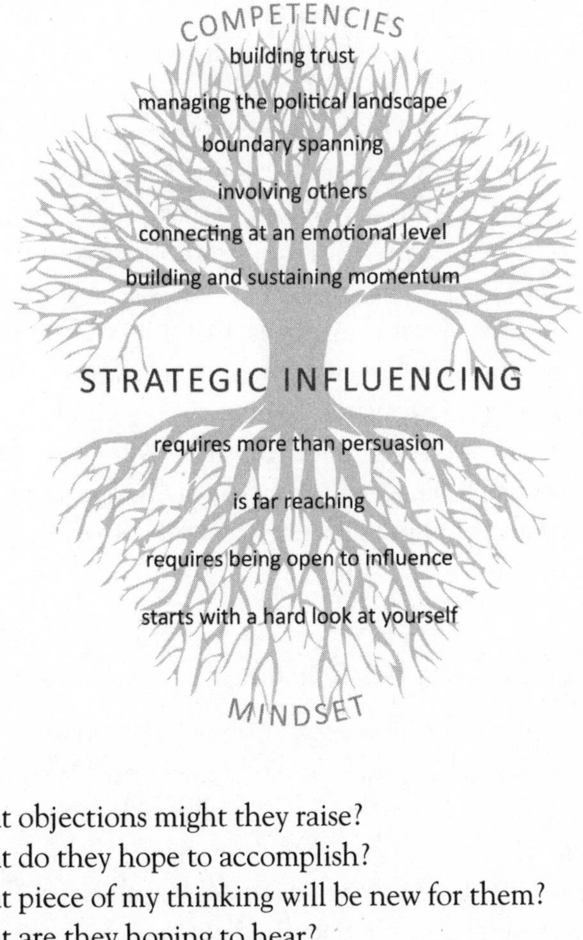

- What objections might they raise?
- What do they hope to accomplish?
- What piece of my thinking will be new for them?
- What are they hoping to hear?

Research on influence has in fact fueled the notion that influence occurs in finite, persuasive instances. As a case in point, much of the literature on influence is about direct influence tactics—specific ways of interacting directly with people to win them over to one's ideas. These streams of research do not mention the many indirect ways in which influence can occur, for example, through organization systems, processes, and culture (Yukl, 2012). Our education systems, including MBA programs, have also supported this view. How much of a curriculum is devoted to developing strong logical analysis that can be communicated through a presentation, versus navigating the emotions, values, and life experiences of colleagues to build long-term, trusting relationships with them? After all, your colleagues are humans. They aren't machines driven only by logical analysis.

Influence is actually quite different from persuasion. It does not happen in one interaction, but instead is built over time, on a solid platform of credibility and relationships. Time and experience with people are important for relationship and trust building, as they provide the opportunity to assess others' integrity and competence, to know if their ideas are in service of the future of the organization or just their own future. These assessments contribute to the relationship foundation on which influence is built. In addition, strategic influence is not over when you get the "yes" from others. In fact, with this type of change, conversations must continue as change is planned, implemented, and adapted over time.

Strategic Influence Is Far Reaching

Strategic influence is also expansive in relationships. Leaders may tend to keep their circle close to those with whom they have trust or those who are most directly affected by the work. But real strategic change is far reaching throughout the organization, and therefore, so is the work of strategic influence. Figure 4.2 depicts a lesson leaders have learned as they've developed their skills in this area: strategic leadership happens in the white space on organization charts—the areas between the formal structural groupings and the areas between the structure and the outside world.

Kevin Hart had to connect across multiple parts of the organization and work outside the structure in order to accomplish his key strategic objectives. This idea is related to the concept of organization as biological system versus hierarchy. Real change comes about through the connections that exist and are

Figure 4.2   Strategy Happens in the White Space

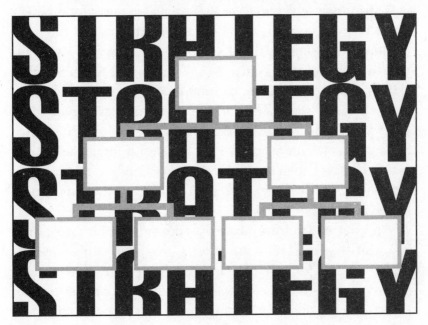

leveraged, as opposed to the reporting relationships. The work of influence therefore is to create and ignite new connections in the service of the strategic changes required. Because the current strategy has given rise to a formal and informal structure of connections that support it, if a new vision or strategic direction is to become a reality, leaders must break down walls that exist between those groups, so that efforts can be blended. These walls can take many forms.

One set of walls may be hierarchical, as boundaries exist between levels in an organization and strategic influence must be exercised to break down these barriers. Influencing upward is a necessary yet delicate art, as subordinate-level executives and managers have information and perspectives from their interactions with customers that are important for their superiors to hear. But someone who exercises strategic influence upward is attempting to change the direction that might have been set by those same individuals in the first place. It's an easier task when senior managers open themselves up to be influenced by asking for different perspectives and seeking input from those throughout the organization. Unfortunately this does not always happen. Downward strategic influence may seem to be easier. After all, isn't it true that all you need to do to influence your direct reports is to tell them what you want? From that point of view, you might not even think of downward influence as strategic at all insofar as it might involve the implementation of strategic initiatives. If influence is to be mutual, however, then methods of downward influence should not undercut the kinds of relationships in which two-way communication is enhanced.

Another set of walls may exist across different parts of the organization—different functional groups or different geographic regions, for example. Strategic leaders are acutely aware of the competition that can exist between peers: competition for resources in the organization, for attention, for power, for praise, and for the next promotion. So influence attempts can be met with skepticism and mistrust, especially if relationships have not been built before the influence attempts are made. Strategic leaders create opportunities for alliances that do not form naturally because the organization's structure or the work itself militates against them. These leaders reach out to people not because they need help on some particular task, but because they are looking for possible connections across the organization and beyond. That is, they build what one Leading Strategically program alumnus calls "unnatural relationships." This is no easy task, as it can be inhibited by organizational culture, structure, and measurement and reward systems.

Geographic and cultural differences also create walls within organizations. Different regions of global organizations are serving different markets and operate in a sea of cultural influences. Despite many similarities resulting from being in the same business and organization, market and cultural dynamics create differences that build barriers across groups.

Finally, a strategic leader who is working to ensure an organization's sustainability in the ecosystem cannot ignore the importance of influencing that ecosystem. This includes any stakeholders with an impact on the organization: customers, suppliers, strategic partners, community, governments and regulating bodies, analysts, even competitors. Executives might consider their organization's relationship with the external world as more reactive, such that their job is to be the most agile reactor to what is happening in the environment. While that certainly is true, it is limiting to think that an organization cannot reach out and influence its environment. Consider, for example, the impact various government regulations can have on an industry. If organizations do not attempt to influence those regulations, they can suffer. Porter and Kramer (2012) in fact argue that capitalism must undergo a significant shift such that leaders realize that their organizations are acutely interdependent with their environment and surroundings and must contribute to them so that the organization has a fertile ground on which to survive. Figure 4.3 summarizes the types of far-reaching boundaries that must be crossed to effectively create and implement the organization's strategy.

Figure 4.3   Boundaries to Cross for Effective Strategic Leadership

Vertical

Horizontal

Stakeholder

Demographic

Geographic

It's as Important to Be Open to Influence as It Is to Influence Others

Does love lead to labor, or does labor lead to love? This is the question posed by researchers interested in understanding the connection between the effort people expend toward something and their attitude toward it. Their findings (Norton, 2009) have come to be called the "IKEA effect," referencing the retailer based out of Sweden that designs and sells ready-to-assemble furniture. The researchers found that customers of IKEA actually value their furniture more than furniture purchased elsewhere, even if it is poorly assembled. The reason? After expending effort in making it their own, they feel more attached to it. Indeed, the effort a strategic leader expends in thinking about a strategic change, analyzing whether it is possible and good for the organization, and planning what might be needed to make it happens serves to increase his or her attachment to the idea. The challenge is that it becomes more difficult to remain open to new information that disconfirms the idea. Strategic influence becomes a delicate balance between being enthusiastic and charismatic about something yet open to the possibility that your own thinking may have flaws.

Strategic leadership is not about who knows best. Rather, it involves ongoing, collaborative learning, and that means strategic leaders must create a climate where they not only exert strategic leadership themselves but also encourage strategic leadership from others. Some executives may have difficulty believing this statement, particularly those who believe that being open to influence is a sign of weakness. If true strategic learning is to take place in the organization, however, executives need to be mindful of the ways in which they define their own strength and competence and the impact that those definitions have on others.

Here is a story that provides a powerful example in communicating openness to such influence. Torstar sent its top executives to a customized strategic leadership program, and Rob Prichard, at the time the chief operating office and CEO designee, was one of the attendees. He found himself in a somewhat odd situation: his role in the business simulation in the program was at one of the lowest levels, without much power attached to it. For nearly three days, Prichard enacted his role in the simulation constructively if somewhat quietly. During the debriefing, however, he was explicit in expressing the considerable frustration he'd been feeling as a result of not having his input sought out by the simulation company's CEO. He had realized that he could not influence the simulation's CEO if he never had the opportunity. Few other things Prichard might have done could have sent a clearer signal about his own desire for people to be engaged with the CEO in strategic discussions. He clearly wanted people to engage with him—and influence him—in the strategy process.

Communicating an openness to influence is important for a superior in interactions with those lower in the organization. This openness has several outcomes, including creating a climate that allows ideas critical for strategic thinking to come forward. It is also vitally important in peer relationships, where the competitive pressures can overwhelm such an approach. In a sense, openness to influence with peers is an outcome—a benefit—of having formed "unnatural" and trusting relationships. This is particularly important in the context of a strategic leadership team, a topic we address in the next chapter.

Strategic Influence Starts with a Hard Look at Yourself

Considering both competence and likability, who would you rather work with: a lovable star who possesses both characteristics, an incompetent jerk who possesses neither, a competent jerk, or a lovable fool? This is the question posed by Casciaro and Lobo (2005) in an interesting study reported in *Harvard Business Review*. Not surprisingly, people want to work with lovable stars and don't want to work with incompetent jerks. But quite surprisingly and despite what they might say in direct response to the question, people in reality choose lovable fools over competent jerks. In fact, if someone is strongly disliked, it doesn't matter if she is competent or not: people don't want to work with her. But if someone is liked, people are likely to find ways to use his skills, whatever they may be. Working with someone you dislike takes extra effort, and in many cases this can lead to frustration and even mistrust. When you are dealing with strategic change, this can have devastating effects. So it is critical that strategic leaders interested in effecting change through their influence first take stock in themselves. How are your relationships? Do people trust you? And because being a lovable fool isn't enough for the long run, are you also seen as credible and competent?

Being successful in the strategic influence process requires that people trust you. By allowing themselves to be influenced, they are changing their beliefs, attitudes, and behaviors in ways that you request. There is a level of vulnerability they are likely to feel as they follow you and your direction. In short, you must be trustworthy in your motivation, your concern for them and the organization, and your competence so that they are willing to let you take them and the organization to a place that is different (and better) from where they are today.

A place to begin is to closely examine your competence. Have you put in the effort to learn about your business and industry—beyond your own job function and responsibilities—so that you are aware of important decision levers for the future? Have you ensured you have the time in important roles—versus moving quickly up the ladder—to gain the exposure and experience you need for learning? Are there areas where you need to roll up your sleeves and dig in to learn more to truly arm yourself with the experience and knowledge needed to lead the organization forward? People who advance based on their style and warmth but lack technical and business knowledge can do true harm to the organization.

Similarly, you need to know your motivations and what is important to you for yourself and for the organization. Both are important for you in life, but in strategic leadership situations, people want to know that you have the best interests of the organization in mind. It is important for them that your passion for the organization's future is at the forefront.

People who are clear about their passions and convictions are experienced by others as more authentic, because there is clarity about the reasons behind their actions. That clarity helps you know—and others understand—why you are choosing to tackle some challenges and not others. In addition, passion and conviction allow us to persevere in the face of adversity, and when others see this dedication, it can become infectious. In chapter 3, we discussed Jack Welch's passions, which "often veered toward the lunatic fringe" (Welch, 2003, p. 298). It's difficult to get on that "lunatic fringe" if you don't feel passionate about your work. Exhibit 4.1 provides an exercise to better understand your passion for your work.

In addition to areas of trust and motivation, it is also important to know your own needs, style, and expectations of good leadership, because these areas will drive you to behave in certain ways that may or may not be consistent with others' needs. When your influence extends across geographic cultures, you will be interacting with people who likely have different expectations of good leadership simply due to the different culture influences inherent in their context. Exhibit 4.2 outlines some dimensions of leadership expectations where people from different countries show differing results. Take a minute to answer the questions in this exhibit to better understand your own expectations of strong leadership and how they may drive your behavior with others.

While strategic influence begins with a hard look at yourself, it also involves skills related to building trust with others; we will address these as we turn our attention to the competencies that are critical for strategic influencing. Before we begin, though, take this opportunity to broadly assess your own strategic influencing capabilities with the exercise in exhibit 4.3. We also recommend that in addition to rating yourself, you ask some of your colleagues to give you anonymous feedback on the same items, since effective influence is often best judged by others.

EXHIBIT 4.1
Suggestion for Development: Understanding
Your Passions

Start by understanding the focus of your convictions and passion. Think of yourself as a person, not just an embodiment of your particular role or job. Explore where your passion lies by considering these questions:

- What is the future you are personally hoping to achieve?
- What does it look like?
- What is exciting about that future for you?
- How does it fit with your personal values and aspirations?
- What kind of impact are you hoping to make in your lifetime?
- How do you define success for yourself, personally?

Now spend some time thinking about what is important to you in your work, from many different perspectives. For example, consider these questions:

- What are your own personal values for work? What is important to you regarding the ways in which your organization succeeds, how people work together, the roles various people play, and so on?
- What future state are you trying to reach for the organization? What will it look like? Consider using the writing exercise from exhibit 2.6 to clarify your own personal vision for your work, whether it be for the organization overall or for a particular project you are working on.
- How does your vision for your work match up with your personal aspirations for yourself? What connections do you see?

EXHIBIT 4.2
Suggestion for Development: Dimensions of
Leader Expectations

Think about the following dimensions of leader characteristics. Rank
in order the characteristics according to your own perceptions of
strong leadership. The characteristic that is most consistent with your
perception of strong leadership should be ranked number 1, the second most characteristic associated with strong leadership should be
ranked number 2, and so on. The characteristic you rank number 7 is
the one least associated with strong leadership from your perspective.

Characteristic	Ranking
Autonomous: leader is independent, individualistic, or self-reliant	
Authority oriented: leader influences others by formal status, authority, or position	
Charismatic: leader inspires others around a vision or values and high performance standards	
Face saving: leader maintains harmony and good relationships by indirect communication or avoiding negatives	
Humane oriented: leader is supportive, compassion-ate, and considerate of others	
Participative: leader shares power and decision making	
Team oriented: leader effectively builds and manages cohesive and loyal teams that work to achieve a com-mon goal	

Now think of leaders with whom you work who demonstrate these
strong characteristics. Are you more naturally inclined to respect
them as leaders? Similarly, think of leaders with whom you work

(*continued*)

who tend more toward the characteristics you rank lower. Do you have challenges working with them? In your experience, are there differences in the characteristics displayed by leaders from different geographic regions? In what ways are your expectations of strong leadership driving your behavior with others?

EXHIBIT 4.3
Evaluate Your Strategic Influencing Skills

For each of these behaviors and characteristics, use the following scale to assess your need to improve in that area:

1	2	3	4	5
Considerable Improvement Needed		Moderate Improvement Needed		No Improvement Needed

• • •

Understand your impact on others and how that affects the quality of collective work.

1   2   3   4   5

Build a network of relationships with people who are not part of the routine structure of your work.

1   2   3   4   5

Intentionally discuss and build trust with others.

1   2   3   4   5

Assess and navigate the political landscape without limiting your credibility.

| 1 | 2 | 3 | 4 | 5 |

Build bridges across diverse groups.

| 1 | 2 | 3 | 4 | 5 |

Understand the needs, styles, and motivations of others, and use that information to communicate with them and influence them.

| 1 | 2 | 3 | 4 | 5 |

Ask questions of others' perspectives to deepen your own understanding of their view.

| 1 | 2 | 3 | 4 | 5 |

Create ways to openly discuss difficult topics where there are conflicting views.

| 1 | 2 | 3 | 4 | 5 |

Create enthusiasm and understanding about a vision of the future in the hearts and minds of others.

| 1 | 2 | 3 | 4 | 5 |

Use aspirational language and stories to draw people to your concepts.

| 1 | 2 | 3 | 4 | 5 |

(continued)

Create champions throughout the organization to further your project
   or cause.

| 1 | 2 | 3 | 4 | 5 |

Celebrate and advertise successes to build and sustain momentum.

| 1 | 2 | 3 | 4 | 5 |

Be open to influence from others.

| 1 | 2 | 3 | 4 | 5 |

Developing Your Strategic Influence Capability

With the mind-set discussed above, you are ready to tackle critical
skills necessary for strategic influence:

- Building trust
- Managing the political landscape
- Spanning boundaries
- Involving others
- Connecting at an emotional level
- Building and sustaining momentum

Building Trust

Dwight D. Eisenhower highlighted the importance of trust when
he said, "A platoon leader doesn't get his platoon to go by getting up and shouting and saying, 'I am smarter. I am bigger.
I am stronger. I am the leader.' He gets men to go along with him
because they want to do it for him and they believe in him" (*Public
papers of the presidents of the United States*, 1960, p. 684). When

Eisenhower commanded the Allied troops in Europe during World War II, even his greatest critic and nemesis on the British side, Field Marshal Bernard Montgomery, said of Eisenhower, "His real strength lies in his human qualities. He has the power of drawing the hearts of men toward him as a magnet attracts the bit of metal. He merely has to smile at you, and you trust him at once" (Montgomery, 1958, p. 484).

Influencing others strategically is virtually impossible if you don't have trust in your relationships. There are many definitions and understandings of trust, and this is often related to character and integrity. In fact, studies of religion and philosophy, literature, business and government ethics, and psychology (Zauderer, 1992) have identified many behaviors central to a leader's integrity.

More recently, the work of Dennis Reina and Michelle Reina (2006) has been helpful in providing a structure and road map to build trust in the workplace. Since trust is frequently related to integrity, it carries such emotional meaning that it is difficult to believe trust can really be rebuilt once it is broken. People often believe that trust is shattered in grand events—lies uncovered, unethical behavior, and choices—and in fact this can and does happen. However, according to the Reinas' research with thousands of leaders, more frequently trust is both built and broken over time based on small subtle acts and common mistakes. Behavior along three dimensions can lead to trust being built or trust being broken:

- *Contractual trust*, the trust of character, exists when people mutually understand that they will do what they say they will do. In this area, people discuss their expectations to arrive at something that is reasonable and realistic for all parties, setting and agreeing on boundaries where needed. They are also consistent, and they meet their obligations based on the expectations that have been set.
- *Competence trust*, the trust of capability, exists when people respect each other's skills and abilities, seek input, involve each

other, and allow people to make their own decisions. It also is promoted when we support people in learning new skills.

- *Communication trust*, the trust of disclosure, is the willingness to share information in a timely manner, admit mistakes, tell the truth, keep confidences, and give and receive constructive feedback that opens dialogue when challenges happen. It also involves a respect for people when speaking about them (e.g., by not gossiping).

Aegon, one of the world's largest life insurance and annuity companies, is headquartered in The Hague, Netherlands. It operates in the Netherlands, the United Kingdom, the United States, Asia, Latin America, and Central and Eastern Europe. It has grown significantly by making acquisitions, including the purchase of Transamerica in 1999, and it operates in the United States under the Transamerica brand.

Clay McBride oversees the data management function for Aegon USA Investment Management, the asset management arm of Aegon USA/Transamerica. This function is responsible for ensuring the accuracy of investment data that are shared internally and externally, a critical function for businesses in the financial industry. When McBride assumed that role, he had a team of seven people, and quality measures indicated the data that were being shared were 65 percent accurate. He realized that this level of accuracy is not acceptable for the department: it created a lack of trust in the information provided and resulted in a high level of rework and inefficiency.

McBride set out to rebuild the trust by directly attacking the errors. He and his team created the mind-set that 100 percent accuracy was the goal. They reframed their thinking to consider themselves more of a production type of function and knew that if 35 percent of their product going out the door had errors, they were not providing the kind of value needed for the organization to be successful. The team began to exercise strong oversight of the data and discover root causes and solutions to problems they were seeing (competence trust). They were transparent about their quality scores, publishing them to each other, their internal customers, and their external customers (communication trust). This opened up the relationships they had with these stakeholders in new ways and created confidence in the data they were consuming. It also ultimately helped them to deliver on the promises they made to their customers (contractual trust).

At the beginning of this process, it was clear that the front office and the traders had less trust in McBride's team. However, by addressing each area of trust, McBride's team is now seen in a different light and is more of a partner in the business. In addition, by being more efficient and productive with less rework, McBride has not needed to replace team members who have left through attrition; his team is more effective and efficient with four members now than it was with seven before. This, of course, has increased the trust and respect of their work in senior management's eyes.

Exhibit 4.4 provides some reflection questions to assess your trust building and breaking behaviors along these dimensions.

With respect to communication trust, research at CCL supports the fact that people are often relatively unwilling to be open and honest with others, even though they want others to be open and honest with them. They prefer that others lay their cards down first, and then they might choose to share more once they've heard from others. However, laying down one's cards creates a feeling of vulnerability that many wish to avoid. According to the Reinas, though, taking the first step to open communication is in fact a high-leverage way to build trust. It creates a climate where others feel freer to share their thoughts and feelings too. Exhibit 4.5 gives some suggestions for getting started.

In a global environment, there are definitely nuances to building trust across cultures. The leader dimensions outlined in exhibit 4.2 (Dimensions of Leader Expectations) were developed as part of an extensive study on cross-cultural leadership, the Global Leadership and Organizational Behavior Effectiveness (GLOBE) project (House, Hanges, Javidan, Dorfman, & Gupta, 2004).

EXHIBIT 4.4
Suggestion for Development: Trust Self-Assessment

According to Dennis and Michelle Reina (2006), the following behaviors are examples of ways to build three dimensions of transactional trust: contractual, communication, and competence trust. Place a check mark next to the five behaviors you exhibit most frequently. Place an X next to the five behaviors you exhibit least frequently that may compromise your trustworthiness. Find ways over the next two weeks to display the behaviors you marked with an X more frequently.

[Items below are adapted from Reina and Reina (2006).]

Contractual Trust	
	I discuss my expectations with people so that we arrive at clear and explicit understanding of our mutual expectations of each other.
	I ensure that roles and responsibilities are clearly defined in my working relationships.
	I make sure objectives of a project are clearly defined, and measures of success are understood.
	I give as much weight to others' needs and interests as I do to my own.
	I keep my agreements or renegotiate when I am unable.
	My behavior matches my words.
Communication Trust	
	I willingly share pertinent job information with others.
	I create a climate where people feel safe to tell the truth.
	I admit and take responsibility for my mistakes.
	I give and receive constructive feedback.
	I appropriately maintain confidentiality.
	I speak about and to others with respect.

	Competence Trust
	I acknowledge my own strengths and weaknesses.
	I delegate to others, even though they may not meet my expectations.
	I allow people to make decisions, even if I do not think it is the best decision.
	I involve others in matters that have an impact on them.
	I actively develop my own skills.
	I take action to help others develop their skills.

EXHIBIT 4.5
Suggestion for Development: Creating Trust

If you want others to be open and honest with you but you feel hesitant to do the same, consider trying these ways to create a more trusting environment:

- Begin your trust-building efforts outside work—for example, at your church, in a community organization, or in other community service work that you do.

- When you find yourself strongly agreeing with what has been said because it links to personal aspirations or hopes you have, voice that agreement and the reasons.

- When you find yourself disagreeing with what has been said, tactfully voice that disagreement and your reasons.

- Rather than waiting to voice your thoughts and opinions until others have had their turn, try a different tactic: be the first or second person to put your cards on the table.

(continued)

As you do each of these things, observe others' reactions. Do they tend to share more or less of their own thoughts and feelings? Is the climate or feeling in the meeting more open?

If you have presented your thoughts and feelings in a positive way (even if you disagree with the prevalent view), you'll likely notice that others are more open to saying what is on their mind. Once you have tried this outside work, pick a particular meeting or group of people you work with to try your new skills. Again, observe others' reactions to see the ways in which they are more open with you.

In this study, over seventeen thousand people from sixty-two societies were asked about their expectations of effective leadership. The results indicate that perceptions of a good leader are culturally based, meaning that some behaviors may be associated with effective behavior in one culture but not in others. For example, of the dimensions in exhibit 4.2, only charismatic and team-oriented behaviors are universally and similarly valued across cultures (although some individuals may not value these and in certain contexts they may not be appropriate). The remaining dimensions (autonomous, authority oriented, human oriented, face saving, and participative) are valued differently in different cultures. For example, Nordic Europe, Germanic Europe, and Anglo countries tend to place more value on participative behaviors than do Eastern Europe, Middle Eastern, Confucian, and Southern Asian countries. Because people have different ideas about the essence of good leadership based on their cultural experiences, they will pay attention to different things in your behavior, including different kinds of behaviors that break and build competence, contractual, and communication trust.

So what is a person to do? One suggestion is to discuss the level of trust you are experiencing and feeling with a person. Ultimately making trust explicit in conversations helps to build trust and repair situations where trust has been broken. The three areas of trust that Reina and Reina identified provide a helpful structure for those conversations. The assessment in exhibit 4.4 is also a useful frame for discussions with others about the underlying trust in your relationship. Small mistakes and missteps that break trust over time are common. What isn't common is talking about those small mistakes and being intentional about rebuilding trust where it has been broken.

Managing the Political Landscape

Let's go back to Kevin Hart's strategic influence challenge: changing the way Kaiser Permanente approached facility expansion to achieve the organization's aims of rapid growth and significantly upgraded facilities. Hart had several different stakeholder groups involved in this endeavor: senior management, the information technology organization, the leadership teams of the eight regions, the medical groups, and also the organized labor groups. Hart realized the importance of his relationships with each of these groups and their relationships with each other, and so he engaged the help of a mentor to understand how to navigate the politics of the situation.

A book on strategic leadership would be remiss if it did not discuss one of the surest realities of organizational life: politics. At its best, politics is often viewed as a necessary evil in organizations. Stanford professor Jeffrey Pfeffer has studied power and politics in organizations, and he defines political behavior as activities to acquire, develop, and use power and other resources to obtain one's preferred outcomes when there is uncertainty or disagreement about choices (Pfeffer, 1981). Because politics is an effort in service of obtaining one's preferred outcomes, the exercise of political behavior can be seen as self-serving. But it is important to realize that those preferred outcomes can also be good—they are not necessarily harmful to the organization. It's just that judgments differ about the value of the outcome to the organization, and that's why those with dissenting opinions can interpret the behavior as self-serving.

If strategic goals were always clear, if the information necessary for crafting strategy were always available, if all groups in the organization held the same values, if decision-making processes and accountability were always clear, then there would be less conflict over the strategic direction and how to achieve it. However, these conditions do not exist, particularly in organizations that strive to be more inclusive in their strategy-making and strategy implementation processes. Similarly, because strategies represent both a guide for decision making and action and a plan for where resources should be invested, they are associated with power in the organization. Therefore, shifts in strategy equate to shifts in power, and conflict is sure to be generated by those shifts. The nature of strategic leadership involves bringing about change amid diverse and often contradictory opinions, so uncertainty abounds and the political landscape is a very real element of the strategic leader's life. Hence, politics is one necessary mechanism by which people and groups within organizations can reach agreement on these complex decisions.

But here is the problem. Because politics is a natural part of the strategic leader's life and political behavior can be seen as self-serving, organizational politics can limit the leader's credibility and ability to influence. This conundrum leads to a basic question for strategic leaders: How can they influence others effectively, given the reality of organizational politics, while maintaining their credibility and remaining authentic? The best leaders are quite skilled at this, and in fact, according to Gerald Ferris (quoted in "Six Aspects of Political Skill," 2007), a management and psychology professor at Florida State University, "If you have political skill, you appear not to have it. . . . Truly skillful execution of the behaviors associated with politics is usually perceived as genuine, authentic, straightforward and effective. Leaders who are not politically skilled come off as manipulative or self-serving." The developmental exercise in exhibit 4.6 can help you address this challenge for yourself.

EXHIBIT 4.6
Suggestion for Development: Politics and Credibility

Here are some ideas to keep in mind about maintaining credibility as you find your way through the political landscape:

- Because political behavior is often viewed negatively—or at best, suspiciously—examine your own motivations with care and honesty. Knowing who you are, why you do what you do, and how your behavior affects others is critical to ensuring that you are operating with the organization's best interests in mind.

- In communicating to others, speak about long-term issues that are fundamental to the organization and how your ideas help achieve these. Letting people know you are striving for the same outcome as they are will help them to connect to your proposals.

- Recognize that you might not achieve optimal results when the political landscape is difficult, but achieving satisfactory results is better than achieving nothing at all. It also shows that you are willing to give as well as take.

- Keep your end point in mind, and be open to other ways to get there. You might have to try several different ways or only one way that is very different from what you imagined. But usually that end point can be achieved in many ways, so do not get frustrated if your method of achieving it does not survive.

- Over time, show through your results that you are furthering the goals of the organization.

- Be careful about labeling others as political when you perceive them to be acting in self-serving ways. You might not have all the information, so strive to understand how they view their ideas as furthering the organization—not just themselves. In short, model the behavior you would like others to show toward you when they don't fully understand your intentions.

Ferris, Davidson, and Perrewe (2010) note the importance of trust, credibility, and apparent sincerity as a cornerstone of political skills. Their work, as well as the work of Bill Gentry and Jean Leslie (cited in "Six Aspects of Political Skill," 2007), points to these additional skills as well:

o *Social astuteness.* The actual words that are exchanged between people represent only a small portion of what is actually going on and the meaning of strategic situations. Leaders must be astute observers of situations, accurately reading between the lines by paying attention to nonverbal communication such as body posture, facial expressions, and tone of voice. They use this information to better understand and address the concerns others may have.

o *Thinking before acting and speaking.* In the heat of a discussion on the future direction of the organization or resources to achieve plans, it can be difficult to choose your words wisely. Politically astute leaders, however, do think before they speak and act, recognizing the emotion contained in these discussions. They are aware of their own worries about the situation, as well as those of others. They don't take things personally but work hard with their colleagues to get through the conflicts in a manner that doesn't leave lasting scars.

o *Networking ability.* Strategic influence doesn't just happen. Instead, leaders need to be deliberate and purposeful with their influence, meaning you must step back and reflect on your relationships with others while assessing the landscape of relationships around the organization. Then you use that information and learning when you step in to shape and enhance those relationships. Essentially you need to be strategic with your influence. The tool described in exhibit 4.7 of mapping one's network and using this to plan out influence attempts inside and outside the organization is helpful in this regard. In Kevin's case, after assessing the political landscape, he realized the regions had been operating independent of each other, so he informally formed a cross-regional, cross-functional team to oversee the planning and implementation of the seven hospitals. Previously individuals in this group would have been responsible only for facilities in their own region. He created a group that shared ownership of the whole and worked with this team to determine the feasibility of the overall project.

o *Managing up.* Although it is important not to ignore any stakeholder in the political landscape, skillfully managing one's superiors is critical because they hold the ownership of the current strategic direction. It's important to be seen as contributing to the benefit of the organization, including such simple things as ensuring your bosses' needs are met and following through on commitments. But it is also important, when you want to influence a chance in your superiors' thinking and actions, to consider timing. Floyd and Wooldridge (1996) suggest considering, for example, if the current strategy is new or not yet fully implemented. In that case, senior leaders are more likely to give it the benefit of the doubt and are less open to influence regarding a different direction. In Kevin's case, his cross-regional, cross-functional team was composed of people who were close enough to the work to fully understand what would be required to implement such an ambitious plan. These people were also credible in others' eyes, given their previous accomplishments. In their planning, they uncovered some serious challenges that could not readily be resolved and developed a proposal to scale the plan back a bit by delaying the opening of two hospitals to the next year. The breadth and depth of their analysis in looking at the situation as a whole was critical to successfully making the case to executives that these two hospital openings should be delayed.

Spanning Boundaries

In 2010, CCL was invited to Iraq to assist with the critical transition from Operation Iraqi Freedom to Operation New Dawn, representing the move from a military mission for the United States in Iraq to a diplomatic and civilian role run by the State Department (Chrobot-Mason, Ernst, & Feguson, 2012). The culture, processes, systems, and leadership between the US Army and

EXHIBIT 4.7
Suggestion for Development: Use Network
Mapping to Plan Your Influence

The first step in finding your way through the political landscape is to understand it. Consider a particular challenge you are dealing with and trying to influence around. Draw a "political map" to demonstrate who might be connected or aligned around potential solutions to this challenge. Position those with similar opinions on the matter close to each other on the map, and highlight those with the most power to affect the outcome. Consider all the expected opponents, supporters, and those who might be affected or whose help you might need, even if they might not have a strong opinion. Simply thinking through the various stakeholders in this way can be helpful. Once you have completed your map, go through the following steps:

- Look at the map to see who is grouped together. Why are those people aligned? What common goals, perspectives, and beliefs do they share?

- Strengthen your support system by asking those members who are close to you on the map to express support for the idea and give it visibility where possible.

- Generate interest among those who do not have strong opinions by talking about it with them, sharing the data and information you have, inviting their input, and developing contingencies to address the concerns they have.

- Lessen the resistance of those who are opposed by anticipating their arguments and building in compromises or solutions to address those arguments. If possible, talk to them and others to ensure that you fully understand their positions. In communicating to them, work to articulate the advantages they can reap from adopting your position.

- Consider the potential of work assignments. Are there people opposed to your ideas whom you can assign to various projects or task forces so that they will come to understand the issue differently? Or are there potential key supporters who have not yet been involved enough to understand the issues? Perhaps there is a way to get them involved through various work assignments.

- Find ways to support the legitimacy of your arguments by bringing in outside experts. Have these experts work with those who do not have strong opinions or are opposed to the ideas.

State Department were dramatically different, yet the two had to work in close collaboration to ensure the success of the transition and the role of the United States in Iraq going forward. General Lloyd Austin and Ambassador James Jeffrey were keenly aware of the boundaries they had to span across their organizations in order to carry out their work successfully. As General Austin said, "I knew we had to build a team of teams with the Ambassador and the Embassy. If we achieved unity of effort, we would have a chance to reach all of our objectives. We really thought about this, and we felt that if we worked at cross-purposes, it would be nearly impossible to accomplish both of our mission sets" (p. 4).

Strategic influence is expansive: it happens in the white space on organization charts, exists in an environment of cross-cultural work, requires virtual teams interacting with other virtual teams, involves a diverse workforce, and can expand beyond the organization itself. Strategic leaders must not just get individuals to align with their vision; they must also ignite disparate groups to work together because strategy is reflected in the coherence and alignment of the collective actions of groups across the organization and even outside the organization. This isn't easy to do: basic psychological principles serve to create cohesion inside a given group, resulting in an us-versus-them mentality. How might leaders turn that into an us-and-them mentality? General Austin and

Ambassador Jeffrey decided to accelerate the process of building a team of teams by holding a one-day seminar for their key personnel that would begin the process of boundary spanning.

Ernst and Chrobot-Mason (2011) describe three strategies and six practices to use when spanning boundaries. The first strategy is to provide opportunities for groups to understand and manage the boundaries around them. It may seem a bit odd, but this first strategy serves the purpose of strengthening the group's identity and sense of itself in the whole, so that it can then effectively interact and explore possibilities with other groups. Two specific practices to manage boundaries are buffering, which creates safety and cohesiveness by clarifying the team's purpose in the system, and roles and responsibilities to accomplish the work, and reflecting, which fosters the respect of other groups by sharing assumptions and perceptions of the role each group plays.

The seminar in Iraq began with the groups working separately to develop their own vision for success, as well as articulating their strengths and weaknesses in achieving their vision. Interestingly, when the groups came together to share their work, they found that their strengths and weaknesses were almost opposite of each other. For example, the military has strengths in the area of planning, while the State Department has strengths in the areas of communication. This realization laid the groundwork to see the possibility of the two departments complementing each other in achieving the full mission, as opposed to viewing the differences as obstacles to overcome.

Once the boundaries between groups are explicit through these practices, the groups can focus on forging common ground—that is, determining what they share in common in the service of the strategic transformation. One practice here is connecting, that is, building trust between the groups by providing opportunities for them to get to know each other better. Another practice is mobilizing, or developing a sense of shared purpose by exploring how they both fit into the larger picture of the strategic transformation. In the workshop, the two groups built on their respect of their differences and each group's articulation of success to develop a shared vision of success.

Finally, groups can move toward something new together through the strategy of discovering new frontiers. One approach here is weaving, or integrating the differences between the groups to create interdependence. And finally, through the practice of transforming, the groups reinvent how they work together to achieve the new strategy. In Iraq, the groups continued working together throughout the day to articulate each other's specific roles and responsibilities in the new vision. They identified particular high-priority issues and worked together to solve some of the shared challenges in those issues.

The work did not end with that day's session. To the contrary, the session simply laid the foundation for what was to come. As they began to implement the plans they developed, General Austin and Ambassador Jeffrey agreed to meet twice each week to ensure alignment at the top and role-model what they expected from their teams. These meetings were held face-to-face, alternated between locations, and became the architecture of what was called their "Battle Rhythm." They also set an expectation of inclusiveness such that any key issue was a shared issue, even if it looked at the outset as if it was primarily a military issue or State Department issue. They ensured that any communication was presented as one voice. For example, all briefings with Washington and the Iraqi government were done together. The story of the transition from a military operation to a civilian run, diplomatic operation in Iraq is a potent example of boundary spanning practices in action. Figure 4.4 provides some other practical tips that can guide how you use boundary spanning to create and implement your strategy.

Involving Others

In chapter 2, we discussed the importance of involving others in strategic thinking and collaborative sense making. Involving

Figure 4.4 Boundary-Spanning Practices

Buffering: Defining the team and its identity to *create safety*

Example practices:
- Provide group members with the resources, time, and space needed to develop into a cohesive unit.
- Clearly define the roles and responsibilities of group members.
- Protect the group from external interference and demands.
- Clarify boundaries to accurately differentiate the work of different organizational members.

Reflecting: Examining perspectives to understand differences and similarities and to *foster respect*

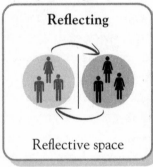

Example practices:
- Sensitize groups to each other's needs and priorities.
- Facilitate the exchanges of information and viewpoints across organizational lines.
- Serve as an ambassador across groups by representing the unique perspective of one group to others.
- Help members of different groups surface assumptions and beliefs about each other.

Connecting: Linking and bridging to create a third space to *build trust*

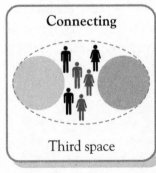

Example practices:
- Create a positive and welcoming environment for people to get to know each other on a personal level.
- Build social networks across the organization.
- Provide opportunities for individuals to discover commonalities across group lines.
- Create links between members of separate organizational groups.

Figure 4.4 (*Continued*)

Mobilizing: *Developing community* between groups by creating common purpose and shared identity

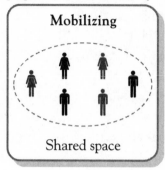

Mobilizing

Shared space

Example practices:

- Develop an inclusive vision and shared goals, and inspire members to unify toward the vision.

- Assist groups to feel a strong sense of belonging to the organization and its mission.

- Engender accountability to the work of other groups and to the shared goals.

- Encourage groups to set aside their differences and work for the common good.

Weaving: Integrating group differences within a larger whole to *create interdependence*

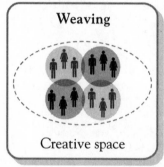

Weaving

Creative space

Example practices:

- Express the value of the unique contributions of each group and the synergies between them.

- Provide opportunities for people to integrate their distinctive resources to achieve greater success.

- Creatively reconcile conflict between people to uncover new solutions.

Transforming: Bringing groups together in emergent, new directions to cross-cut boundaries and *enable reinvention*

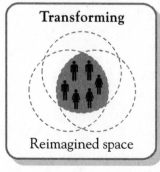

Transforming

Reimagined space

Example practices:

- Encourage different groups to reinvent how they work together when a new direction is required.

- Marshal wide-ranging expertise and experience across the organization to realize new opportunities.

- Create an environment where deeply held values, beliefs, and perspectives are open to change.

others in that process allows diverse and important perspectives to be represented so that the overall strategy is better than it would be if it were developed in isolation. Involving others has another benefit: it helps generate commitment to the final product when others participate in developing it. This is especially true in Nordic, Germanic, Anglo, and Latin European countries. While participation may be somewhat less valued in Eastern Europe, the Middle East, Confucian Asia, South Asia, and sub-Saharan Africa (House et al., 2004) it is still valued and worthy of consideration, especially given the importance that a broad perspective has on the quality of the strategy itself.

The concept of involving others in the process for the purpose of engendering commitment is probably familiar to you. We suspect, though, that when most managers think of involving others as a way of exerting influence, they are thinking of influencing direct reports. Think about how involving peers, bosses, and even those outside the organization might be helpful in your strategic influencing efforts.

Consider the case of Andrew Cole, former vice president of human resources for American Power Conversion (APC). APC makes power control devices and is now a division of Schneider Electric. Prior to the acquisition, though, Cole learned that the CEO was concerned about a lack of bench strength in the company. APC was not in a position to grow through acquisitions because it did not have leaders in place to take over those acquisitions. Despite a long history of success in terms of strategy and implementation, APC executives had paid little attention to leadership development. Cole was tasked with an executive development initiative.

In the early stages of this initiative, Cole realized its complexity. One of his biggest concerns was that he did not want to be seen as the driver of the initiative. He worried that it was risky to have this seen as his project, so his first step was to have the CEO invite several executives (Cole's peers) to join in a pilot program to try out some leadership development experiences. The plan was for the group to assess the program and experience and determine what they would need to do to support these efforts internally if they chose to continue down this path. In addition to getting more input on the process, Cole wanted to engage these executives in leadership development activities so that they would feel more committed to those activities. Although he had some ideas about what leadership development should look like in APC, he put those ideas aside in favor of bringing his peers and his boss into the development process.

Involving others in the process helps to generate commitment in at least three ways. First, involving others helps to create a common understanding of the entire picture. Through their participation, people have access to much more information than if they heard of the final product in a presentation; for example, they see and help analyze all the data, hear others' opinions, develop the pros and cons of various approaches, and understand the criteria in the decision making that led to the final direction. They develop an implicit understanding of the situation and proposed approach that is vital when it comes to strategy and direction, because executives rely on it to guide their day-to-day activities and they use it to evaluate and engage in conversations with others.

As a case in point, Cole had been in conversations with us about the linkages between APC's leadership development work and other initiatives in the organization. He had not yet discussed those linkages with the CEO. While the CEO was attending CCL's Leadership at the Peak program, he began to see the connections himself. He called Cole immediately afterward, and they began discussing it. He had come to a deeper understanding of the leadership strategy by participating in the work itself, as opposed to hearing Cole talk about it, and he was more committed to the breadth of the work when he understood it more fully.

You might even consider the benefits of involving those outside your organization in strategy development and implementation so as to engender their commitment to your ideas. For example, executives frequently use the tactic of running ideas by board members before actually presenting them at a board meeting. This allows the executive to gauge where the board member stands on the issue. It also allows the opportunity for the board member to have input to the idea before it is finalized.

A second way in which involving others serves to advance the work is it helps to develop consensus around the direction chosen so that the group will pull together to make it happen. They share beliefs and enthusiasm about it that makes them more likely to support each other and assist in the influencing process throughout the organization. In fact, one of Andrew Cole's objectives, beyond simply involving others in the pilot to get their ideas and their own commitment, was also to create champions of the process. He knew that ultimately these executives could be helpful by influencing others if they themselves were committed to the objectives. In fact, he knew his early efforts at involving others and creating champions were successful when he saw executives including their own people in the leadership development efforts.

Finally, involving others sends a message that others' input and perspectives are valued—that they add something to the organization beyond getting the work done. It feels good to them to have their thoughts and opinions listened to and acted on. These feelings of being valued have strategic importance beyond creating a more caring culture. When people know that they are needed, they are more likely to feel compelled to participate in the strategy-making and strategy-implementation processes in ways that go beyond what you can anticipate. They will keep their eyes and ears open for strategically relevant information, and they will exert the effort to bring forward that information to ensure it is considered. They will work harder to solve problems related to strategic issues. They will trust the judgment of others who value them and therefore will be more committed to directions set forth by those leaders. They will exert the effort necessary to implement the strategies and directions of the organization.

One of the biggest barriers to involving others is that they may come up with something different from what you have intended;

they may have ideas and plans that are different from yours. So involving others can feel risky because you might have to let go of your way of doing things in order to include others' ideas. The danger of not letting go of your ideas in favor of others' ideas is that others may feel manipulated. Asking for their ideas but not accepting them is a sure way to show they aren't valued.

Balancing this risk can be difficult, particularly for thoughtful and bright people who are generally good at solving problems (a description of most executives). In chapter 1, we discuss the importance of viewing strategy as a learning process and that it involves discovery more than determination. That is a helpful concept to keep in mind when involving others, and many executives find that it helps them when approaching situations where they need to involve others and demonstrate the value others bring to the process. Rather than determining a solution or an answer, they find ways to let the solution emerge through the work. In fact, framing the project as an experiment might be helpful, as we suggest in exhibit 4.8.

EXHIBIT 4.8
Suggestion for Development: Reframe a
Project as an Experiment

Think of an initiative or project that you are about to undertake. Consider viewing it as an experiment as opposed to a project. In what ways do you think about it differently? What questions or hypotheses can you form about it? What do you want to learn? Now consider the role others will have in your experiment. What information and perspectives might they have that will inform your hypotheses? Why are their views important in the learning process? What will they bring to the experiment that you could not bring yourself? How can you communicate the value that they bring?

Connecting at an Emotional Level

Strategic direction, alignment, and implementation require tremendous amounts of persistence and effort, demanding commitment from the heart. Earlier in this chapter, we discussed the importance of engaging your own heart by being clear about your passions. You also need to engage the hearts of others. Certainly elements we've discussed already (e.g., demonstrating others' value by involving them in the process) will help to engage people's hearts. In this section, we explore three additional ways to generate that commitment. All of these elements are related to the GLOBE leadership dimension of charismatic, a dimension that is universally associated with effective leadership in different cultures.

Engendering the commitment with others begins by learning what is important to them. Your logic for taking a particular direction in your organization likely makes sense to you, since it is based on your own assessment of what is important. Realize that your assessment will be different from that of others and that they will be starting from a different base that might invalidate your logic. For example, while achieving aggressive profitability targets might be one of the most compelling factors for you personally, people in your organization might be more concerned with changes necessitated by that goal and how those changes will affect them personally. Consider how those changes might affect the distribution of resources in the organization. Perhaps one or more areas will find their budgets cut, possibly in ways that seriously threaten the attainment of their goals. Try the exercise in exhibit 4.9 to see ways to reach out to others in your organization.

Once you have put yourself in the shoes of your stakeholders, you'll be in a better position to connect with them. You can frame your conversations in ways that let them know you've thought about what is important to them, considered how this strategic issue will affect them, and developed ways, where possible, to mitigate the negative effects. You'll also be in a better state to discuss the positive aspects of the future in terms that are important to

EXHIBIT 4.9
Suggestion for Development: Putting Yourself in Their Shoes

In considering others' perspectives related to a strategic challenge or initiative you are undertaking, use the following questions to put yourself in the shoes of your stakeholders:

- Think of yourself as one of your employees. What are your goals? What concerns have you raised in the past? In what areas is the uncertainty harder to tolerate? How will this strategic change affect you on a daily basis? Is there a way to mitigate the downsides of those impacts?

- Now think of yourself as one or more of your peers. What are your goals for your area? What concerns have you raised in the past that might be relevant here? How can you be helpful in achieving this goal?

- Now think of yourself as your boss. What are your goals and aspirations for the organization? How will this change help achieve those goals?

- Now think of yourself as one of your suppliers. What role do you play in the success of the organization? Similarly, what role does the organization play in your success as a supplier?

- Now think of yourself as one of your customers. How will this change make working with the company better? What challenges have you experienced in the relationship? What is important to you, and in what ways will this initiative impact that?

Once you develop your own answers to these questions, have discussions with these various stakeholders and ask them the questions directly. How close were your original answers? What did you learn from the conversations about what it is like to walk in the shoes of your stakeholders?

them. People are generally more willing to go along with the pain of change if they know they will be better off for it.

A second way to engage the hearts of people and engender commitment to strategic goals is to connect to the organization's aspirations. Thomas J. Watson Sr. once said, "Whenever an individual or a business decides that success has been attained, progress stops" (Watson, n.d.). Having aspirations for a different and better future allows work to have purpose and meaning, as people want to feel that their efforts are making a positive difference.

An important first step in connecting to the organization's aspirations is to have a good understanding of the personal aspirations of others. It's also important to then link those personal aspirations to the aspirations of the organization; in a way this is similar to the boundary-spanning tactic of mobilizing. A story from Torstar CEO Rob Prichard illustrates this connection. The businesses within Torstar had been separate and independent operating companies that saw their future as distinct from one another. Prichard began to speak of the organization as a whole, as one entity. He communicated the rationale for the operating companies to be together and interdependent in a way they had never thought of before. He also talked about what their collective goals and aspirations should be. In doing this, he created a sense of mission for all the people of Torstar so that they were committed to the entity and its future in ways they hadn't been before.

For some strategic leaders, it is simply a matter of remembering to talk about the organization's aspirations and link them to more specific goals and aspirations of those they are influencing. However, for most strategic leaders, talking about the why requires a bit more preparation. In many cases, it requires thinking more fully about what you are doing in the first place, as in the exercise in exhibit 4.10. In fact, talking about the why links to the concepts discussed early in this chapter about first determining what is important to you and what your aspirations are. If you have that understanding, then this element of influence simply involves communicating that understanding to the rest of the organization.

EXHIBIT 4.10
Suggestion for Development: Linking
to Organizational Goals

Think of a project or initiative you are working on. Consider the following questions:

- What is the overall goal of the project or initiative?
- How does that goal link to the organization's goals?
- In what ways will the organization be in a better place because of this work?
- What steps are you taking to achieve the goals?
- What might people expect to see as a result of this work?

After answering these questions, craft an elevator speech (which can be delivered in one or two minutes) that you can use again and again with various stakeholders to clearly convey how the work links to the broader goals of the organization.

A third practice strategic leaders use to capture the hearts of people is to enliven their language through the power of stories, metaphors, and images, as these elements of language have staying power beyond the traditional rational and analytical descriptions of the future. The Disney organization is well known for its use of ideas and words to create a culture that connects with people inside and outside the organization. Employees at amusement parks, whatever their jobs, are taught to think of themselves as members of a cast that is putting on a show and of their jobs as roles in the performance. Those words and that perspective have strong influencing power.

The executives we work with understand this power of language; however, many of them often lament that their strengths lie in a kind of quiet impact, as opposed to a charisma that draws attention to them and their ideas. And some are quite turned off by those who are more charismatic, feeling that there is little substance beneath the style. No one would suggest that these executives lose their substance in favor of style. But we do encourage them to consider how they talk about the organization's goals and various strategic initiatives in order to engage others in a substantial way. And there are some simple ways to do this that do not need to threaten a person's core being or style.

For example, how often do you find yourself telling stories to make a point? Stories are powerful because they create images in their hearers' minds. The human brain naturally links information to form stories and images, so using stories is a simple way to harness that power. Images help us make connections we may not typically make between different content elements and therefore can enhance understanding and recall. Images and stories also develop our ability to connect on an emotional level, as they engage the emotion centers of the brain. In all these ways, they are critical to the strategic influencing process. The developmental suggestion in exhibit 4.11 outlines a simple way to begin to use stories and to see the power that those stories might have.

Finally, we close out this section with some advice from a master storyteller. In an interview with *Harvard Business Review*, Robert McKee, a well-known screenwriting coach, offered executives advice about telling a story ("Storytelling That Moves People," 2003, pp. 51–55). Compelling stories tell about the struggle of a protagonist against one or more antagonists. Stories without struggle do not engender trust because they don't match life's realities. But stories that do tell of a protagonist who struggles and then prevails in the face of those obstacles are dynamic, realistic, and exciting.

As you craft a story to influence others around a strategic issue, consider the following questions:

- Who is your protagonist? A customer? One or more employees? A supplier? A key strategic partner?

EXHIBIT 4.11
Suggestion for Development: Making Stories

Try this exercise to practice your skills at using vivid language:

1. List three bullet points or phrases that describe your organization's greatest strengths. Then put that list aside.

2. Tell a story about a time when your organization was at its best. Our bet is that the three bullet points will be reflected in the story, but consider the different impact of the story as opposed to the bullet points on someone you are trying to convince to join your organization.

To adapt this exercise to a strategic challenge or issue whose outcome you are attempting to influence, try thinking of the future state the organization would achieve if it were to adopt your approach. What characteristics would you see in the organization should that happen? Now craft a story that describes how people will work together, how your customers will view you, how the competition will react, and so on. Consider sharing your story as you talk about your approach.

- What does your protagonist want? What is the core need?
- What is keeping your protagonist from achieving that desire—that is, what is the antagonist? Forces within? Doubt or fear? Confusion? Tough competition? Organizational culture? Personal conflicts? Social conflicts? Lack of time?
- What is it like for your protagonist to deal with these opposing forces? How would the protagonist decide to act in order to achieve that desire in the face of these antagonistic forces?
- Do you believe the story? Is it neither an exaggeration nor a soft-soaping of the struggle?

Using these questions can help you develop a compelling, inspiring story that serves as a powerful influencing tool in your toolbox.

Building and Sustaining Momentum

Building relationships as a foundation is vital for a particular influence or persuasion attempt to be successful. Similarly important is what you do after you get the yes. Strategic influence is not a one-time event; rather, it is a process that begins with the foundation of understanding yourself and forming relationships with others and continues through to building and sustaining momentum in the midst of strategic change.

Work can get off track in many ways, so a critical element of influence is ensuring that daily pressures do not become distractions to the long-term goals. One can do this by setting appropriate expectations along the way, searching out and celebrating successes, and sending consistent messages.

One of the challenges organizations experience with strategic investments is that these investments might not show results right away and this can run counter to people's expectations, so it is important to preempt this phenomenon by setting appropriate expectations along the way. We see the impact of this type of situation in the business simulation in the Leading Strategically program. At the start of the simulation, it is clear that investment in factors critical for the company's long-term success has been low and participants are quite willing to invest in these areas. But when they receive results after the first year, they are surprised that the company is doing no better—and, in fact, it is doing worse by many measures. When the information is distributed, you can almost hear the participants gulp and start reconsidering their course. They expected to see success after the first year, and the results do not meet those expectations.

The typical Western organization demands results right away, so executives are conditioned to make quick assessments of the value of various investments and initiatives. If they don't see early success, they are tempted to cut their losses and move forward. However, there are at least two reasons that success might not show itself right away in strategic change. First, these are long-term initiatives. Effectively creating a quality culture and instilling quality in the processes of the organization, for example, have been shown to take three to five years (Hendricks & Singhal, 1997). It is unrealistic to expect to see a return on that investment in a one-year time frame.

The second reason that results may not show themselves right away is that when organizations go through significant change, performance drops because the people in the organization are learning new ways of operating. Execution cannot be flawless right away if the change is significant. There will be missteps as people learn and the organization adapts. In fact, one might argue that a drop in performance means the change is progressing exactly as planned.

The danger of this dynamic is that people in the organization often interpret a lack of immediate success as failure, and this interpretation is a key threat to building momentum and expanding the stretch of influence. The strategic leader must preempt those interpretations by setting appropriate expectations inside and outside the organization. Exhibit 4.12 provides an exercise in looking backward and forward to interpret results properly.

In the absence of immediate results of strategic change, people may tend to doubt the direction. When that doubt becomes public, it can create a counterforce that is difficult to overcome. So a second practice to sustain momentum is to search out, celebrate, and communicate the successes of efforts that are under way. The point is not to stage events and programs but to show tangible evidence that you are on the right path.

One reason that executives don't do this is that they see the successes as expected and therefore simply move on. Achieving success, of course, is what they are paid to do. But while these executives believe that success in a strategic initiative means all is operating as expected, they are not remembering that others may still be on the fence and so the influence process is not complete. Those on the fence need to see tangible evidence that the initiative is working.

In addition, since strategic change is typically ambiguous, people who are already in agreement with the change may still be unclear as to what they should be doing differently. They are in

EXHIBIT 4.12
Suggestion for Development: The Progress
of Performance

Think back to a strategic initiative you led or worked on in the past. Since hindsight is twenty-twenty, reflect on the progression of performance in that initiative:

- What went exactly as planned?

- What missteps occurred?

- How did those missteps affect the key performance measures of your unit and your organization?

- How were the missteps interpreted? In what ways did you and others react to them?

- Could any of the missteps have been anticipated? Why or why not?

Now think about a strategic initiative or challenge you are facing. What do you believe are the prevailing expectations about your key performance measures and how this initiative links to those measures? Think critically about the potential dips that might occur in those performance measures as the organization and people shift their work, their focus, and their mind-sets. The most important part of this exercise is to communicate with others—both inside and outside the organization—to set appropriate expectations about what will happen. Look for every possible opportunity to do so.

a learning mode, and encouragement and reinforcement of their actions are important parts of that learning process. They may just need to hear that they are moving in the right direction and are working toward the right outcomes, even if they can't see the whole picture just yet.

Finally, it's important to consider the extent to which you can influence or even stop other potentially distracting messages from being communicated. If your approach to the strategic issue requires a change in people's behavior, it's a good idea to iden-tify any other organizational systems, processes, or structures that might encourage different behavior from what you want to see. Exhibit 4.13 provides some suggestions along these lines.

EXHIBIT 4.13
Suggestion for Development: Minimize the Impact of Distractions

As you begin to see successes with your strategic initiative, gather together those who have been part of those successes to explore their experience of alignment:

- What are the key three to five things they are doing to generate these successes?
- In what ways are the organization's measurement and reward sys-tems, information systems, structure, and other processes facilitat-ing their work?
- Are there ways in which these variables are limiting their work by distracting them or others from it?

The information you gather can be used in many ways. Ideally you would change anything that is sending inconsistent messages, but that may not be realistic given your level in the organization and competing organizational priorities. At a minimum, use this informa-tion to set appropriate expectations in others about what is realistic given these messages. And as you generate more and more suc-cess for the organization, use this information to influence upward regarding the impact of the structure, systems, and processes on that success.

Connecting Influencing to Thinking and Acting

Strategic influencing cannot be isolated from strategic thinking and strategic acting. For example, becoming clear about your passions is similar to how organizations become clear about their key drivers. But in this case, the clarity you are seeking is for yourself, not your organization, and you cannot have that kind of clarity for yourself without engaging in some significant strategic thinking. Similarly, being very deliberate about building your relationships with others requires reflection to understand and invest in unnatural relationships, as well as to find your way through the political landscape and keep your credibility intact.

Skill in exercising strategic influence tactics and building momentum for the strategic initiative also requires a combination of reflection and analysis to better understand where, when, and why this skill should be applied. Finally, and perhaps most obvious, the overlap between thinking and influencing is best exemplified when you involve others in the strategic process. That is, in chapter 2, we discuss the importance of involving others in the strategic thinking process to make common sense. Not surprisingly, involving others in the process has influencing benefits too.

There are also many overlaps between acting and influencing. Consider, for example, the work of creating alignment by setting clear priorities across the enterprise (see chapter 3). One component of this work is to ensure that you are not sending mixed signals. It's important to send consistent messages to ensure that your influence attempts don't cause confusion. Similarly, we can also draw a connection between strategic influencing and the need to foster agility. When viewed from the influence perspective, what better way to foster agility than to focus on creating true commitment across the organization to these strategic imperatives? With that commitment, people will go above and beyond what is needed in their problem solving and effort expended to make sure the initiatives are successful.

Earlier in this chapter we discussed some of Andrew Cole's efforts to engender commitment to the executive leadership development initiative at APC. Cole chose to engage in a pilot process through which other key leaders were invited to participate in leadership development activities. One purpose was to create buy-in to those efforts (strategic influencing), which he did. But even conceiving of the first step as a pilot represents strategic acting. Cole knew that leadership development was not optional, but exactly how to carry out that required development was not clear. He took action in the face of uncertainty and then invited people to review the process and make it better for the future. Herein lie elements of strategic thinking. As people engaged in the process, they shaped it and made it better for themselves and the organization.

This overlap in thinking, acting, and influencing does not happen by chance. In fact, they must complement each other if leaders and organizations are to enact strategy as a learning process. And as you will see in the next chapter, thinking, acting, and influencing also work together within strategic leadership teams.

Chapter 5

Strategic Leadership Teams

With Beach Boy–like roots in a Southern California suburban home garage, Linkin Park is one of the most successful musical groups of this still-new century. It won the American Music Award in 2008 and 2012 for best alternative rock band, and *Billboard* ranks it as the third best-selling artist/group of the decade. Of particular relevance to this book is the fact that Linkin Park is even more popular internationally than it is in the United States, an achievement that is no mere coincidence. No other American band has been more intentional about appealing to the international market than Linkin Park. Similarly, no other band has been so strategic in aggressively using social media to connect with its fans. And these distinctions are not the product of some backstage manager's cunning. They represent the mind-set of the band members themselves, who collectively are charting their strategic path in a technologically changing global market. Linkin Park is not just a group of musicians; it's a *strategic leadership team*.

While collaboration in making and implementing strategy happens in myriad ways and in a variety of forums, one that demands particular attention is the strategic leadership team (SLT). In our work with executives and organizations, we define these as teams whose work has strategic implications for the organization. Teams that are formally chartered to develop strategy or do strategic planning certainly represent SLTs, but other teams also qualify. Similarly, we are not necessarily referring only to the top team in an organization. Top teams are clearly SLTs (though they don't always function as such), but they are not the only ones.

The Definition and Role of Strategic Leadership Teams

An SLT is a one whose work has strategic implications for a particular business unit, product line, service area, functional area, division, or company. Just as strategic leadership is different from general leadership (see chapter 1) and strategic influence is different from general influence (see chapter 4), SLTs are differentiated from other teams in the organization by the work they do. If the work of the team is in service of the long-term success of the organization, then the team is a strategic leadership team.

It might be useful to consider a few examples of SLTs. One example is a team that is tasked with developing the next generation of products in a firm that has innovation as a strategic driver. The work of an SLT might also be linked to the overall strategy and direction of the organization in less direct ways. Consider, for example, the top people in a particular functional area of the organization who view their role as ensuring that the function supports the strategy of the organization. Some examples of teams in this category that our Leading Strategically program executives have served on include a distribution operations leadership team, a sales management team, and the senior finance staff. A final example is a team that is chartered to design a new process for the organization, such as a continuous-improvement team. Such work has strategic implications because it has impact across different organizational units.

The SLT is a critical element in the strategic leadership process because teams represent the confluence of information in an organization. That is, people come together and bring multiple perspectives, different sets of data and information, and different experiences. In effective teams, this breadth of information is blended in ways that can't happen with any single individual. In a sense, teams have the potential to fill the white space on the organizational chart where strategic leadership happens.

SLTs Exist Throughout the Organization

CCL has conducted research with thousands of executives who have led or served on SLTs. Using an instrument called the strategic team review and action tool (STRAT), SLT leaders and members rated several dozen aspects of the SLT's functioning and leadership, as well as members' interactions with each other. Illustrative items include, "Members of this strategic leadership team trust and respect each other," and, "This strategic leadership team understands the threats and opportunities in the external environment." (See appendix B for the complete set of items.) Our findings with STRAT validate the pervasiveness of SLTs in organizations.

In related research, an informal poll of readers of CCL's electronic newsletter asked them to tell about the SLTs they serve on (Beatty, 2003). While more than half of the respondents indicated that they were below the senior management level, 97 percent of the respondents indicated that they had served on at least one SLT in the past five years. As our respondents described the type of work their SLTs did, we found that they were engaged in the actual work of the organization: improving processes, running cross-functional initiatives, and supplying leadership at the functional level, to name a few. Based on this informal evidence, we believe that strategic leadership indeed occurs at levels below senior management.

That SLTs exist, however, does not mean they always function effectively. Sometimes they do not function well simply because members do not think of themselves as furthering the sustainable competitive advantage of their organization. This might happen when members get caught up in day-to-day activities and pressures and let their perspectives on the overall value they provide to the organization slip into the background. It's often helpful for these teams to step back and refocus, gain the big-picture perspective, and bring it into the foreground again. Exhibit 5.1 may prove useful in this effort.

EXHIBIT 5.1
Suggestion for Development: The Role of Your SLTs

Consider the work you do and the teams you serve on. List the SLTs (there may very well be more than one) that you lead or are a member of. For each SLT, answer the following questions:

- What is its mission or charter?
- What value does the team provide to the organization?
- What would the organization miss if this team suddenly disbanded?
- How does this team help your organization ensure its competitive advantage in the industry?
- How do you know when your team has been successful? How do you measure your success? In what ways do these measures align with your mission or charter?
- In what ways are the members of the team interdependent? Could you and the other team members operate independently and still be successful in the work of the team? Why or why not?
- Describe the two or three most important ways this team has impacts on other organizational units.

Consider asking the other SLT members to answer these questions and then spend some time discussing everyone's responses so that you have a shared sense of the role each SLT plays in your organization.

The Top Management Team as an SLT

Although SLTs exist throughout the organization, none probably has greater strategic impact on the organization than its top management team. Much has been written about top management teams in organizations, with no clear consensus as to whether this group is or should be a true team (Katzenbach, 1997), or whether leadership at the top rests on the shoulders of the CEO alone or should be shared by that individual and the broader top team (Katzenbach, 1998; Nadler, 1996).

In any case, the top management team has been an interesting entity for researchers and practitioners alike. You have probably observed your organization's top team and asked some of the same questions that researchers have—for example, are the members really a team or just a bunch of individuals who get together to share information? There is no doubt that working as a team at the top of an organization is not an easy thing to do. Katzenbach (1997) offers the following reasons why this is true:

- A meaningful, concrete purpose for a team at the top is difficult to define.
- Tangible performance goals (clear, specific, recurring, and measurable) are hard to articulate.
- The right mix of skills is often absent; instead, members are chosen based on their formal position.
- The time commitment is too high for most busy executives.
- Real teams rely on mutual accountability; executives, however, have excelled by being individually accountable.
- Nonteams fit the power structure; that is, executives are used to a hierarchy that provides clarity about leadership and decision making.
- Nonteams are fast and efficient; executives typically have little patience for the work of energizing and aligning teams.

Despite these difficulties, at least some of the work of the CEO and top management requires teamwork. In fact, Katzenbach (1998) argues that the best CEOs know how to distinguish between work that requires teamwork from the top management group and work that does not. These CEOs are also able to adjust their leadership for the group according to the situation.

The question remains whether the strategic leadership responsibilities at the top of the organization are such that the top management group needs to function as a team. And our answer is yes: the top management group should approach this work as an SLT because crafting a strategy for the organization and leading the organization through the learning process require the interdependence of members at the top of the organization and cannot be done in isolation. Exhibit 5.2 provides some hints on how to be successful in creating a top-level SLT.

EXHIBIT 5.2
Suggestion for Development: Creating an SLT at the Top

Creating a climate where the top management group functions as a strategic leadership team is difficult. The following suggestions (based on Katzenbach, 1997) can be helpful:

- Ensure that the strategy-making work is defined and viewed as a collective work product. That is, emphasize that the team members must apply different skills, perspectives, and experiences to produce the strategy in ways that are not possible by the members working on their own.

- Shift the leadership role. This might be particularly difficult in a top management team, as people clearly look to the CEO as the leader. However, on real teams, the leadership is viewed as a process, not a position. That is, it shifts from person to person depending on who has the knowledge or experience most relevant to the issue at hand.

- Build mutual accountability. Executives are typically accustomed to being held individually accountable. In order for team-based strategic leadership to occur, the executives will need to approach this in a different way. Katzenbach offers the following distinguishing phrases to make the point: "We hold one another accountable" as opposed to, "The boss holds us accountable" (1997, p. 89).

Why SLTs Struggle

Have you ever been part of a team that included talented individuals with resources and commitment but whose performance was less than expected? In some way, when they came together, the members encountered obstacles to their effectiveness beyond any individual's skills and abilities. Maybe it was a team that consciously or unconsciously adopted a norm of not challenging the leader's opinions. Frequently in these situations, poor decisions result since no one raises relevant information and perspectives. This is one of the many ways in which a team's ability can be less than the sum of the abilities of its individual members.

Although we do not consider athletic teams to be SLTs, they do provide some vivid examples of the whole being more—or less—than the sum of its parts. On one hand, there is the gold medal win by the US Olympic hockey team in 1980. It was an inspiring win because this group of individuals was not supposed to win given their talents and capabilities, yet combining those individual talents and capabilities into a team created more than anyone expected. Years later, in 1998, the US team was even better than the 1980 "miracle" team. That's because policies governing team membership had changed by then, and the roster was populated with all-stars from the National Hockey League. But the 1998 team did not advance past the quarter-final round. This "dream team" composed of great individual athletes just wasn't good enough as a team.

As it was with the US hockey team, it is a challenge for teams of all sorts to become more than the sum of their parts. There are other challenges, too, that all teams face that become even more consequential in the case of SLTs—for example (Beatty & Smith, 2013):

- *Disagreements on the team concerning the importance or urgency of proposed changes.* Some may wonder whether any change is needed because things seem to be going fine; others may believe that while minor changes might be appropriate, no major change is warranted.

- *Disagreements on the team about key priorities and investments needed to achieve the vision.* This almost certainly will occur if the team has struggled to create a shared vision and can also occur if the team is generally aligned around a vision and strategic intent but does not have a shared understanding concerning resource allocation. Often teams try to do too many different things because they fail to agree on those few most critical priorities on which the team should focus its resources. Data collected from the Center for Creative Leadership from more than twelve thousand SLT members over the past twelve years indicates that in a ranking of team strengths, the ability to be discriminating about what the team will and will not do is consistently at the bottom of the list.

- *Feelings of threat to one's position, resources, or other personal interests.* A proposed change might involve a shift in power or resources to one's own area of responsibility and/or identification. Alternatively, a change might be experienced as a competitive threat because of the status, rewards, or promotion potentially going to its initiator. It isn't easy to subjugate what seems to be in one's personal interest to the broader needs of the whole organization.

- *Difficulty in complementing a short-term focus on results with a longer-term focus on building capabilities, both individually and organizationally.* Most work teams have a history of putting their efforts into what needs to be done today. Developing individual and organizational capabilities, however, almost always involves trade-offs between the needs of today and those of tomorrow. And strategic change inherently requires commitment to developing new capabilities. In CCL's survey of team strengths, striking an appropriate balance between near-term and long-term needs was ranked third from the bottom.

Strategic leadership teams are also often composed of individual all-stars, such as successful senior executives and people with considerable technical expertise and experience. In our informal poll, only 40 percent of respondents rated their teams as effective or very effective in meeting their responsibilities (Beatty, 2003). That means that 60 percent of the teams were perceived to be less than effective. In contrast to a sports team, the ineffectiveness of an SLT reverberates throughout the entire organization and can have a lasting impact beyond the life of the team. In the most serious situations, ineffective SLTs can threaten the very existence of the organization, with impacts on people's jobs and lives. At a minimum, when SLTs have difficulties, such as balancing tactics and strategy or communicating throughout the organization, the consequences are likely to be greater than when individuals have these problems.

SLTs involve more people and more resources, and they reach deeper, wider, and further into the future of the organization. Their impact is felt more widely than the impact of any individual. That's why it's important for SLTs not to parallel the record of the 1998 US Olympic hockey team—great individual players but disappointing team performance.

One CEO we worked with told us a story about how a team in his organization had failed. The organization had just been through an employee opinion survey, and several issues were identified for exploration. Cross-functional teams were formed to gather and analyze information and make recommendations to senior leadership regarding possible actions. Each of these cross-functional teams represented a different SLT, and their success was important to the company's senior leadership. The senior leadership tried to demonstrate that importance in many ways. Most visibly, a different senior executive championed each of these projects. That role included selecting team members, scheduling and facilitating team meetings, providing information and resources to the team, and coaching the team.

One team's task was to examine benefits provided to employees, a problem area identified from the opinion survey. The team was populated with middle-tier employees; it did not include junior staff members or senior management (with the exception of the executive champion). It was expected that the team would make recommendations in the interest of the broad employee base and company overall. But that is not what happened.

First, not everyone on the SLT understood that it was a recommending body rather than a decision-making body. In addition, since the team did not access financial information available to it, it did not evaluate the financial impact of its decisions on the company. Finally, team members emphasized their personal and parochial wants and needs in their deliberations rather than looking at the issue from the perspective of the broader employee population.

The team did come up with eight recommendations, but only two were implemented. What's more, senior management had already identified those two ideas. In the words of the CEO, the other six recommendations were "either absurdly expensive or just totally inconsistent with something that a responsible company would do." The CEO commented that his employee population is very bright—95 percent of them have college degrees, and several have doctorates. Thus, the issue was not the intelligence of the individuals on the team. Rather, the team had failed to think, act, and influence strategically.

Making Strategy a Learning Process in SLTs

The conceptual framework used throughout this book provides an ideal way to highlight the critical role SLTs play in making strategy a learning process in organizations. In this section, we examine the role of SLTs in assessing the internal and external environment; supporting organizational aspirations as reflected in mission, vision, and values; identifying strategic drivers and developing the business strategy; developing a leadership strategy to support the business strategy; and performing or successfully executing the tactics supporting the strategy.

Assessing Internal and External Environments

All teams must have access to the information they need to understand the competitive environment, and the information they use must be valid and timely. SLTs in particular must check that they are relying on measurements and data that are consistent with the drivers of the organization, and not simply data that have "always been used" for this type of decision. SLTs should also ensure that they have information about the external environment and industry, as well as the internal environment of the organization:

- Are the measurement and information systems set up to give the team access to these types of information?
- Does the SLT have norms that encourage taking a strong look at all of these types of information?
- Does the team actually use that information when it is available?

A classic example of a team that might limit the information coming to it is a top management team that does not have sensors out in the organization to really know what is happening, what the employees believe to be important, and which processes are working and which are not. This team is overlooking important pieces of data that are vital in assessing the health of the organization.

The questions in exhibit 5.3 will help you evaluate your SLT's effectiveness in assessing the internal and external environments.

SLT Mission, Vision, and Values

A critical foundation of maintaining sustained competitive advantage and vitality is ensuring widespread and shared understanding and embrace of the organization's most important aspirations. This helps create a strong sense of collective identity and answers for people questions like, "Who are we? What makes us different? What do we care most strongly about?" It is vital for SLTs to be

---

EXHIBIT 5.3
Suggestion for Development: Assessing the
Internal and External Environments

Use these questions to evaluate your SLT's effectiveness in assessing the internal and external environments:

- Does this SLT regularly and realistically assess the organization's strengths and weaknesses, or is it privy to such assessments conducted elsewhere in the organization?
- Does this SLT understand the threats and opportunities in the external environment?
- Does this SLT keep abreast of technological, cultural, and market trends?
- Does this SLT have a global perspective?

---

aligned with the organization's aspirations. You can gauge your own SLT's effectiveness on this dimension by answering the questions in exhibit 5.4.

Strategic Drivers and Business Strategy

SLTs generally can only be as strategically effective as the organization's overall strategy itself is both well reasoned and clear. An exception of sorts to that generalization pertains to SLTs that play a significant role themselves in the actual identification of strategic drivers and development of business strategy. In either case, an indispensable element of team effectiveness for SLTs is the ability and willingness to make choices among many seemingly good alternative possibilities of activities in which the team could invest its energy and resources or, even more important, ask the whole organization to invest in. Strategy is inherently about

EXHIBIT 5.4
Suggestion for Development: Assessing
Mission, Vision, and Values

Use these questions to evaluate your SLT's understanding of and commitment to the organization's most important aspirations:

- Does this SLT have a shared vision of our organization's future?
- Does everyone on this SLT understand how the team's assignment supports the overall organizational mission?
- Is this SLT clear about the organization's basic purpose and core values?
- Is everyone on this SLT proud of the way it handles issues of right and wrong?
- Does this SLT exhibit a high level of integrity in its actions?

trade-offs, and the effectiveness of SLTs in developing and communicating business strategy (both the disseminating and receiving aspects of communication) will be a function of the team's ability to focus and align its work with organizational priorities. You can explore your SLT's effectiveness in developing strategic focus with the questions in exhibit 5.5.

Leadership Strategy

One of the most important elements of leadership strategy pertains to the desired culture in an organization, and that translates in an SLT to examining the influence processes within the team itself. Who are the most influential members on the team and why? For example, are power differentials within the team so great that only some points of view will be attended to—regardless of their merit? Do team members trust each other? If they don't, then mutual influence and effective collaboration become quite difficult.

EXHIBIT 5.5
Suggestion for Development: Strategic
Drivers and Business Strategy

- Is the organization's strategy discriminating? Are organizational members clear about what they will do and clear about what they will not do?

- Is there widespread agreement on this SLT about the most important organizational priorities (key success factors) needed to drive sustainable competitive advantage?

- Is the SLT clear about precisely how it supports one or more key drivers of organizational success?

Without trust, team members will have minimal impact on each other. The team will be far less likely to make common sense effectively or to collectively embrace bold strategic decisions with the levels of commitment essential to championing them throughout the organization. Because SLT members often come from different parts of the organization, they have relatively little interpersonal experience together and are also likely to run into apparently competing departmental interests and priorities.

Trust and strong relationships must also exist between the team and other key teams in the organization. It's important to identify, for example, the ways in which the work of one SLT is interdependent with that of other SLTs. Do these teams understand each other's goals and roles? Do they understand the constraints each faces? Do they understand their potential points of overlapping responsibility or authority? Do they know how the success of the organization is dependent on its teams collaborating effectively?

A third area for consideration is the extent to which the team sends consistent signals throughout the organization. How often have you believed that one thing was decided in a meeting, only to hear later that other team members are talking about it in different ways? These are not necessarily deliberate acts; people may not be purposefully spinning the decision in ways that work for them (although that happens too). Even when based on innocent but meaningful differences in understanding, the resulting mixed messages spread through an organization can confuse others about actual strategic direction and priorities. Here, too, the issue is even more important for SLTs than for other teams. That's because people across the entire organization will understand and interpret communications from the perspective of their own primary group (e.g., manufacturing, marketing, or sales).

This type of situation is common in the simulation used in CCL's Leading Strategically program. Say, for example, that three executives from headquarters staff agree to disseminate the decision that the fictional company used in the simulation will become a global company. Sometimes they even announce this in front of the entire group of corporate officers.

Sounds simple, right? When the headquarters executives then visit separate regional meetings, those regional executives often ask for clarification. It's interesting to see—once you go beyond sound-bite descriptions of decisions (e.g., becoming a global company)—how radically different interpretations of a decision can come from people on the same headquarters team—people who have presumably reached a common decision. For example, being a global company could mean anything from, "Be aware of what is happening in other regions, but it doesn't really affect your own decisions," to, "You should be talking to the other regions and making these decisions in common, because we don't want to duplicate efforts throughout the organization."

Finally, it may be as important for an SLT to be open to influence from others as it is to be influential itself. We have discussed how important it is for individual leaders to be open to influence, and this is critical at the team level too. This can help improve the quality of thinking, decisions, and buy-in within an SLT, and it can do the same with regard to the reactions of individuals and teams outside the SLT. Members should pay particular attention to the norms in their SLT regarding their openness to information and perspectives from the outside.

These aspects of culture and dynamics in SLTs also affect the team's ability to make common sense, one of the strategic thinking competencies addressed in chapter 2. Because making common sense inherently involves collaborative work, it is vital for SLTs to make it a team competency.

The ability of an SLT to engage in making common sense is a function of many things, including the authority dynamics on the team. Ironically, a strong leader can have an adverse impact on the quality of a team's thinking. We recently worked with a chief information officer and his direct reports, all of whom worked in a global organization. He was energetic, bright, and passionate about his work and was well respected by his team. However, his energy and enthusiasm were detrimental because people were reluctant to challenge him. SLT members can be reluctant to challenge a leader for other reasons as well; for example, they may have been punished for doing so in the past.

An SLT's ability to make common sense is also dependent on the team's norms and skills in having open and honest conversations. Most likely you have had the experience that during a team meeting, there is a pause in the conversation. You look around, and you know that people are not happy, yet no one speaks. The team is limiting its collective thinking by failing to discuss the undiscussable. There are many potential reasons behind such scenarios. For example, the leader may discourage open conversation by reacting negatively when tough topics are raised. One approach SLTs can take is to adopt norms that encourage open and honest conversation. At the same time, team members need a level of trust that allows them to feel supported when they do take the risk to be honest. Exhibit 5.6 lists some questions your own SLT can use to assess the part it plays in supporting your organization's leadership strategy.

EXHIBIT 5.6
Suggestion for SLT Development: Leadership Strategy

- Is this SLT encouraged to experiment with new or different ways of doing things?
- Does this SLT have constructive interactions with other groups across the organization?
- Does this organization foster executive growth and development?
- Does getting ahead here depend on performance, not politics?
- Are cooperation and collaboration rather than competition fostered?
- Is an appropriate level of risk taking encouraged?
- Are there few undiscussable subjects here?
- Are different opinions welcome?
- Is information shared well within this SLT and with others across the organization?
- Does this SLT work well together?
- Is this SLT composed of diverse individuals with complementary talents?
- Is there a positive sense of energy and excitement around here?
- Do members of this SLT trust and respect each other?

Performing

In order for an SLT to perform effectively, it's important that the team have access to diverse strategic perspectives. Often the easiest and best way of doing this is through careful determination of SLT composition. Careful selection of team membership at the outset allows multiple perspectives to emerge and interdependencies to be identified. If critical perspectives are not present, the ensuing conversation cannot be as robust as necessary.

Earlier in this chapter, we told about an SLT that failed in its assignment to review the results of an employee opinion survey and recommend possible actions to senior management. The CEO specifically cited team composition as an issue in that team's failure. The team included people who were senior-level professionals, but they were not in management roles and so did not have the experience necessary to understand issues from an enterprise-wide perspective. As the CEO said, "We made assumptions about this level of employees' ability to think more strategically than they were probably ever trained to think." Given the necessity for strategic and enterprise-wide thinking, he wished the organization had assigned managers and directors to the team.

You can think of team composition in a strict sense (Who specifically is assigned to this team?), but you can also think of it more creatively. For example, does a team employ or access temporary members—people who are brought in for a short period because their expertise or viewpoint is needed? In examining the extent to which a team has all the necessary information and perspectives available to it, it's important to consider how permeable its boundaries need to be.

Let's look first at the extent to which the team has a clear understanding of its latitude of action. You might be surprised to learn how much confusion can exist about this, even within the very top team in an organization. We were working with the executive team of a firm, and one area that the group felt needed improvement was strategic planning. Among the executives on this team, however, perceptions differed about what specifically the issue was. Some members felt that the strategic direction was clear but that they had little built-in accountability to ensure progress in that direction. Others felt that they had not set strategic direction at all but instead were only doing annual planning. As the discussions evolved, deep philosophical differences emerged regarding the role of the executive team in setting strategy: Should they all be involved in it, or should it be reserved for a smaller group of the senior-most executives? The executive team could not make progress on improving the company's strategic planning processes until it had a common understanding of its role in the process. This type of confusion in a strategic leadership team is not uncommon.

Have you ever been part of a team in which, after a couple of meetings (or when things get tough), members look at each other and ask, "Why are we here? What is our task? Do we have control over this issue?" This situation arises when a team is not empowered and does not clearly understand what latitude it has for action. This is a critical element in a team's ability to act strategically.

SLTs need to know their boundaries—what they can do and what they can't do—in order to act strategically. If they don't have this understanding, they will have difficulty creating strategic clarity for others in the organization.

Even when boundaries are clear, the SLT must also make timely decisions. Is this a team that spends most of its time talking about issues but never charting a course to deal with the issues? In many ways, this area of team functioning is the team corollary to an individual's ability to deal with uncertainty in the decision-making process. Some teams analyze and analyze before coming to some decision. That's an overemphasis on thinking, if you will, that can be detrimental in the long run.

Effective SLT performance also depends on the team's ability to balance and integrate short-term action with long-term action. This ability (or lack thereof) becomes most apparent when something unexpected happens in the organization—for example, the quarter's results are lower than expected. Does the team immediately cut investments that were to have yields in the long term, such as investments in quality or leadership development? In chapter 3 on strategic acting, we discuss the importance of a learning orientation for individual strategic leaders. The same is true for teams. For teams to act strategically, they must foster a climate of learning in the team itself. That climate can be affected by certain norms—how mistakes are handled, for example. Do members examine the mistakes in a nonjudgmental way for their learning value, or do they jump to apportion (or avoid) blame? Has portraying individual competence become such a dominant norm that there's a spirit of one-upmanship? Is it a risky place to say, "I don't know"? SLTs should also consider the extent to which they encourage—or discourage—strategic action in others. For example, what impact does the team have on the climate for innovation in the organization? Are there norms within the team regarding how others' failures are handled that reach out to the rest of the organization? For example, if the team is quick to ridicule other parts of the business that have failed, that will send a message to organization members that failure is too risky. Also consider the way in which the team as a whole facilitates coordinated action throughout the organization. Inherent in this aspect of team performance is the need for everyone to be in agreement regarding what that action should be. Exhibit 5.7 lists a number of questions you can use to assess your own SLT's effectiveness in successfully executing the tactics supporting your organization's strategy.

EXHIBIT 5.7
Suggestion for SLT Development: Performing

- Does this SLT respond effectively to opportunities and threats in the environment? Does the organization?

- Does this SLT strike an appropriate balance between dealing with short-term and long-term needs? Does the organization?

- Does this SLT waste its own or others' energy on unproductive activities? Does the organization?

- Does this SLT have the appropriate composition to achieve its purpose?

- Does this SLT have access to the information it needs to make decisions and take the actions needed to accomplish the team's purpose?

- Does this SLT have direct (or at least indirect) control of the resources it needs to accomplish its purpose?

How the Harlequin Leadership Team Made Strategy a Learning Process

It might be helpful to see how one particular SLT approached strategy as a learning process. We'll use Harlequin's senior team as our focus here.

Assessing the Competitive Environment

In 2001, Harlequin was in a strong and enviable position. It was the world's leading publisher of romance fiction and controlled the majority of the North American market. It had enjoyed twenty years of profitable growth. But the leadership team was not satisfied with the status quo. After all, the majority of the market in women's romance fiction represents only a small portion of all women's fiction.

While only modest sales growth was expected in its basic niche, opportunity for growth in the broader market was significant.

Organizational Identity and Aspirations

Shortly after taking over as Harlequin's CEO, Donna Hayes refocused the company on its core expertise and identity: a book publishing company (it had diversified in several ways). She also challenged the members of the leadership team to set significantly higher targets in their respective business areas, their record of solid performance year after year notwithstanding. Finally, Hayes challenged the identity of the team itself. Specifically, she redesignated it the Harlequin leadership team (formerly the Harlequin management committee). More than just a name change, the new label symbolized how the whole team (and not just the CEO) now would be responsible for leading Harlequin.

Business and Leadership Strategy

Shortly after taking over, Hayes held a two-day retreat for the Harlequin leadership team. As part of that retreat, the team identified key drivers in the publishing industry and metrics for evaluating progress and success. Their work reflects what we mean by "systems thinking" and "making common sense." Hayes and the Harlequin leadership team also took steps to ensure that their deeper strategic understanding and philosophy of leadership cascaded throughout the organization. In new all-employee meetings, Hayes and Harlequin's chief financial officer and human resource vice president clarified Harlequin's strategy for everyone in the organization. Formal leadership development opportunities were provided for the first time to levels below the executive.

Performing

For the next year, each of Harlequin's businesses focused its efforts on its respective strategic drivers. Each monthly business group meeting was organized to highlight current efforts and progress with regard to these drivers. Attention focused on the extent to which business tactics were consistent with the strategy and these key drivers.

By virtually all measures, the following year was a very successful one for Harlequin. Its earnings were much higher than during the previous year. It placed four books on the *New York Times* best-seller list at the same time—a first for Harlequin and a notable achievement for any publishing company. A key factor in this success was enhanced strategic thinking, acting, and influencing in the Harlequin leadership team itself. For example, members engaged more collectively on substantive issues than before, the team was more open to ideas from anyone on the team, strategic priorities were clearer in the team and throughout the company, and there was a higher level of energy on the team. After one year, the team had achieved virtually across-the-board improvement on items measuring strategic team effectiveness.

One year after its first strategic retreat with Hayes as CEO, the team met to review its progress. As noted, the year had been a successful one by all measures. But it also was a year of continuing reflection on the industry and Harlequin's place in it. It was during this year, in fact, that Harlequin's new vision (mentioned in chapter 2) became crystallized: world domination of women's fiction. In the context of the competitive analysis of a year before, the rationale underlying that new vision was becoming clearer. The expansion of its market to the broader field of all women's fiction offered growth opportunities otherwise unavailable.

That vision represented both a bold aspiration and radical redefinition of company identity. In effect, it represented a change from being a very big fish in a relatively small pond to becoming a big fish in a much bigger and different pond (somewhat different organizational competencies and key strategic drivers likely apply in different genres of women's fiction). To succeed, Harlequin's leadership team knew that it needed to make strategy a learning process and continue strategic thinking, acting, and influencing.

Setting a Solid Foundation for SLT Effectiveness: A Case Study

In this last section of the chapter, we look at creating conditions that will enhance the chances for success of your own strategic leadership team. First, we look at the importance of laying the right foundation for SLT success based on lessons learned from a five-year (and continuing) educational initiative at the US Air Force Academy. This case study reveals generalizable lessons discerned from years of experience using SLTs in a major organizational transformation initiative. We conclude the chapter with an overview of several developmental tools for SLTs that are provided in the appendixes.

At first it might seem that work of an essentially educational nature would have little applicability to other contexts, especially to business settings. In fact, though, the general lessons we've learned from this work seem applicable to virtually any context or setting. As evidence, we provide a brief background concerning the nature of the work. A brief overview of the content of the work will make it easier to appreciate what is important to know about processes applicable to most any SLT.

We begin with the concept of outcomes, an idea that has become pervasive and important throughout all of education, including the undergraduate level. Outcomes refer to what a student is supposed to get from a completed course of study beyond some mastery of the content (facts) of assorted subjects. For example, is there evidence that college improves students' ability to communicate effectively? Does it develop their ability to think critically? Does it develop teamwork?

To be sure, colleges have long claimed they developed skills and values like these, and other outcomes as well. Mere claims of educational benefit or appeals to institutional reputation, however, no longer suffice. A college's very accreditation today depends on demonstrating that its students actually achieve the school's specified learning outcomes like communication ability and critical thinking.

Consider figure 5.1, which depicts the outcomes at the US Air Force Academy. There are nineteen outcomes grouped into four broad categories. These outcomes are not entirely independent of each other (e.g., critical thinking and decision making share similar sub-competencies), and the cumulative effect of the four-year experience designed to develop these outcomes is the academy's mission: producing leaders of character for the nation.

Toward that end, cadets take a four-year course of instruction including required courses in the humanities, social sciences, basic sciences, engineering, and physical education, as well as character and leadership seminars, athletic participation, and diverse military training experiences. It is the academy's nineteen outcomes, however, that are the developmental targets of the instruction cadets receive and the experiences they have. Every required activity at the academy supports the development of several of these outcomes, as well as assessing their achievement. The outcome labeled Respect for Human Dignity, for example, is supported in the academic curriculum by behavioral science, English, and

Figure 5.1 Learning Outcomes at the US Air Force Academy

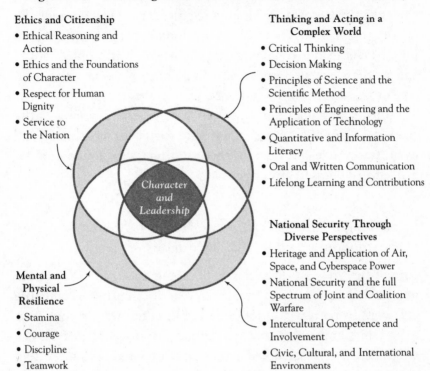

Ethics and Citizenship
- Ethical Reasoning and Action
- Ethics and the Foundations of Character
- Respect for Human Dignity
- Service to the Nation

Thinking and Acting in a Complex World
- Critical Thinking
- Decision Making
- Principles of Science and the Scientific Method
- Principles of Engineering and the Application of Technology
- Quantitative and Information Literacy
- Oral and Written Communication
- Lifelong Learning and Contributions

Character and Leadership

National Security Through Diverse Perspectives
- Heritage and Application of Air, Space, and Cyberspace Power
- National Security and the full Spectrum of Joint and Coalition Warfare
- Intercultural Competence and Involvement
- Civic, Cultural, and International Environments

Mental and Physical Resilience
- Stamina
- Courage
- Discipline
- Teamwork

Source: US Air Force Academy (2013).

history courses. (This does not mean that other courses or experiences do not support that outcome, merely that these courses have a formal institutional responsibility in its development and assessment.) Each of the nineteen outcomes has a corresponding set of courses specifically identified to support its development and assessment.

When these outcomes were adopted in 2006, the academy concurrently decided to invest responsibility for the institutional stewardship of these outcomes in a set of cross-disciplinary teams, each composed of representatives from the distinctive sets of academic courses and other activities formally identified to support the respective outcomes. The academy refers to them as outcome teams, and in every sense, each outcome team qualifies as an SLT (but with different degrees of effectiveness, as we will see). For example, the Respect for Human Dignity outcome team includes faculty representatives from the freshman psychology course, a junior-level leadership course, a junior-level philosophy course, and a senior-level literature course; it is chaired by one of the academy's academic department heads.

With that background, let's look at several key lessons the academy learned from its experience with outcome teams and what its example can teach us about setting a solid foundation for SLT effectiveness in any organization.

Foundational Principle 1: Ensure There Is Shared Understanding About an SLT's Purpose

One of the greatest obstacles to outcome team (OT) effectiveness at the academy was the widespread inclination to construe OT work in narrowly functional and habitual ways rather than in systemic and strategic ways. In many, if not most, cases, OT assignments were perceived as administrative tedium rather than transformational (strategic) work. Despite communication efforts to the contrary, often the message heard about OT responsibilities was, "We need to collect unnecessary and unhelpful quantitative data, then put it in a three-ring binder that some unknown bureaucrat will probably never look at anyway."

In truth, the work of OTs, and the role of outcomes in education more generally, has required a profound reframing of how faculty members construe the purposes of education. This reframing has been driven by sweeping changes over the past decade that accrediting agencies have imposed on all colleges and universities in the country: in essence, to demonstrate that each institution's educational practices actually do achieve its stated outcomes. Outcome teams are the most distinctive and critical element of the academy's strategy for meeting this mandate.

In terms of any particular college teacher's experience, this mandate requires adopting a point of view something like this: "My task [as, say, a professor of history] is to use the Civil War to develop my students' critical thinking and communicative abilities, as well as to instill an appreciation for our national heritage—and credibly demonstrate I've done all that." In that way, serving on an OT required adopting perspectives and behaviors often outside the comfort zone of most faculty members' more disciplinary-focused training and experience. Even more, becoming an effective OT required developing a shared understanding on the team of that new view of the faculty's collective educational responsibilities.

There were other challenges to developing shared understanding on OTs. Probably the most difficult was lack of shared understanding (and commitment) among the heads of the twenty or so academic departments providing representatives to the various OTs. These department heads—very senior leaders in the academy's hierarchy—had themselves officially voted in the novel OT-based approach to education, but in many cases, they did not communicate to their department members that it was important and valuable to work on OTs. Another challenge involved high levels of turnover among faculty OT members, which exacerbated team cohesiveness and shared understanding.

While educational philosophy, practices, and politics represented strategic challenges to the academy's OTs, it is important to understand that SLTs in any context are likely to be challenged in their own ways in developing shared understanding of their roles and strategic purposes. Almost by definition, it's a requirement of SLT effectiveness to reframe the way it looks at how the organization and the SLT members' respective functions within it need to work together for the organization to be strategically successful. Experience at the US Air Force Academy suggests that in all new SLTs, there will be a strong tendency to persist in seeing things through old rather than new lenses even when parroting the new words.

Foundational Principle 2: SLT Members Must Translate Organizational Strategy into Specific Team Tactics

Having a shared understanding of an SLT's purpose does not guarantee SLT effectiveness. We have described some of the obstacles and inertia that thwarted an understanding and embrace by OTs of the US Air Force Academy's new strategy for educational excellence and thus affected the OTs' ability to fulfill their related purposes. Each SLT must translate its shared understanding of the organizational strategy into specific tactics needed to carry out the strategy.

Consider the case of the Critical Thinking OT at the academy. One important tactic this OT implemented in support of the broader strategy was to administer a nationally standardized test to random samples of freshmen and senior cadets. It tested students' ability to think critically by presenting a series of problems that were not difficult technically (e.g., the problem did not demand complex math skills) but nonetheless challenged the student's ability to make reasoned judgments about the credibility of various propositions. For example, does a brief description of the relationship between two variables provide enough information to conclude that one caused the other? One reason this test was selected was that its methodology involved students' writing short answers to standardized problem scenarios that were graded by faculty at the same school using rigorous and specific scoring protocols. While this required more work than a machine-scored test, the feature was deemed useful to the OT's ability to understand even more completely what developing critical thinking looked like in practice. In becoming deeply familiar with the rationale used to score the test's standardized scenarios, faculty learned how they could apply it in designing discipline-specific versions to better develop and test critical thinking in their respective courses' exams. The OT considered this an important new tactic in accomplishing its purpose.

In an analogous way, all OTs need to translate organizational strategy into team tactics. That is challenging because aligning SLT tactics with organizational strategy may require changing familiar patterns of thought and action.

Foundational Principle 3: SLTs Should Make Strategy a Learning Process

The example of how the Critical Thinking OT discovered ways to write course exam questions that could better assess required course content and critical thinking is also a good example of making strategy a learning process. We underscore the word *process* because no one on the OT believed that discovery would immediately result in educational practices that could thereafter be implemented widespread in cookie-cutter style to ensure good critical thinking in students. It was one further step in an ongoing process of making systematic, data-based improvements in teaching, lesson after lesson, exam after exam, semester after semester. For example, insights about how test questions could be better crafted to assess critical thinking naturally would lead to insights about how course subject matter could be presented differently in the classroom through different kinds of homework, class discussions, and so on. Similar cycles of assessment-based improvement efforts occurred in all of the OTs, as in experiments assessing the effectiveness of digital videotape feedback of students' oral presentations to improve subsequent oral presentation quality.

SLTs should think of their work in implementing tactics aligned with overall strategy as hypotheses to be tested and refined over time rather than as procedures to be standardized and set forever in concrete. SLTs need to keep learning from experience and thereby help their organizations continuously adapt to the changing competitive environment.

Foundational Principle 4: Senior Organizational Leaders Must Credibly Demonstrate Their Commitment to the SLTs' Work

For several years, much of the resistance within the US Air Force Academy's OTs to this additional duty was that it seemed to many team members that their OT work was not strategically important to senior leaders. To be sure, those senior leaders made occasional public affirmations about the importance of the OTs in carrying out the academy's mission, but there never seemed to be any real or tangible evidence of true senior-level interest or support beyond the rhetoric of periodic "all-hands" meetings. This situation changed rather dramatically in 2012 as a result of two new institutional practices implemented that year.

One was adoption of a balanced scorecard approach to strategic planning. In the new institutional scorecard, the most important goal (that for which all other dimensions of institutional performance played a supporting role) was ensuring that the academy's educational and training activities develop leaders of character who embody the nineteen outcomes. And as is inherent in a scorecard approach, metrics were developed to indicate levels of institutional effectiveness in key success areas. In this case, metrics would be provided to the academy's senior leadership on how effectively the OTs were developing and assessing the respective outcomes. The adoption of an institutional balanced scorecard that was transparent to the entire organization was a big step in demonstrating that senior leaders were diligently monitoring the performance of the OTs and not just paying lip-service to them.

The other new practice that elevated the perceived importance of OT work was a significant change in the format of the monthly meeting of faculty council, the formal leadership body of the faculty that included the dean and heads of the academic departments and major faculty staff agencies. Starting in fall 2012, every monthly meeting of the faculty council included presentations by the leaders of two OTs on the status of their teams' work, as well as follow-on dialogue among members of the whole faculty council about progress in developing and assessing those outcomes. Part of the rationale for the inclusion of this new emphasis on OTs in faculty council meetings was recognition that oversight and guidance of OT work were among the most strategic activities the council could be engaged in.

In emphasizing the importance for senior organizational leaders to credibly demonstrate their commitment to SLTs in ways that go beyond, for example, comments in public forums, we are not implying that the latter are unimportant or insincere. It is our experience, though, that senior leaders sometimes act as though they believe that if they say something is important, then others throughout the organization will follow through with action. Such assumptions become particularly questionable when those senior leaders fail to set clear priorities about what is most important. When everything is said to be important, nothing is. And in that situation two things happen: credibility suffers, and people become confused. Both of those detract from organizational effectiveness. That's why senior leaders must take actions (not just say words) that tangibly enhance the likelihood of SLT success.

Developing Your Own Strategic Leadership Team

To close out this chapter, we turn to several tools to help you develop your own SLT. They are based on the STRAT instrument mentioned earlier in the chapter. STRAT allows SLT members to rate the team on several diverse aspects of the team's overall strategic effectiveness. Its purpose is to generate conversation within the team about the team's effectiveness.

You also should notice that the STRAT items can be categorized in terms of the various elements of the strategic process presented throughout this book. Exhibits 5.3 through 5.7 used designated subsets of the STRAT items to look at how SLTs impact respective elements of that process.

Appendix B provides general instructions for completing the STRAT instrument as well as the specific STRAT items.

In appendix C, we provide specific tips for using the STRAT instrument with your team, instructions for preparing your team to complete STRAT, and procedures for scoring and debriefing STRAT with your team.

Appendix D provides comparison data for the STRAT items. We've collected data on how nearly ten thousand managers and executives rated their respective SLTs on the STRAT items. The item averages and standard deviations based on this data are shown in this appendix.

We invite you to use these tools with your SLTs to assess and improve their strategic effectiveness. We believe you will find, as we have, that nearly every SLT has at least one or two things it can do differently to be even more strategic. We also believe you will find, again as we have, that because SLTs are embedded in the organization's context, there are certain organization-level variables (e.g., culture, structure, systems) that have an impact on these teams. The next chapter will help you better understand the influence of those variables so that you and your team can be more strategic within their context.

Chapter 6

Leadership Strategies for Superior Performance

Up to now we've been focusing on the skills and perspectives individual leaders and leadership teams need to be highly strategic. In this chapter, we turn to the broader organizational context and the process of crafting leadership strategies to foster high-performing organizational cultures.

Unleashing Performance Potential

In the pursuit of superior performance, business strategy and leadership strategy go hand-in-hand. They are the science and the art of achieving the full performance potential of the organization. If business strategy indicates how the organization plans to position itself for superior performance, leadership strategy acts as the human enabler to unleash the potential of individuals and groups throughout the organization. *Leadership strategy* makes explicit how many leaders we need, of what kind, where, with what skills, and behaving in what fashion individually and collectively to achieve the total success we seek (Pasmore, 2009).

Our experience working with and studying organizations across the world suggests that superior-performing organizations tend to practice strategic leadership as an iterative, ongoing learning process. As organizational leaders become increasingly competent at scanning the horizon for future opportunity, translating that vision of future opportunity into coherent organizational strategies, unleashing the human potential to execute consistently on strategic priorities, and adapting to external change and internal conditions, they are more likely to reap the full performance potential of the organization.

Bridging the Strategy/Performance Gap

Our interaction with over twenty thousand senior leaders every year brings to light that the science of strategy—the process of developing the strategic lens to guide organizational decision making—is quickly learned and relatively well understood at the cognitive level. Although this process is not necessarily easy, our leaders are becoming more sophisticated at applying strategy models to understand the competitive environment and formulate business strategies to pursue our organizational missions. Even so, we often hear such comments as the following:

> *Our people lack direction:* "So much fuss with the international markets and new strategies takes us away from our traditional customers here in Spain. I guess someone knows where we are going but I sure don't."
>
> *Our people lack alignment:* "Everybody is doing their own thing, fighting for their own markets and interests so of course I will defend my territory too."
>
> *Our people lack commitment:* "I liked the old company better. . . . It made some sense to me, and the new orientation is really not so motivating."

Increasingly we see gaps between the strategic intent of business executives and scenarios that are played out by people throughout the organization. In fact, studies show that up to 95 percent of employees are actually unaware of or do not understand their organization's strategy. When strategy lacks meaning for people, it is highly unlikely that they will assimilate the strategic directives and perform to their highest potential. Gaining commitment and aligning individuals with the overarching organizational aim require investing time and energy into crafting people-oriented strategies that bring the business model to life.

The power of linking this level of personal commitment with the strategic imperatives of the organization is crystal clear when speaking to Francesc Mateu, director of Intermón-Oxfam in Catalonia, Spain: "There is an identity which is quite strong here. Not everyone perceives it in exactly the same way but people are absolutely committed to helping others through our work, eliminating poverty and spreading certain values. This is what our work means to us and this is what our strategies help us do."

The Desire to Perform

To gain true commitment to achieving organizational aims, leaders must craft strategies that address the beliefs, processes, systems, and structures that influence the behaviors of people: how they interact with each other; how they do their work; and, most important, how they feel about the work they do—in short, the recognition that business is personal and that people behave according to deeply ingrained values that give meaning to what they do.

Strategic leaders motivate others through personal connection and inspire them to work together in pursuit of a superordinate goal that each individual can somehow identify with.

Intermón-Oxfam's director of people and organization, Pilar Orenes, sees a deep personal connection of leaders with the organizational aims and feels that this helps them connect with and motivate others to achieve the strategy: "The fact that our leaders love the work we do opens the door to connecting with people throughout the organization. People strive to perform because we all believe that our work is important. We see its importance when we aid others, and we feel its importance."

The Conditions to Perform

No behavior occurs in a vacuum. Individuals and teams always exercise leadership in particular organizational settings that can vary dramatically in the way they encourage the strategic leadership we've been describing. While there is little conclusive evidence regarding standard leadership practices applicable across organizations, there is strong evidence for three conditions that are important for the performance of individuals that has impacts on the performance outcomes of the organization at large: the motivation to perform, the ability to perform, and a work context that provides an opportunity to perform (Blumberg & Pringle, 1982; Dinwoodie, 2011). When leaders create a work context that brings together the motivation, ability, and opportunity to perform and nest that in a solid strategic framework, they have a high probability of achieving the performance potential inherent in the organization. We define *performance potential* as the latent organizational vitality that leaders harness in pursuit of the strategic objectives of the organization.

The director of Talent at Banco de Credito of Bolivia, Miguel Solis, recently described it this way at the closing ceremony of an executive leadership program: "We see so clearly the desire of you, our leaders, to succeed. We provide training, coaching, and support for you to be strong managers and wise leaders. Our joint commitment, together, must be to find those business opportunities for you to perform and for your people to perform so that Banco de Credito continues to perform."

Unleashing the full performance potential of the organization requires intentionality. Strategic leaders view performance as a resolute requirement, and they intentionally create the conditions for people to achieve performance success within the organization.

The Culture to Perform

The extent to which organizational conditions facilitate or inhibit the successful execution of business strategies stems from the combined effect of an organization's culture, structure, systems, and processes. The culture that leaders define and shape over time determines the behavior of individuals within the organization (Hofstede, Neuijen, Ohayv, & Sanders, 1990; Schein, 1992; Cunha & Cooper, 2002; McGuire & Rhodes, 2009; Dinwoodie, 2005, 2011). It falls on leaders to shape a culture that elicits strong identification on the part of individuals with the organizational aims and motivates them to release their collective potential in the pursuit of superior performance.

Again, Intermón-Oxfam serves as an example: "Our work has changed so much as we expand throughout Latin America and Africa. What remains constant is our culture of dedication and commitment to doing our work well so that we benefit others. How we do our work, the systems we use and structures we operate under must always evolve to support us as our external environment and strategic objectives change," says executive director Jose María Vera.

In the following section, we look at the elements that are critical for senior leaders to consider in order to craft leadership strategies that tap the performance potential of the organization and enable individuals to execute successfully on the business strategies.

Leadership Strategies of Superior-Performing Organizations

At the beginning of this book, we highlighted the increasing complexity of today's business environment and the difficulties that leaders face to implement their strategic plans and achieve superior performance. Surveys of CEOs show that one critical factor for determining the fate of the organization is the quality of their leadership talent. Similarly, HR analytics expert McBassi & Company (Bassi & McMurrer, 2011) concludes, "Superior human capital is an extremely powerful predictor of an organization's ability to outperform its competition."

Superior-performing organizations invest in human capital and back up that investment with leadership strategies that bring together four crucial elements: strategic drivers, leadership culture, talent systems, and organizational design. Figure 6.1 illustrates the critical elements to consider when formulating leadership strategies that act as enablers of business strategies.

Many organizations fail to execute sound, smart, complex strategies because their leadership is simply not capable of implementation. The leadership culture must function at a level of complexity at least on par with the requirements of the business strategy. This is fundamental but often not seen or understood by senior leaders. A sound leadership strategy will inform you whether leadership is capable of executing the business strategy, and when in balance with unfolding business strategies, it will ensure success in the long term.

Figure 6.1   Leadership Strategy Formulation Process

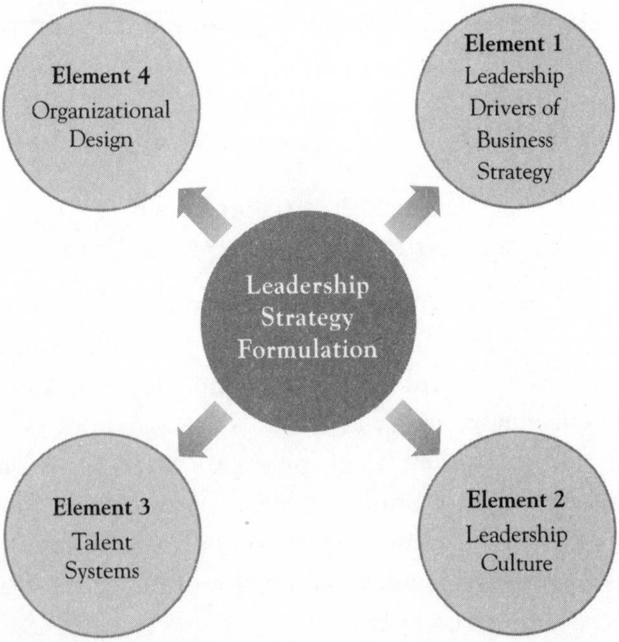

Element 4
Organizational Design

Element 1
Leadership Drivers of Business Strategy

Leadership Strategy Formulation

Element 3
Talent Systems

Element 2
Leadership Culture

The following sections consider these elements of leadership strategy and illustrate from our work with Credicorp Group how the strategic leadership process is playing out in one of the fastest-growing financial institutions in Latin America.

Element 1: Leadership Drivers of Business Strategy

The first step in formulating a leadership strategy is to review the business strategy for implications regarding new leadership requirements. At this stage, we seek to understand the key strategic drivers that have a direct impact on the ability of people in the organization to execute the business strategy and to create, develop, or enhance the individual leadership competencies and organizational capabilities that will enable the business to succeed (Center for Creative Leadership, 2013). In short, we prioritize and invest in the areas that ensure our capability to execute the strategy.

Equipping Leaders to Execute Strategy As leaders prioritize the drivers that are critical for superior performance within their industry, they must simultaneously ask, "What is absolutely essential for leaders and the collective leadership of the organization to accomplish in order to execute successfully its business strategy?" Just as leaders scan the internal and external environments to identify the business drivers to invest in as they strengthen the organization's competitive positioning (e.g., innovation, quality, customer relationships), so too must they identify the leadership competencies and capabilities that require strategic investment. They must prioritize and make decisions about building the capability of leaders—the leadership drivers—to collectively implement business strategies.

The individual and group competency sets necessary to achieve this will be different for each organization depending on its unique strategic orientation. This may include capabilities such as fostering imagination, creating collaboration, developing ownership, guiding engagement, fostering feedback, or promoting public learning.

Drivers are the levers that—if pulled—will catapult the organization toward success. The strategic drivers from a leadership perspective absolutely must support the execution of the business strategies. In the words of Walter Bayly, CEO of Banco de Credito and chief operating officer of Credicorp Group, "Let's be clear— we invest in developing our leaders in order to meet our business goals. Our leaders drive our business performance, and so we must understand what drives our leadership capability."

After over one hundred years of sustained growth and a dominant position in the local market, the executive team at Credicorp, a multinational company in the financial services industry, realized that the time had come for a radical change of business model to pursue the growth opportunities emerging across the Americas. This change in vision led to growth strategies of internationalization, mergers and acquisitions, diversification, redefinition of product portfolios, and penetration into new market segments—in short, significant business challenges that put leadership competencies to the test.

It is no small challenge to move from a dominant position in the local market to going head-to-head with domestic, regional, and global players across the Americas. In order to make this shift in strategic orientation, we worked with the senior leadership team to define the key drivers from a leadership perspective that would be critical to develop as the organization began to execute on its business strategies. They recognized that managers who had been extremely successful in the past would face a whole new level of complexity and uncertainty as the strategy was executed.

In light of the new strategic vision, we identified a set of eighteen individual competencies that would be critical to strengthen across leaders at every level in the business if they were to face the changing nature of their leadership challenges. We further identified three core leadership drivers to strengthen across the entire organization in order to execute successfully on the strategy. As the business strategy was being fine-tuned, we crafted strategies to begin transforming the leadership culture in meaningful ways. We took steps to move from high-performing individual achievers to connected leaders who collectively influence strategically to drive change across the organization. "By linking the development of leaders throughout the organization with our strategic drivers we are laying fertile ground for strategy execution. In this sense leadership development is a strategic investment that is vital to achieving our mission," says Bayly.

Element 2: Leadership Culture

At this stage in the leadership strategy formulation process, we seek to understand the current state of the leadership culture that is driving the behaviors of people and decision making throughout the organization (Center for Creative Leadership, 2013). We then consider the type of culture that will be necessary for leaders to create to foster organizational success in the future.

The way in which leaders interact, make decisions, and influence others in the organization is what we refer to as *leadership culture*. The beliefs, practices, behaviors, and patterns of interaction that leaders exhibit have a direct impact on the work context and cultural fit throughout the organization.

Cultural Fit Drives Performance In a study by Bersin & Associates and the Center for Creative Leadership (Lamoureux, Campbell, & Smith, 2009) executives from hundreds of companies indicated that creating a performance-oriented culture is one of the most difficult challenges that leaders face when they attempt to manage people in the organization. Thus, the leadership strategy must give particular importance to determining the elements of leadership culture that will favor effective interaction and decision making and at the same time benefit the overall performance outcomes of business.

In every organization, leaders create formal and informal elements of culture that define the work context and influence the way people in the organization behave. Culture represents "how things are around here." It reflects the taken-for-granted values, beliefs, underlying assumptions, and collective memories that accumulate in an organization over time. It conveys a sense of identity to people in the organization and provides unwritten (and often unspoken) guidelines for how to interact. Studies show that strong identification with the culture leads to the desire to exert extra effort to the benefit of the organization at large (Haslam, 2001; Haslam, Powell, & Turner, 2000; Ouwerkerk, Ellemers, & de Gilder, 1999; Kreiner & Ashforth, 2004; McGuire & Rhodes, 2009; Dinwoodie, 2011) and can be directly linked to achieving positive performance outcomes (Kreiner & Ashforth, 2004; Dinwoodie, 2007, 2011).

Strong identity and cultural fit can also help smooth the relational tensions that come from increasing internal complexity, allowing leaders to channel individuals' energy toward productive and innovative organizational aims (Cox, 1991; West, 2002; Dinwoodie, 2006, 2011). Conversely, the lack of organizational identity or a culture that discourages people from giving their best on behalf of the enterprise at large can lead to poor performance outcomes and even put the long-term viability of the organization at risk (Dinwoodie, 2011).

We often say that in the pursuit of executing our business strategies, culture trumps strategy every time (figure 6.2). That being the case, it is essential for leaders to recognize that they are responsible for shaping and evolving the culture so that people collectively engage in behaviors that support the strategy and contribute to good organizational performance.

The leadership culture has a profound impact on the strategy formulation and execution processes. Leadership strategy must articulate how leaders are expected to interact in the organizational context and how they will influence the behavior of other organizational members.

Figure 6.2   Culture Trumps Strategy

Dependent, Independent, or Interdependent Leadership Cultures McGuire and Rhodes (2009) observe that as the competitive environment forces organizations to evolve from hierarchical, to autonomous, to integrated business models, the leadership culture tends to evolve from dependent, to independent, to interdependent forms of interaction and decision making. As the business model evolves over time, so too must the culture, which guides the behaviors of organizational leaders. The differences in leadership culture typologies are depicted in figure 6.3.

Intentionally or not, leaders create culture that determines whether relationships between people will be more or less authoritative (dependent culture), individualistic (independent culture), or collaborative (interdependent culture). The extent to which the culture has a positive or negative impact on performance depends on the nature of the challenges that they face. For example, the captain of a boat may decide that an authoritative-dependent culture is the most appropriate approach when a storm hits and orders must be given and followed without question. Drivers on the same racing team may create an independent

Figure 6.3   Leadership Culture Typologies

Interdependent — Leadership is a **collective** activity

Independent — Leadership emerges out of **individual expertise and heroic action**

Dependent — **People in authority** are responsible for leadership

culture as they compete against each other for an individual title. Members of a soccer team may decide that a collaborative-interdependent culture may be the best approach to harness the best of each player to the benefit of the team. When leaders shape culture in a strategic way, they consciously consider what cultural context will be most effective to meet the organizational challenges dictated by their strategic objectives.

The changing nature of today's business environment appears to be pushing organizations toward leadership cultures that increasingly require interdependent, connected, collaborative interaction. This was eloquently expressed at the close of a leadership retreat in 2011 by Bob McDonald, chairman of the board, president, and CEO of Procter & Gamble:

> The world is shifting in such magnitude that there is not enough physical resource for us to view our market places in the traditional ways. . . . In a fundamentally interconnected world our leaders face new and greater challenges that require new and greater leadership strategies. . . . Our future performance will increasingly

require our top leaders to think and act inter-dependently and above all to influence the men and women throughout our company to think and act inter-dependently to move towards a higher organizational aim.

As we worked with the senior leaders of Procter & Gamble from around the world to determine what an interdependent culture would look like across the top tier of executives, it was fascinating to see how soon the concept caught fire. It quickly became evident that there were certain strategic initiatives that could move forward only by first generating a space for collaborative dialogue and decision making across different geographical regions, different functional areas, different areas of the business, and even different cultural norms. We witnessed a true exercise in leading across differences in order to benefit the higher organizational aims.

CCL research shows that 86 percent of senior executives believe that the ability of leaders to span organizational boundaries in an interdependent way is extremely important to achieving business success. The same senior executives believe that only 7 percent of the leaders in their organizations are very effective at collaborating across boundaries. Figure 6.4 illustrates the critical gap between the importance and the effectiveness of leaders at collaborating across organizational boundaries.

A critical part of the leadership strategy formulation process is to determine the extent to which the leadership culture is (or is not) adequate for executing the business strategy. For many organizations, the existing state or the future state analysis of culture may highlight the need to redefine the way that organizational leaders interact and make decisions.

The leadership drivers and developmental activities in Credicorp are tailored specifically to the challenges that leaders face as a result of the shift in business strategy. As the business model evolves to accommodate the complexities of internationalization, how will the culture change to promote the collective

Figure 6.4   Leadership Gap Collaborating Across Organizational Boundaries

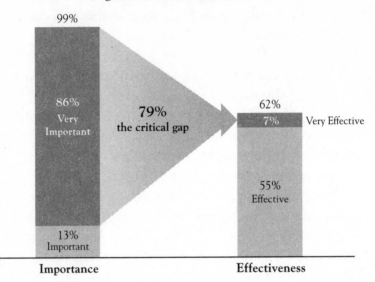

Source: Yip, Ernst, & Campbell (2009).

pursuit of the organizational vision? According to Walter Bayly, "Developing our leaders means shaping our culture so that people can perform. It is about finding a fit. I have learned in business that if it doesn't feel right, isn't right. And our leaders must create the right performance-culture mix for our people to thrive. What are those elements of culture? That is for our leaders to discover."

Top leaders from across Credicorp did just that in a strategic business simulation that allowed them to appreciate the necessary and vital connection between business strategy and leadership strategy. Through the simulation, they tested hypotheses related to strategic drivers and different approaches to leadership culture and reflected on the impact their decisions had on business performance. Over the course of the simulation, they learned that as they developed a more interdependent, collaborative approach, the quality of their business decisions improved and they achieved increasingly superior performance results. They saw the direct impact of consciously changing policies and practices related to cultural elements such as information sharing, organizational focus, goal orientation, compensation, meaning of success, risk taking, mistake making, identity, and knowledge generation. They saw how effective collaboration across different regions, functions, and leadership levels strengthened the sense of direction, alignment, and commitment across the organization and subsequently improved performance results.

Above all, senior managers at Credicorp learned that shared experimentation, reflection, and learning are critical activities for executives to engage in when determining the cultural element of leadership strategies.

Element 3: Talent Systems

At this stage in the leadership strategy formulation process, we seek to understand the organization's current talent systems and leadership architecture and make sure that they are aligned with the organizational competencies and leadership culture (Center for Creative Leadership, 2013).

The Criticality of the Talent Pipeline *Talent* seems to be the buzzword these days when senior leaders approach the Center for Creative Leadership searching for mechanisms to bring business strategy to life in their organizations. Executives identify managing talent as one of the most complex and most frequent challenges organizations face (Smith & Campbell, 2010). They tell us that developing individual and collective talent is both the critical success factor and the limiting factor to executing on the strategic priorities of the organization and achieving superior performance.

Talent management is oriented to ensuring that the organization has, retains, and develops the right people to fulfill its mission and pursue the organization's vision. It delves into issues related to recruitment, compensation, training, succession, human capital, resource constraints, downsizing, and growth. Figure 6.5 illustrates the overwhelming opinion of executives from hundreds of

Figure 6.5   Top Talent Challenges

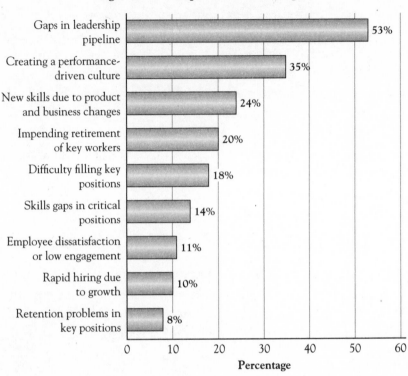

Source: Lamoureux, Campbell, & Smith (2009).

organizations that gaps in the leadership pipeline are the number one challenge related to managing talent in their organizations.

Talent management initiatives must meet today's business needs and, more important, ensure sustainability over time. Thus, the leadership strategy must address short-, medium-, and long-term plans to attract, retain, and develop the talented people who are critical to meeting the organization's strategic objectives.

A solid leadership strategy must be forward thinking and match the talent requirements with the strategic priorities of the organization. Leaders must address questions related to whether they have enough of the right people with the right capabilities to take them toward their vision of the organization's desired future. This we refer to as *talent sustainability*. Exhibit 6.1, which draws

---

EXHIBIT 6.1
Key Questions to Evaluate Talent Sustainability

Consider the strategic objectives of your business, and then assess the existing and future state of the talent pipeline. Do you have the right number of the right people with the right capabilities to achieve the mission and take the organization toward the desired future?

- How well do your talent management efforts align with your strategy and support moving toward a performance-oriented culture?

- Which talent management processes are effectively helping to produce the results (and leaders) you need? Which processes are less effective?

- How integrated are your different talent management systems and processes?

- Is there a compelling reason for talented individuals to join, and stay at, your organization?

- Do you continually and effectively develop the talent in your organization?

- Is there a development road map that addresses the business and leadership challenges that different levels in the organization face?

---

from work by Smith and Campbell (2010), may be a useful starting point for asking probing questions to test the degree to which your talent systems will be sustainable as leaders pursue the strategic initiatives of the organization.

Build the Talent Pipeline When Courtney Harrison, a vice president of human resources for Juniper Networks, a leading company in network innovation, was asked about the key players for building the talent pipeline, her answer was immediate: "All leaders at every level must play a role in identifying and developing our

Figure 6.6 Key Roles in Succession Management

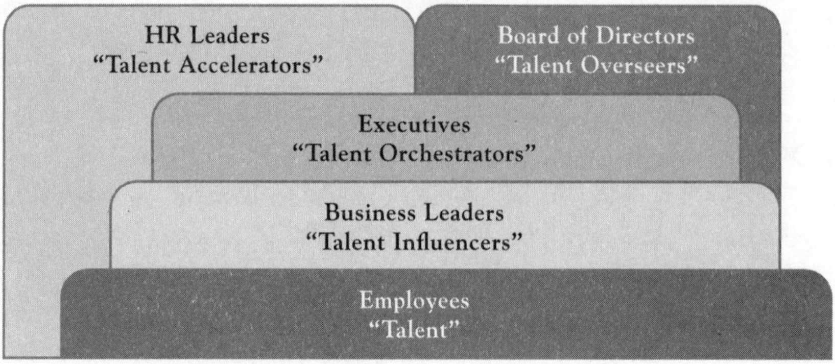

HR Leaders
"Talent Accelerators"

Board of Directors
"Talent Overseers"

Executives
"Talent Orchestrators"

Business Leaders
"Talent Influencers"

Employees
"Talent"

Source: Lamoureux, Campbell, & Smith (2009).

current and future talent. Their responsibilities vary depending on the level of the leader in terms of their relationship with the employee as well as their level of influence within the Juniper-wide system. Regardless of leadership level, it is critical that all of our leaders make strengthening our talent pool a day-to-day priority as our talent is Juniper, today and in the future."

We agree with Harrison: leaders at every level in the organization are charged with contributing to the sustainability of the talent pipeline. Figure 6.6 illustrates several of the specialized roles that leaders can play in building talent and managing succession as the organization evolves.

Independent of the specific role that individuals play in the talent-building process, we find one common factor across the superior-performing organizations that we work with: a passion for people. Leaders who genuinely care for the well-being of people tend to attract, retain, and develop the individuals who will contribute to the sustainable pursuit of the organization's aims. This factor too should be addressed by the leadership strategy. As Harrison further notes,

The passion for our people is an underlying foundation for our leaders at Juniper as you cannot teach someone to authentically care about the success or development of another person. The passion for people's success needs to be instinctive and inherent in all of our leader's day-to-day behaviors and decisions. But passion alone will not ensure success for the development of a large pool of talent. That passion also needs support. It needs to be nested in our company's values, processes, systems, and metrics to include a continuous feedback loop as a means of making sure we are continuously learning and adapting to the changing needs and opportunities for our talent. All of these need to be in place and aligned if talent development is to play an effective role in the execution of our business strategy.

A robust, sustainable leadership strategy addresses with a clear focus processes, systems, and metrics similar to those illustrated in figure 6.7 (McCauley, Smith, & Campbell, 2007).

Managing talent for organizational success and sustainability requires addressing multiple organizational systems and processes. Perhaps the most critical of these is ensuring senior executive commitment and engagement in the talent management process. Senior leaders need to champion and embrace the importance of talent management across the organization, communicating to everyone that they believe talented employees are critical for organizational success. To do that credibly, senior leadership must be directly involved in talent management work, and the leadership strategy must ensure that effective talent management practices are put in place throughout the organization.

Credicorp provides an interesting example of an organization that prioritizes the leadership development aspect of talent management to see that the talent pipeline progresses hand-in-hand with the business strategy.

To ensure alignment between leader development and the organization's strategic objectives, the director of talent management reports directly to the senior leadership team. This way, she has knowledge of the business strategies and contributes directly to investment decisions important to leadership development at

Figure 6.7   Model for Talent Sustainability

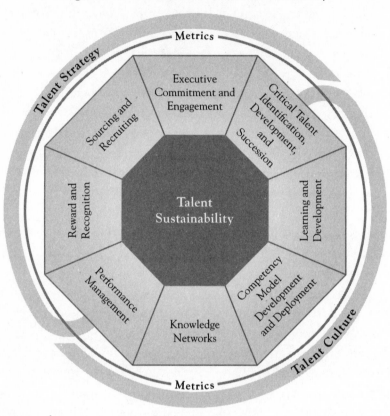

Note: See appendix E for a detailed explanation of each component in the model.

all levels in the organization, from high-potential young leaders up to the senior leadership team. Walter Bayly summarizes the importance of the role this way: "Ursula [Credicorp's director of talent management] is like our eyes into the talent of the organization. We know the people and of course we know what they do and how well they perform. She 'sees the people'—she sees why they behave the way they do, what motivates them to perform and how to strengthen their leadership skills so that they can perform. The talent managers in her department provide the glue between where we want to go as an organization and developing our leaders to enable us to get there." In this sense the director of talent acts as a true talent accelerator and provides a critical link between the talent element of leadership strategy and the business objectives.

Element 4: Organizational Design

At this stage in the leadership development process, we seek to understand the current and desired states for the enterprise's organizational design—its structure, systems, and processes—as they inhibit or strengthen the ability of the culture and leadership to evolve as is necessary to achieve the strategic aims (Center for Creative Leadership, 2013).

Multiple Design Options As organizations engage in transformative change initiatives, successful leaders intentionally design the internal structures, systems, and processes that facilitate new forms of decision making and interaction among people throughout the organization.

Organizational design is the result of a strategic thought process that invites leaders to understand the current and desired states for the organization's components—its structure, systems, and processes—as they inhibit or strengthen the ability of the leadership to transform the organization. The thought process regarding the right organizational design to meet the existing and future organizational aims typically brings together criteria regarding strategic orientation, desired culture, and developmental needs that will result from internal structural changes. Figure 6.8 represents the high-level considerations involved in generating design options for the organization.

As with the other elements of leadership strategy, the role of leaders is to consider multiple options and then determine the organizational design that will best serve the strategy formulation and execution processes.

Structure, Systems, and Processes: Means to a Strategic End An organization's structure is typically depicted as a chart that clarifies

Figure 6.8   Considerations for Organizational Design Options

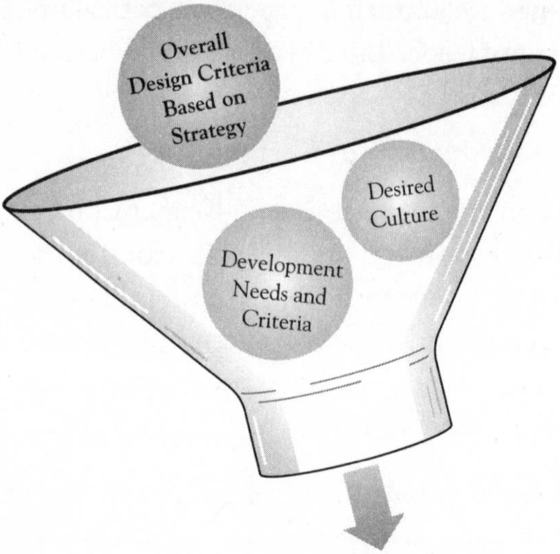

Overall Design Options

formal authority relationships and patterns of communication within an organization. Most people take structure for granted and fail to realize that it's just a tool for getting things done. Structure is not an end in itself, and different structures might exist for organizations performing similar work, each structure having distinctive advantages and disadvantages.

We believe that structure should serve strategy, not vice versa. How can you be sure that this is the case in your organization? One company whose top team we worked with, a $1.3 billion high-tech company, has studiously avoided publishing any organizational chart. A big reason for this is the belief, held by many of its senior executives, that organizational charts by their very nature curtail creativity and initiative. As the company has grown larger, however, increasing numbers of people inside and outside the organization have begun to call for greater clarity about roles and responsibilities. For example, how do you know who to go to? Who's in charge? The lack of structure creates confusion, uncertainty, and conflict. Yet the senior team still wonders about the answer to a basic question: Have we been successful because we've avoided creating organizational charts, or in spite of it? These are important questions that require decisions regarding the most coherent structure to support the changing strategic framework of the organization.

As with structure, organizational systems and processes should also to be designed to serve strategy. The way that people behave in the organizational setting is greatly affected by the processes and systems that leaders create to establish and communicate priorities, determine individual and group-level responsibilities, facilitate learning and knowledge sharing, generate relational networks, and, of course, control activities going on throughout the organization. Exhibit 6.2 serves as reminder of the internal systems that leaders should pay close attention to when formulating the leadership strategy.

Best-Fit Organizational Designs The organizational structures, systems, and processes must be designed through the lens of the strategic leader whose aim is to ensure that people behave and interact in ways that move the organization in line with the strategic objectives. Achieving a fit between strategy and structure requires that leaders understand which structures are more or less appropriate for certain strategic thrusts and business models.

The structure of the organization is evident in the design of its top two or three levels (Center for Creative Leadership, 2013). For example, in a functional structure, the key areas of marketing, research, production, finance, human resources, information technology, and legal typically report directly to the CEO. Similarly, in an organization where different lines of business require autonomy of scope, investment, and decision making, leaders of independent business units tend to report to the CEO. A customer-focused structure would find individuals representing key customers or customer segments near the top of the organizational chart. In a process-based structure, the leaders of areas such as supply chain, customer fulfillment, and quality enhancement hold strategic positions. A matrix structure would find a balance of functional groups and business units at the same high level of the structure.

EXHIBIT 6.2
Five Systems to Consider for Leadership Strategy Formulation

Consider the five types of systems that are common to virtually all organizations:

- *Reward systems*, which define formal and informal practices that determine who and what gets rewarded
- *Communication systems*, which identify channels and processes through which goals and plans, information about individual and organizational development, and progress toward strategic objectives are made explicit and understood
- *Learning systems*, which ensure that resources are designed, acquired, evaluated, and distributed for both individual and organizational development
- *Social network systems*, which connect the web of relationships, information flows, and patterns of influence that make things happen
- *Control systems*, which stipulate policies, processes, procedures, and authorities for decision making, resource allocation, and other organizational commitments

To what extent has sufficient time been invested in understanding the strategic importance of each system? Are the systems complementary? Do they guide people's behaviors in ways that line up with the strategic priorities? Do the systems help or hinder unleashing the full performance potential of individuals and teams?

Leaders should ensure that the systems and related processes help guide the behaviors of organizational members so that members channel their efforts into endeavors that support the successful implementation of the business strategy.

There is no perfect organizational design; certainly it is not a matter of one size fits all. Rather, the design of the organization is a trade-off between options, each with advantages and disadvantages. There are of course certain structures that logically have a better fit than others with the strategic orientation of the organization. Exhibit 6.3 illustrates the correspondence

EXHIBIT 6.3
Examples of Best-Fit Organizational Structures

When making decisions regarding the organizational structure that will best support achieving the strategic objectives, consider the following correspondence between strategic orientation and structural design:

Strategic Orientation	Possible Best Fit
Geographic growth based on local knowledge	Business unit
Diverse portfolio (holding company)	Business unit
Channel optimization	Business unit
Growth through replication	Functional
Efficiency, low cost	Functional
Brand dominance	Functional
Technological leadership	Technical groups
Superior customer focus	Process driven
Serving unique client requests	Project based
Growth through product innovation	Matrix
Leveraging strengths of different specialties	Matrix

In the process of formulating leadership strategy, decisions regarding the most effective structure to unleash the performance potential of the organization are paramount to achieving success.

between strategies and some best-fit designs that may be helpful when making important decisions about the organizational design (Center for Creative Leadership, 2013). Although it is not an exhaustive list of structural typologies, it may aid leaders in thinking about the strategic intent underlying the organizational structure before imposing systems and processes on organizational members.

Since the design of the organization has a profound effect on its culture, it is important to think about the culture required to support the strategy before choosing a design. Steep bureaucratic hierarchies make lines of authority clear, encouraging dependent behavior, which might impede collaboration across the silos that are created. Matrix or team-based structures promote collaboration but make decision making more difficult since multiple parties must be involved. Exhibit 6.4 is a guide to help leaders link the desired leadership culture with the organizational structures and processes that may be associated with those cultures (Center for Creative Leadership, 2013).

As executives in Credicorp moved toward making the strategic vision a reality, they came to the conclusion that they would have to regularly evaluate the extent to which the organizational design created the degrees of dependence, independence, and interdependence that would best support the execution of the business strategies. As Bayly stated, "Credicorp is diversifying and entering into new lines of business in new markets. Our leadership strategy must guide us in structuring our business and shaping the culture that is right for the different industries that we enter. Our organizational structures, our systems, our processes, our management styles must help our people act and interact to be effective in their industries, with their clients and ultimately in the communities where we wish to do business."

EXHIBIT 6.4
Leadership Culture, Structure, and Process

Consider the relationship between different leadership cultures and the organizational structures and processes that may be associated with those cultures. Challenge basic assumptions about the strategic intent of the organization, performance expectations, and the behaviors that senior leaders believe will be required to unleash the performance potential. Then settle on the organizational structure that senior leaders truly believe is the best fit for achieving success.

Desired Leadership Culture	Structures	Processes
Interdependent	Matrices, teams, shared resources (consulting firms, construction firms, R&D)	Emergent, constantly evolving arrangements
		Membership in multiple teams, units, locations, or functions
		Focused on shared outcomes (usually customer)
		Careers linked to a series of team-based projects
		Few permanent boundaries
		Joint innovation and collaborative creativity
		Learning from experimentation but difficulty in achieving repetition
		Breadth of knowledge sharing
		Rewards for creativity, innovation, collaboration
		Processes change frequently

Independent	Autonomous business units	Hub and spoke operations of autonomous but connected parts
	Professional associations (region-based multination-als, legal firms, holding companies)	Independent professional work under shared umbrella organization
		Independent profit-and-loss units within a larger corporation
		High levels of autonomy and discretion in decision making
		Careers that are self-deter-mined or within units
		Depth of knowledge acquisition
		Rewards for expertise, indi-vidual achievements
		Processes that are minimized to allow local discretion
		Maintenance of professional standards and meeting perfor-mance targets critical to retain-ing membership and autonomy
Dependent	Functional	Top down
	Bureaucratic, hierarchi-cal (airlines, banks, military)	Centralized
		One right way; perfection through repetition
		Execution emphasis (versus planning, innovation)
		Careers that are seniority driven, usually within one's function
		Rewards for rank, loyalty, longevity
		Well-defined processes
		Maintenance of quality and other standards is critical to success

Consider whether your leadership strategy ensures coherence between the leadership culture that will be most effective and the structure and processes that will determine the behaviors of organi-zational members as they execute the strategy.

The Leadership Strategy Plan

Successful organizations tend to pull together the work done around linking business strategies with key leadership drivers, determining desired leadership culture, building solid talent systems, and crafting organizational design in a plan that outlines the actions to be implemented.

A leadership strategy plan integrates the considerations given to the four elements of leadership strategy and makes recommendations about the types of leadership development solutions that are needed to close the gap between the existing and desired organizational states in order to move towards successful strategy execution.

In appendix F, we provide a leadership strategy plan template that outlines the major topics that should be addressed when drafting such a plan.

Some Final Thoughts

This chapter describes the importance of crafting leadership strategies that are consistent with business strategies. It also spells out in some detail the distinct components that a robust leadership strategy should contain. There are a few important considerations to take into account during implementation of the leadership strategy plan. First, it is important to identify both the organizational and human capabilities needed to implement the actions related to leadership drivers, the culture, talent systems, and organizational design. Significant change to these elements will almost certainly require capability development within the organization. A second important consideration is to diligently assess the current state of leadership readiness compared to the capabilities that leaders will require to execute the plan. Third, a robust leadership development architecture to close the gaps between leader readiness and the necessary capabilities should be considered as a core element of the implementation phase. Finally, eliciting support from the top executive level is a critical success factor for moving from leadership strategy formulation to leadership strategy execution.

Senior leaders must model the strategic leadership process and ensure that the practices are extended throughout the organization. Kaye O'Neal, regional director of human resources at The Wendy's Company expresses it like this: "Leadership strategy is a multilevel process that spirals down and around the entire organization. The tactics of one level become the strategic challenges of the next. As the strategic challenges cascade from level to level and spread across the organization, so too must the leadership process."

We now turn our attention to individual and organizational developmental processes to build leadership capability.

Chapter 7

Developing Strategic Leadership

One of the most common concerns that we hear from senior executives when we explore ways to support leadership development in their organizations is how their leaders can become "more strategic and less tactical." Correspondingly, one of the most common questions that we hear from up-and-coming organizational leaders when we coach them for greater effectiveness is, "How in the world do we become more strategic and less tactical?"

In this chapter, we turn our attention to what leaders can do to develop both individual and collective capabilities and practice leading strategically at the individual, group, and organizational levels.

An Illustration

Becoming more strategic is related in many ways to moving beyond a strictly tactical focus. We have found that a mere exhortation to others to "become more strategic and less tactical" rarely proves helpful. The challenge for most people is discerning what it means to be more strategic, and progressively learning how to think, act, and influence others in those ways.

If we are to develop strategic leadership in ourselves, our people, and throughout the organization, it would be helpful to know what it looks like when leaders are actually doing it. In chapter 1, we noted that individuals and teams enact strategic leadership when they create the direction, alignment, and commitment needed to achieve the enduring performance potential of the organization.

When we study organizations that appear to be successful at creating direction, alignment, and commitment and attaining superior performance, we observe that they tend to view strategic leadership as a collective, continuous learning process—a learning process that consistently engages both individuals and the organization at large. Organizations that invest in developing certain critical competencies of individual leaders as well as developing the organizational capabilities to execute on business strategies are generally well positioned to perform well over time.

Developing Leaders and Leadership at Credicorp

Let's take a further look at Credicorp and the developmental architecture that it is creating to support its organizational transformation process by aligning leadership strategies with the shifting strategic orientation of the organization. The perspective of senior leaders regarding the radically different challenges that their leaders would face in the future informed the design of a radically different approach to development in the organization. In the words of Ursula Alvarez, the director of talent management,

> We know that we must reach our numbers, and we will only reach our numbers through our people. In our formula for success, *Performance = People*. We now know which human factors or talent drivers to focus on in order to strengthen individuals and also the organization to meet our challenges.

Developing Individual Competency and Collective Capability Inherent in Alverez's statement is the crux of an approach to learning and development that is critical for leaders of organizations that are engaged in business model transformation. It illustrates the necessity of investing in both *leader development* to enable people to perform to their highest potential and *leadership development* to build the collective capability to perform in line with strategic objectives. Exhibit 7.1 raises some developmental considerations to be taken into account to build individual talent and organizational capability. We explored many of these questions when we worked with Credicorp to craft its leadership development solution.

EXHIBIT 7.1
Developmental Considerations

Consider the leadership challenges that individuals at different levels in the organization face. What individual competencies do leaders need to develop in order to meet their strategic challenges? Influence others in a strategic way? Achieve individual performance expectations? Consider the strategic challenges that the organization faces to strengthen its competitive positioning. What organizational capabilities need to be developed to create direction, alignment, and commitment across the organization? Strengthen the collective leadership practices and leadership culture?

From Leader Development to Leadership Development

Leader Development	Leadership Development
Focus: Individual	Focus: Collective
Process: Leaders influence others	Process: Creation of direction, alignment, and commitment (DAC)
Development: Leader skills and perspectives	Development: Collective leadership practices and culture
Assessment: Career progress or performance	Degree of DAC, achievement of performance potential
Build Talent	Build Organizational Capability

The dual leader and leadership development approach is critical to building the depth and breadth of strategic leadership in the organization.

Following this dual developmental approach, a core leadership development program was designed around a set of key individual competencies and delivered to the top five hundred leaders across all business units in the organization. This provided the base for a common skill set, knowledge base, and behaviors to be modeled by leaders throughout the organization. It also allowed us to get a snapshot of the leader profile at Credicorp and compare it to the nature of the business and leadership challenges that the organization was encountering as its leaders executed on the new strategies. Every individual in this leadership pool worked with an executive coach in order to tailor an individual developmental plan aimed at strengthening the competencies most important for their success at Credicorp.

Equally important to Credicorp's developmental architecture are advanced leadership courses differentiated by the leader level that were designed to strengthen the organizational capability to perform. These programs are tailored to the type of challenges that we observed leaders facing at different levels in the organization as they operationalize business strategies into organizational practices. From young high-potential contributors, to middle managers, to senior leaders, to the executive team, they engage in collective developmental activities to build the organizational capability that supports strategy formulation and execution.

Learning Through Application, Support, and Accountability A strategic business simulation was developed for top leaders to practice using the strategic leadership model (SLM) and jointly apply the concepts to leadership challenges that they face in their day-to-day management responsibilities. The opportunity for senior leaders to formulate hypotheses regarding leadership strategies to improve their ability to interrelate and consider the impact of those strategies on projected performance outcomes is a priceless learning experience. Through the simulation, they challenge themselves individually to become stronger strategic thinkers; the leadership team to improve on their ability to communicate effectively, influence others, and make collaborative decisions; and the organization to translate learning from the strategic simulation into the enterprise-wide knowledge sharing.

Every leader in Credicorp is a member of a learning and developmental support network in which they share with each other their developmental challenges and feed-forward the action items that they intend to carry out in order to strengthen their leadership capacities. They act as accountability partners to both challenge and support each other in implementing their developmental plans. This support network benefits each individual while at the same time developing the collective capability of each level of leaders in the organization.

Credicorp leaders actively help each other gauge the degree to which their colleagues perceive a positive (or negative) evolution in their leadership development as they take steps to strengthen their leadership behaviors. Furthermore, an executive mentoring program is gradually being introduced so that organizational wisdom is shared throughout the different levels of the business and leaders. This knowledge sharing provides important examples of how leaders can develop the capability to influence effectively across the organization.

The Impact of Leadership Development at Credicorp

As we continue to roll out this developmental architecture, we listen closely to participants and observe several interesting phenomena. One is a realization by individuals that the change in strategic direction requires them to build new competencies if they are going to be successful in meeting their challenges. We hear young high-potential leaders saying things like, "Wow! I guess it's true that what got me here may not get me to that next level. I sure didn't hear that at business school, but I get it now. It's not just about me; it's about how I impact others."

A second phenomenon we are seeing is the evolution toward a more interdependent, collaborative approach where leaders realize that achieving the objectives set for their portion of the business is intimately linked to the success of stakeholders in other parts of the business. To quote a quickly rising middle manager, "Wasn't it comfortable when I could just manage my team and focus on meeting our key performance indicators? I now spend most of my time thinking about how we will influence other departments to collaborate, influence top decision makers for resources, influence suppliers to forge partnerships, influence distribution channels to reach new customers. I now see the connections and I'm starting to see how they work."

Finally, leaders are demonstrating a genuine interest in aligning efforts to meet a greater organizational aim. As the HR director of a business unit commented after participating in the strategic business simulation, "I can see that we will be more competitive when I am sharing my talent pool with other business units across Peru or in Bolivia or in Miami. I see that because I now understand that 'we' means Credicorp. That my talent pool is our talent pool."

The Credicorp example illustrates how strategic leadership development occurs at both the individual and collective levels and highlights the importance of paying attention to both levels to truly develop strategic leadership capabilities throughout the organization. It further demonstrates how the developmental process is progressive and evolves in unison with the emerging business challenges of the organization that create new strategic challenges for the leaders in our organizations.

Developing Strategic Leaders

Strategic leaders must invest time and energy into fine-tuning their ability to think, act, and influence in general, as well as strengthening competencies specific to the leadership challenges that today's business environment brings to their plate.

Strengthening Your Ability to Think, Act, and Influence Strategically

For years people have argued about whether it is possible to develop strategic abilities. Beatty and Byington (2010) bring to light that while leaders possess certain cognitive capacities, strategic leadership involves much more than just that. Thinking, acting, and influencing strategically involve social processes that are not necessarily innate or natural to everyone. We say that leadership is actually a contact sport and the art of relating effectively with others requires learning and practice. We can in fact evolve our leader logic in ways that advance our ability to convert strategic intent into effective leadership behaviors.

Leader development begins with visioning and assessment. Before jumping into specific developmental activities to become more strategic, we encourage you to do several things. First, take some reflection time and imagine yourself leading strategically. What will it look like when you are there? How will it feel? What behaviors will you demonstrate? What will be their impact on others? What will other people's perception of you be? How will you know when you are doing it?

Second, revisit the assessment tools previously discussed relating to your present skillfulness at thinking strategically (exhibit 2.3), acting strategically (exhibit 3.4), and influencing strategically (exhibit 4.3). Then prioritize and ask yourself what the two or three areas or personal leadership drivers are for you to focus on that will have the greatest impact on your strategic effectiveness. If you invest your time, energy, and resources in developing these areas, will you move toward the vision you have of yourself leading strategically? If so, you can start to formulate a developmental plan to become more strategic.

Beatty and Byington (2010) note that those who are aspiring to develop in this area need challenges that prompt growth as opposed to knowledge acquisition. Given the breadth of skills required of strategic leaders, the best developmental path will include challenges in multiple domains over the course of a person's career, even lifetime. Certain transitions in one's career inherently bring the need for a shift toward stronger strategic leadership capacities (e.g., promotion from team leader to middle management or the move from functional manager to general management position). Professional progression tends to be an evolutionary process, and the seeds of strategic leadership should be sown over time. Exhibit 7.2 highlights some work-related experiential challenges that can contribute to building individuals' leadership capacity and developing a broader strategic understanding of the organization.

EXHIBIT 7.2
Professional Challenges That Build
Strategic Leadership

Think about yourself or someone you are responsible for supporting in his or her professional development. What are some of the gaps in the development of the person's capacity to lead strategically? What are some work-related situations that would force the person to stretch herself or himself professionally and fill those gaps? How might evolution from one work-related challenge to another help develop the person's ability to formulate and execute on business and leadership strategies?

Consider the extent to which the person is prepared to engage in one or more of the following work experiences that have been shown to hold fruitful challenges for developing strategic leadership:

- *Leading a team:* Engaging with others, eliciting their ideas, and engendering commitment to the team's work
- *Taking a rotational assignment in an unfamiliar part of the business:* Learning how different parts of the organization work together as a system
- *Leading a project that requires coordination across parts of the business:* Learning to influence without authority
- *Serving on the board of a nonprofit organization:* Learning to view the organization as a whole

- *Leading a strategic initiative that is forging new ground in the organization:* Dealing with the complexity, sense making, prioritization required, and engendering commitment to the change

- *Taking an assignment in the strategic planning department:* Facilitating planning that results in the learning required for effectiveness

- *Managing a function:* Creating coherence between different groups and working with other functions, including competing for resources based on business needs; developing a functional strategy that blends with the overall business strategy

- *Managing a business, with profit and loss responsibility:* Learning to balance between future goals and present needs (Charan, Drotter, & Nobel, 2001; Goldman, 2007; Kates & Downey, 2005; Lombardo & Eichinger, 1989; McCauley, 2006)

Ultimately the goal is to provide a succession of increasingly complex developmental assignments, paced so the individual can reflect on and learn from them and apply the lessons to the next assignment.

Developing Individual Strategic Leadership Competencies

In chapter 6 we observed that in superior-performing organizations, the leaders tend to be good at addressing leadership imperatives that in today's business scenario are particularly pertinent. When senior leaders ask us how to be more effective regarding challenges related to leading change, shaping culture, spanning boundaries, and leveraging polarities, we encourage them to start by assessing how confident they feel about certain competencies that we have seen to be important to enacting strategic leadership at the individual level.

Exhibit 7.3 is a reflection exercise that helps determine which strategic leadership competencies are particularly relevant for individual development in the pursuit of becoming a successful strategic leader.

EXHIBIT 7.3
Strategic Leadership Competencies
Relevant for Success

Start by asking yourself: How critical is each of the following leader-ship competencies for me to meet the strategic leadership chal-lenges that I am facing? Then reflect on the behaviors that you exhibit related to those critical competencies. Ask yourself and others where you have existing strengths to build on and what areas require further development on your part:

Business perspective: To what extent do I understand the perspec-tives of different areas in the business and have a firm grasp of external conditions affecting the organization?

Strategic planning: To what extent do I develop long-term objectives and strategies? Am I effective at translating vision into realistic business strategies?

Organizational decision making: To what extent do I make timely decisions? Do I readily understand complex issues? Do I develop solutions that effectively address problems?

Manage conflicting perspectives: To what extent do I recognize that every decision has conflicting interests and constituencies? Am I able to balance short-term payoffs with long-term improvement?

Act systemically: To what extent do I understand the political nature of the organization and work appropriately within it? How effec-tive am I at establishing collaborative relationships and alliances throughout the organization?

Influence across the organization: To what extent am I good at inspiring and promoting a vision? Am I able to persuade and motivate others? Do I skillfully influence superiors? Am I able to delegate effectively?

Build collaborative relationships: To what extent do I know how to build and maintain working relationships with coworkers and external parties? Do I negotiate and handle work problems without alienating people? Do I understand others and get their cooperation in nonauthority relationships?

Promote organizational transition: To what extent do I support strategies that facilitate organizational change initiatives and position the business for the future?

Adapt to new conditions: To what extent can I adapt to changing business conditions and remain open to new ideas and new methods?

Initiate organizational innovation: To what extent am I visionary, able to seize new opportunities, and consistently generate new ideas? Do I introduce and create needed change even in the face of opposition?

Demonstrate vision: To what extent do I understand, communicate, and stay focused on the organization's vision?

Once you have assessed your competency level, ask your boss, trusted colleagues, and perhaps a few enlightened friends how important they think each of those competencies is for you to be successful in meeting your leadership challenges.

Reflect on the questions in exhibit 7.3, seek out some feedback from others, and then prioritize two or three things to focus on improving. To strengthen your strategic leadership competency, set some specific actions that you will implement to sharpen those competencies. Then ask yourself: What mechanisms can I put in place to support myself in implementing actions that strengthen my leadership behaviors?

Behavior change can be tough stuff and certainly much less comfortable than taking a course or reading a book to acquire a new bit of knowledge. We have observed over the years that one of the strongest mechanisms for supporting individuals in changing the behaviors that will strengthen their leadership effectiveness is establishing an active learning and developmental support network—a group of trusted "accountability partners" to challenge and support leaders in their developmental process.

After you prioritize two or three areas to work on that will channel your energy into those relatively few competencies that are both critical to the key strategic challenges you face and that you can develop further, you should actively engage others in your developmental process. People who want you to succeed, can understand the leadership challenges that you face, and can contribute suggestions for your development will hold you true to the actions that you commit to undertake, see you interacting with others, notice the impact your behaviors have on others, and are willing to give you feedback that is both totally honest and totally kind.

This network of accountability partners may include your boss, work colleagues, executive coach, schoolmates, teachers, family members—anyone who is interested enough in you to listen to what you plan to change, offer a suggestion, ask you when you plan to do it, check in with you once in a while, and tell you what they perceive based on what you have done. To these trusted partners, you should "feed-forward" the developmental actions you plan to take and ask them to hold you accountable for following through.

Developing Collective Strategic Leadership Capability

Just as important as developing the strategic leadership competencies of individuals are the developmental activities oriented to strengthening the collective leadership capability of the organization. Chapter 5 discusses ways to build the leadership capability of strategic leadership teams (SLTs) in organizations. The experience and strategic expertise at the SLT level is essential for modeling the leadership mind-set and behaviors that we expect from people throughout the organization. As we have known for thousands of years, "where there is no vision, the people perish" (Proverbs 29:18). The responsibility for establishing strategic vision lies with the senior leaders; bringing it to life in the organization means transmitting the strategic mind-set and strengthening leadership skills of the people throughout the organization.

To determine the right approach to developing organizational capability, it is essential to gauge the readiness for organizational learning. Depending on the prior experience of leaders in both the strategy and leadership arenas, different developmental architectures or leadership solutions can be considered. Leadership solutions for developing organizational capability can range from sending leaders to executive education courses, to tailor-made developmental programs designed around the specific leadership challenges of the organization, to assimilation and ownership of the strategic leadership process by leaders within the organization.

As we saw in the Credicorp example, most organizations that achieve strategic leadership competence craft a developmental architecture that is both broad (extending across the entire organization) and deep (cascading to all leader levels in the organization). The breadth and depth of strategic leadership development determine the extent to which the strategic vision of senior leaders transforms the leadership culture of the organization in its entirety. This often entails a blended leadership solution approach that combines attending open enrollment courses, participating in custom-designed programs, and creating opportunities for practical application of knowledge to real organizational scenarios.

Our studies and practical experience show that superior-performing organizations tend to promote opportunities for group learning related to the constructs of the SLM that is described fully in chapter 1 (see figure 7.1).

As leaders use the SLM to understand the competitive positioning of their organizations and make decisions about how to move that organization from today's current state to tomorrow's sustainable future, they will develop the capability to craft and execute collectively on coherent strategies. Leaders in the organization should regularly assess their collective effectiveness in decision making related to the model and decide where their strengths and improvement needs lie.

Figure 7.1 Strategic Leadership Model

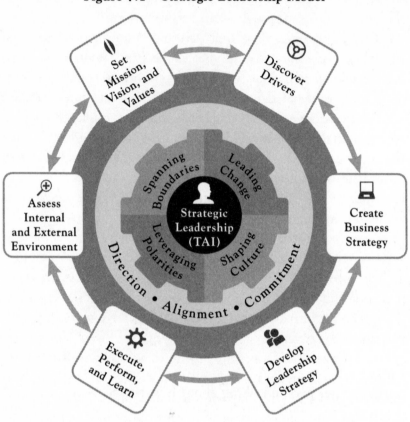

Use the SLM to Frame Strategic Conversations

Beatty and Byington (2010) point out that the benefit of a conceptual model such as the SLM is that it provides a common language for people to use— a shared road map for where the collective is going. Having a common road map is not enough, however. Different members of the collective will inevitably interpret that road map in different ways. For example, many organizations state the importance of "quality" in their service. There are many ways to interpret the word *quality* in a vision, a mission, or even a driver. In order for the collective to develop shared understanding of the framework and its components, members must learn skills of dialogue so they express their understanding, appropriately debate, and ultimately integrate the various perspectives into a common whole. In a sense, then, the framework itself is less important than the dialogue and shared understanding it generates. The shared conceptual model acts as a focal point and helps spark rich conversations among leaders while ensuring that those conversations are strategic in nature.

Having a conceptual framework such as the SLM is the first step in the organizational development process. Equally, if not more, important is an assessment of where the organization currently stands relative to that framework, the ability to practice using that framework when the stakes are not too high, and coaching and support along the way as people attempt to institutionalize the strategic framework.

Assess the Organization's Current State One of the best ways to initiate dialogue is to conduct a survey or quick assessment of the current state of the organization. This helps stimulate conversation and motivates others to work together on areas for improvement.

We use a simple tool we call the Strategic Leadership Practices Survey to get people talking about how the SLM is (or is not) working in their organization. Exhibit 7.4 consists of twelve questions that are linked to the different areas of the SLM. It can be used to assess the strengths and opportunities for improvement related to the organizational capability to effectively deal with critical strategic leadership issues.

Dialogue About the Future State

Once each individual has answered the survey based on her or his perceptions, the leadership team can engage in healthy group dialogue regarding the current and desired future state of the leadership culture. In chapter 5, we considered a series of powerful questions that can build on the survey that will help open rich strategic conversations. The same questions that the strategic

EXHIBIT 7.4
Strategic Leadership Practices Survey

Consider the constructs of the strategic leadership model and evaluate the areas that you believe represent strengths or opportunities for improvement when organizational leaders work together to formulate and execute strategy.

Strategic Leadership Practices Survey Assess the Present State	Strength	Area for Improvement
Assess the internal and external environments. To what extent do we as organizational leaders regularly and realistically evaluate our internal strengths and weaknesses and the external opportunities and threats?		
Clarify mission, vision, and values. To what extent do we as organizational leaders establish an organizational lens that creates a shared vision of the future and understanding of our operating principles?		
Discover and prioritize drivers. To what extent do we as organizational leaders prioritize the key strategic drivers to create focus on mission critical activities?		
Create business strategies. To what extent do we as organizational leaders craft business strategies that will take us from where we are today to our desired future state?		
Develop leadership strategies. To what extent do we as organizational leaders craft leadership strategies that act as enablers to our business strategies?		

Strategic Leadership Practices Survey Assess the Present State	Strength	Area for Improvement
Execute, perform, learn. To what extent do we as organizational leaders effectively translate strategy into practice, learn from our performance outcomes, and revisit our strategic framework?		
Lead change. To what extent do we as organizational leaders foresee the changes to the business environment that will bring increased complexity and new tensions to the organization as leaders engage in transformative business model change?		
Shape culture. To what extent do we as organizational leaders shape organizational cultures that elicit strong identification and a sense of belonging?		
Span boundaries. To what extent do we as organizational leaders implement tactics to span organizational boundaries in order to facilitate interdependent decision making and collaboration?		
Leverage polarities. To what extent do we as organizational leaders reap the upside of priorities that may appear to be diametrically opposed?		
Direction, alignment, commitment. To what extent do we as organizational leaders create direction, alignment, and commitment with the strategic objectives throughout the organization?		
Leadership effectiveness—thinking, acting, influencing. To what extent do we as organizational leaders think, act, and influence strategically to reap the full performance potential of the organization?		

leadership team uses to fine-tune its strategic leadership capability can be used to develop the extended capability of leaders throughout the organization.

Interestingly, we notice that as leaders gain more practice and experience using the SLM to move toward the desired future state, several things happen over time. We tend to see a direct correlation between improvements in the collective capability to think, act, and influence strategically and the extent to which leaders maximize the performance potential of the organization. We also tend to find a strong correlation between the creation of direction, alignment, and commitment and performance indicators such as revenue growth, market share, quality measure, innovation, return on sales, and return on equity.

With respect to creating the experiences to help teams and organizations learn to use the SLM, we have found several developmental techniques to be particularly powerful. They are described below.

Guided Practice Through a Strategic Business Simulation

Simulations are being used more frequently in development experiences, for good reason. The learning retention rate of a standard lecture is quite low compared to the opportunity a person has to practice analyzing data, developing strategic dialogue with their team, making mistakes, and seeing the results. Clark Aldrich, a noted practitioner and builder of educational simulations, says, "A single simulation can teach someone in a variety of ways all at once, and for this reason the medium is actually much closer to how people often learn from real-life experiences" (Morrison & Aldrich, 2003, para. 4).

We use business simulations that involve decisions about the strategy of the company going forward and tactical decisions to implement that strategy. Participants have the opportunity to test hypotheses regarding the impact of decisions taken collectively by the leadership team and determine to what extent their strategic leadership intent is translated into the performance outcomes that they would expect. They can test and retest new strategic hypotheses until they find the strategic framework which best supports the success of the company they are tasked with leading. Figure 7.2 illustrates the evolution of some performance indicators as one executive team formulates and implements strategy as participants in the simulation.

They also reflect on the relationship between the leadership culture that they create and the evolution of hard performance metrics related to the strategic objectives that they set. As illustrated in figure 7.3, leaders can track the direct correlation of creating an interdependent-collaborative leadership culture, improving organizational alignment, and the evolution of sales over a five-year period.

They are further able to evaluate the extent to which they collectively achieve an effective balance of strategic thinking, acting, and influencing and how that translates into maximizing the performance potential of the organization. Figure 7.4 illustrates this relationship.

Figure 7.2 Evolution of Strategic Simulation Performance Indicators

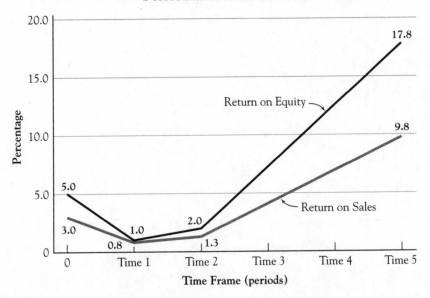

Figure 7.3   Correlation of Leadership Culture, Organizational Alignment, and Sales

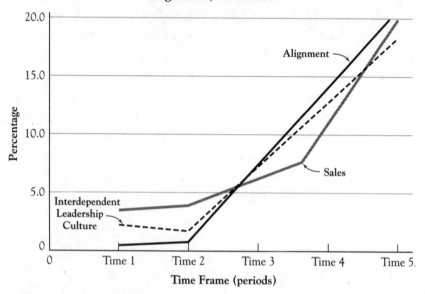

Figure 7.4   Correlation of Collective Thinking, Acting, and Influencing with Maximizing Performance Potential

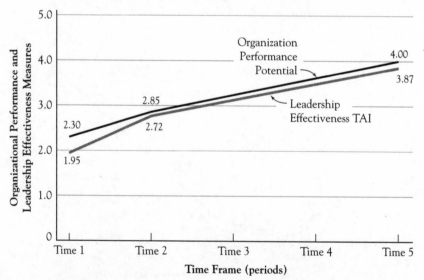

Powering Down to Power Up Simulation sessions provide ample opportunity for business reviews linked to process debriefings, which aid the leadership team in "powering down" to consider necessary improvements to the leadership culture before diving into another round of strategic decision making and tactical execution. The facilitated business debriefings invite leaders to examine important questions related to the SLM framework and the leadership processes that they are enacting. We consider reflection questions such as these:

- How is your team deepening its awareness of the strategic drivers of your organization?
- Have you fully vetted the assumptions about your markets and customers—their behaviors, their needs, their challenges?
- Have you identified your key talent pools that are absolutely needed to implement your strategy?
- What are you doing to develop the organizational capability to perform?

After taking time to collectively think about strategic considerations, talk about the impact of business and leadership decisions that the group is taking and theorize about ways to improve on the strategy formulation and execution process. Participants are ready once again to "power up" and practice acting and influencing strategically as they enter another round of the simulation.

Action Learning

After a group has the opportunity to practice these strategic frameworks and leadership behaviors in the safety of a simulation, the next step is to put them into a work challenge. We recommend using action learning because it is uniquely suited to the fundamental principles underlying the SLM, suggesting as it does that we must both do and learn at the same time. Action learning projects have the dual benefit of strengthening the leadership capabilities of the group that undertakes the project while having a direct impact on an initiative that is strategically important for the organization.

In action learning work, care must be taken in choosing the right project for the team. The project should have strategic significance so that the SLM can be practiced—that is, its outcome must have implications for the long-term effectiveness of the organization. In appendix G we provide criteria for selecting action learning projects with a strategic leadership focus.

It is also important to think through the role of senior management in the process. Ideally, senior leaders will participate in the development process themselves and therefore will be members of the action learning team. They then have the opportunity to model the learning and development that is fundamental to the culture of the SLM. Most important, the work has implications for the organization overall, so the senior management team must buy in. Look for opportunities to build their awareness, buy-in, and readiness to engage in and lead the learning culture that are fundamental to the SLM.

Action learning is best done with an action learning coach who provides guidance along the way. It is unreasonable to expect the group to master everything that the SLM requires after just going through a simulation. They need some additional assessment and support from a coach as they navigate the challenges of their work.

Closing Words

Our primary reason for writing this book was to give managers and executives a more personal perspective about what it means to be strategic as a leader, as well as suggestions about how to foster strategic leadership throughout the organization. But this book does not make becoming a strategic leader easy. You cannot develop by reading a book, pushing a button, or checking a box.

As we saw at the beginning of the book, strategic leadership is a bit like surfing. Both require keeping your balance while learning the best path to follow amid constantly changing conditions. Your challenge now is to start moving on the path to more effective strategic leadership by developing your own and your team's thinking, acting, and influencing skills. This also happens to be your primary role in ensuring your organization's enduring success.

Appendix A

Strategic Driver
Paired-Voting Form

In the paired voting for each cell, record the number of votes for the driver listed in the far left-hand column.

Strategic Driver	A	B	C	D	E	F	G	H	I	J
A										
B										
C										
D										
E										
F										
G										
H										
I										
J										

STRAT: Strategic Team Review and Action Tool

You have been chosen to survey a strategic leadership team of which you are a member. The phrase *strategic leadership team* (SLT) refers to individuals who collectively exert significant influence on the strategic direction of a particular business unit, product line, function (product development, engineering, marketing, and so on), division, or company. SLTs need not be explicitly designated or chartered, can include individuals with varying authority relationships, and can range from four to more than twenty members. The SLT you are to survey may comprise a combination of direct reports, peers you work with often, and people you rarely work with directly.

The Strategic Team Review and Action Tool (STRAT) consists of questions designed to survey a strategic leadership team within an organization. Your task, as a recipient of this survey, is to complete it by answering the questions as they relate to the SLT defined for you. The results of this survey will help you and the members of the SLT analyze strategic leadership in that team and the overall company. A list of the members and observer groups of this SLT has been included with the cover letter for your reference.

Complete the STRAT survey questions by responding to the items as they apply to that strategic leadership team. Please be open and candid in your responses. The report will show a summary of the group's responses. Your individual responses will not be identifiable to anyone else.

Print this survey and complete it using a blue or black pen.

Return it on or before the due date.

Thank you.

STRAT—Strategic Team Review and Action Tool

YOUR NAME:_____

Due Date:_____

SLT NAME: [preprinted when survey is in use]_____

Please respond to the survey items as they apply to the strategic leadership team named above.

For each item, select one option by circling a number to show how much you agree or disagree that the statement describes this SLT, using the following scale:

$$5 = \text{Strongly Agree}, 4 = \text{Agree}, 3 = \text{Neutral}, 2 = \text{Disagree},$$
$$1 = \text{Strongly Disagree}$$

5	4	3	2	1	
5	4	3	2	1	1. This strategic leadership team regularly and realistically assesses its organizational strengths and weaknesses.
5	4	3	2	1	2. This strategic leadership team understands the threats and opportunities in the external environment.
5	4	3	2	1	3. This strategic leadership team has a shared vision of our future.
5	4	3	2	1	4. Individuals at all levels understand how their roles support the organizational mission.
5	4	3	2	1	5. This strategic leadership team keeps abreast of technological, cultural, and market trends.
5	4	3	2	1	6. This strategic leadership team is clear about our basic purpose and core values.

5	4	3	2	1	7. This strategic leadership team thinks globally.
5	4	3	2	1	8. This strategic leadership team encourages others to improve by experimenting with new or different ways of doing things.
5	4	3	2	1	9. There are few undiscussable subjects here.
5	4	3	2	1	10. Different opinions are welcome.
5	4	3	2	1	11. Our strategy is discriminating: clear about what we will do and clear about what we will not do.
5	4	3	2	1	12. This strategic leadership team works well together.
5	4	3	2	1	13. This strategic leadership team is composed of diverse individuals with complementary talents.
5	4	3	2	1	14. This strategic leadership team shares information well with each other.
5	4	3	2	1	15. Members of this strategic leadership team have constructive interactions with others throughout the organization.
5	4	3	2	1	16. This strategic leadership team actively supports executive growth and development.
5	4	3	2	1	17. Getting ahead here depends on performance, not politics.
5	4	3	2	1	18. This strategic leadership team strikes an appropriate balance between dealing with short-term and long-term needs.

(continued)

5	4	3	2	1	19. This strategic leadership team encourages an appropriate level of risk taking.
5	4	3	2	1	20. This strategic leadership team does not waste its own or others' energy on unproductive activities.
5	4	3	2	1	21. This strategic leadership team responds effectively to opportunities and threats in the environment.
5	4	3	2	1	22. Members of this strategic leadership team trust and respect each other.
5	4	3	2	1	23. This strategic leadership team fosters cooperation rather than competition across organizational units.
5	4	3	2	1	24. We share best practices across individuals and departments.
5	4	3	2	1	25. This strategic leadership team exhibits a high level of integrity.
5	4	3	2	1	26. I am proud of the way this strategic leadership team handles issues of right or wrong.
5	4	3	2	1	27. There is a positive sense of energy and excitement around here.
5	4	3	2	1	28. This strategic leadership team has widespread agreement about what are the most important organizational priorities (key success factors) needed to drive our sustainable competitive advantage.
5	4	3	2	1	29. This strategic leadership team has clear responsibility for contributing to one or more of the key drivers of our organizational success.

5	4	3	2	1	30. This team has the right composition to achieve its purpose.
5	4	3	2	1	31. This team has access to the relevant information it needs to make decisions and take action.
5	4	3	2	1	32. This team has direct or indirect control of the resources it needs to accomplish its task.

Using STRAT to Develop Your Strategic Leadership Team

The purpose of the Strategic Team Review and Action Tool (STRAT) is to generate conversation among strategic leadership team (SLT) members regarding what they are doing well and what they could do better. It is not a validated instrument, which means it is not appropriate to say that teams that score higher on STRAT are necessarily better than teams that score lower. Rather than use it as a measurement, we suggest you use it as a springboard for conversations regarding team processes. If you are not the leader of the team, you'll need to gain agreement ahead of time to use STRAT. Spend some time talking with the leader about STRAT and the role of teams in the strategic leadership of the organization. Perhaps you have already had conversations about this particular SLT and discussed what is working well and what is not. Be prepared to answer questions such as these:

- Why should this SLT go through a process like this?
- Why this tool versus another tool?
- Why now?
- What is the benefit of this process?

Typically the process of using STRAT has three steps:

1. Prepare the team for the tool, and distribute it for completion.
2. Score the results so that the team can make sense of them.
3. Review the results with the team.

Step 1: Prepare the Team, and Distribute STRAT

Spend some time before handing out the STRAT tool to prepare the team. A few steps will go a long way toward ensuring the successful use of STRAT:

- *Determine exactly who will complete STRAT.* If all team members can complete it, the data will have more meaning because people will not think, "I understand the results, but I wonder whether everyone else feels this way." Similarly, all members can then feel that they have had input into the data and can participate fully in the conversations regarding the results and any actions taken as a result of those conversations. In terms of protecting team members' confidentiality, more inputs are better. In fact, we recommend you require a minimum of three or four people complete STRAT so that no one can determine the others' responses with certainty.
- *Make sure the team members know the team leader's reasons for using STRAT.* Encourage the team leader—if it is someone other than yourself—to communicate with team members regarding that rationale.
- *Make sure that all members are rating the same SLT.* If your team has a name, include that in the copies of STRAT that are distributed. It's very important that everyone thinks about the same team when they make their ratings.
- *When you distribute STRAT, let members know that their individual ratings will be kept confidential* and that no one on the team will see any other individual's ratings. Assign a trusted and objective person (who is not a member of the team) to collect the STRAT forms and produce the summary of the ratings.
- *Ask members to be as honest as possible when making their ratings* so that the team can benefit most fully from this experience.
- *Suggest that the members keep a copy of their own individual ratings since you will not return that data to them.* It can be very helpful in the discussion of the results if people remember

their own individual ratings (even though they will not be asked to share those ratings).

- *Set a deadline for the return of STRAT.* Typically it takes fifteen to twenty minutes to complete the tool. Most people should be able to find time to complete it within a week. Ask that individuals return it to your assigned person by the deadline. Ask your assigned person to follow up with people to ensure that the forms are collected.

Step 2: Score STRAT

STRAT provides two general types of data that will be helpful in examining the team's results:

- *Average ratings for each item.* Ask your assigned person to average the ratings across all the members for each item and provide that information in a report format. The report will be most helpful if it can list the item number, item text, and the average rating. In addition, if the average ratings can be sorted from highest to lowest, it will be easier to review the data.
- *Frequency distribution for each item.* While an average is helpful, it does not tell how dispersed the ratings are. For example, an average of 3 can be produced in different ways: everyone gives the item a 3, or half the respondents give it a 1 and half give it a 5 (among other possibilities). Those two scenarios are quite different: the second one suggests a fair amount of disagreement among members regarding that item. A frequency distribution shows how many people gave the item a 1, how many a 2, how many a 3, and so on. This information is very helpful when assessing team agreement or disagreement on a particular item.

Reporting frequency distributions poses a slight risk, particularly if the team is small, because it may cause members to ask, "Who gave this a 2?" One way to minimize this risk and still provide the information about agreement or disagreement is to flag items where there is a gap of three or more points between the highest and lowest ratings—for example, the lowest rating is a 2 and the highest rating is a 5, or the lowest rating is a 1 and the highest rating is a 4. You might want to use this method rather than the frequency distribution if your team has five or fewer members.

Step 3: Debrief STRAT

Once everyone has completed the tool and your assigned person has produced a summary of the results, it is time to sit down with the team to review those results. The following two sections give some suggestions regarding that meeting.

General Tips for Debriefing STRAT with Your SLT

- Consider using an outside facilitator, particularly if you are the leader of the SLT. Facilitation requires a level of objectivity that is very difficult to maintain as a team member or team leader. In addition, having another person present to focus on the facilitation allows you to participate more fully in the conversations about the team.
- Ensure that you have enough time to discuss the results and take some action based on that discussion. Allow three hours minimum for this conversation—more if this type of conversation is new for your team or if you have significant issues on the team.
- Consider holding the meeting off-site to minimize distractions and allow people more opportunity for reflection. Also, ask people to turn off cell phones, pagers, laptops, and other distracting devices.
- Set norms at the outset of the meeting to encourage respect for confidentiality and exploration of multiple perspectives. Focus on the issues, not on who said what. Here are some helpful norms to include:

Speak to your own data, and do not ask others to share their scores on particular items. (Of course, people can share their scores, but they should initiate that sharing.)

When there is a confusing data point, consider it a paradox to be understood and not an anomaly that must be incorrect just because it is different from the others. Do this by hypothesizing in the following way: "If I had answered this item in this way, I would have been thinking about the ways in which we . . ."

- Inevitably the group will get into a discussion of what they have control over because several of the STRAT items have root causes that may exist outside the team. This is particularly true if the team is not the top management team in the organization. The danger in these discussions is that the team will feel helpless to do anything to improve the situation. Therefore, encourage them to keep two things in mind:

It is possible to separate out what the team does have control over from what it does not have control over. In fact, put the two sets of items on separate presentation charts to provide a visual cue as to the differences. Encourage team members to focus their action planning on those items over which they do have control.

Items they don't have control over provide members with an opportunity to influence people outside the team. For example, if members feel that the organization's strategy is not discriminating enough and that this is leading to a situation the team is not clear regarding what it should and should not be doing, they can generate a list of clarifying questions and take that list to the top management team.

Possible Flow of a STRAT Debriefing Meeting

If you are facilitating a meeting to debrief the STRAT results, this description of a meeting can help you set the pace. These activities are not inclusive of everything you might do, but they have worked well for us in our work with strategic leadership teams:

1. If the team is unfamiliar with strategic leadership concepts and the implications those have for the team, consider assigning some advance reading, such as this book or selected chapters of it. Even if members are familiar with strategic leadership in general, providing a framework gives everyone a common language to use when discussing their strengths and challenges.

2. Begin the meeting with an icebreaker. For example, ask each team member to share what he or she believes his or her own role on the team is. Examples include devil's advocate and integrator. Also ask team members to share their expectations for the meeting.

3. Frame the purpose of the day. Your purpose might be to generate discussion about how team members are working together, to see whether the team wants to change anything about its interactions and its effectiveness as a strategic leadership team, and, if so, to set plans in place to make those changes.

4. Set some norms for the meeting.

5. Have a discussion about what is important for the team to do effectively given the nature of the challenges it faces. One way to do this is to provide a list of the STRAT items to members and ask each member to pick the three to five they feel are most critical to the success of the team. Summarize the items, and record them on a presentation chart. The team members will be tempted to discuss all STRAT items, but this list will help them narrow their focus.

6. Hand back the STRAT aggregate data and explain how to read this information.

7. It might be helpful for members to have some comparison data. (The norm data that the Center for Creative Leadership has collected for STRAT are in appendix D.)

8. Allow time for members to study the data and to reflect on what they see.

9. Ask each person to complete the following sentences. They might have more than one way to complete each one. Each version should be placed on a separate note.

   I am pleased that the data show our strengths are . . .

   When I look at the data, I am confused by . . .

   Given what is important to this team, I think we need to focus on improving . . .

10. Put up a piece of presentation chart paper for each sentence starter. Ask members to place their notes on the appropriate chart paper.

11. Divide the group into three smaller groups, and ask each group to take one sentence. Their task is to summarize the responses to it by generating the common themes they see in the notes.

12. Have the group that summarizes the strengths report first.

13. Next, have the group that summarizes the confusing points share its report. Leave some time for discussion.

14. Finally, have the group that summarizes the areas for improvement share its report. As part of the discussion, consider the overlap between the sentences—for example:

    Are the areas where we have confusion contributing to our challenges as a team?

    Are there ways we could build on our strengths to help with the challenges we have?

    Is there any way we are overusing a strength, so that it might be working against us?

15. Once there is agreement about the categories under areas for improvement, have a discussion about the root causes of the issues. One simple way to do this is to use the "five why's" technique. That is, ask yourselves, "Why is this happening?" five times, each time building on the preceding answer.

16. Generate as many as three goals you would like to set for yourselves.
17. Assign a champion to each goal—a person who will take the lead to ensure that the group addresses the goal. The champion may need to convene a smaller group to do some work off-line.
18. Discuss the next steps for the team.

Appendix D

STRAT Norm Data

The norms are based on STRAT data collected from 12,364 respondents between January 2001 and December 2010.

5 = Strongly Agree, 4 = Agree, 3 = Neutral, 2 = Disagree,
1 = Strongly Disagree

Rank	Average	STRAT Question Ranked by Average (Highest to Lowest)
1	4.14	25. This strategic leadership teams exhibits a high level of integrity.
2	4.09	6. This strategic leadership team is clear about our basic purpose and core values.
3	4.06	13. This strategic leadership team is composed of diverse individuals with complementary talents.
4	3.98	10. Different opinions are welcome.
5	3.95	26. I am proud of the way this strategic leadership team handles issues of right or wrong.
6	3.93	2. This strategic leadership team understands the threats and opportunities in the external environment.
7	3.86	12. This strategic leadership team works well together.
8	3.85	23. This strategic leadership team fosters cooperation rather than competition across organizational units.
9	3.85	15. Members of this strategic leadership team have constructive interactions with others throughout the organization.
10	3.82	22. Members of this strategic leadership team trust and respect each other.
11	3.80	27. There is a positive sense of energy and excitement around here.

Rank	Average	STRAT Question Ranked by Average (Highest to Lowest)
12	3.78	3. This strategic leadership team has a shared vision of the future.
13	3.72	21. This strategic leadership team responds effectively to opportunities and threats in the environment.
14	3.71	16. This strategic leadership team supports executive growth and development.
15	3.70	9. There are few undiscussable subjects here.
16	3.68	5. This strategic leadership team keeps abreast of technological, cultural, and market trends.
17	3.67	14. This strategic leadership team shares information well with each other.
18	3.66	19. This strategic leadership team encourages an appropriate level of risk taking.
19	3.65	4. Individuals at all levels understand how their roles support the organizational mission.
20	3.65	17. Getting ahead here depends on performance, not politics.
21	3.64	24. We share best practices across individuals and departments.
22	3.64	1. This strategic leadership team regularly and realistically assesses our organizational strengths and weaknesses.
23	3.61	7. This strategic leadership team thinks globally.

(continued)

Rank	Average	STRAT Question Ranked by Average (Highest to Lowest)
24	3.57	8. This strategic leadership team encourages others to improve by experimenting with new or different ways of doing things.
25	3.55	18. This strategic leadership team strikes an appropriate balance between dealing with near-term and long-term needs.
26	3.46	11. Our strategy is discriminating: clear about what we WILL do and clear about what we WILL NOT do.
27	3.38	20. This strategic leadership team does not waste its own or others' energy on unproductive activities.
[No data available]		This strategic leadership team has widespread agreement about what are the most important organizational priorities (key success factors) needed to drive our sustainable competitive advantage.
[No data available]		This strategic leadership team has clear responsibility for contributing to one or more of the key drivers of our organizational success.
[No data available]		This team has the right composition to achieve its purpose.
[No data available]		This team has access to the relevant information it needs to make decisions and take action.
[No data available]		This team has direct or indirect control of the resources it needs to accomplish its task.

Appendix E

Talent Sustainability Requirements

Managing talent for organizational success and sustainability requires addressing systems and processes which include (McCauley, Smith, & Campbell, 2007):

- *Executive commitment and engagement.* Senior executives who believe that talented employees are critical for organizational success, are directly involved in talent management work, and ensure that their organization has effective talent management practices in place
- *Critical talent identification, development, and succession.* Identifying what type of talent is most critical to implementing the organization's strategy, continuously developing that talent, and moving it into roles where it is most needed
- *Learning and development.* Creating opportunities for employees to enhance their capabilities and connections with others in the organization—through feedback, reflection, coaching, mentoring, developmental assignments, and formal development programs
- *Competency model development and deployment.* Delineating the competencies needed in employees and using the resulting competency models across talent processes
- *Sourcing and recruiting.* Developing reliable sources of talent for the organization and practices for attracting that talent to the organization

- *Rewards and recognition.* Using formal and informal rewards to align employee behaviors and activities with organizational strategies and to build a committed workforce
- *Performance management.* Setting performance standards, monitoring employee performance, providing feedback and support for performance improvement, and firing employees who cannot meet standards
- *Knowledge networks.* Developing and making accessible the shared knowledge, expertise, and collective wisdom across the organization
- *Metrics.* Indicators that provide feedback to the organization not only on the effectiveness of various talent systems and processes but also on how well the organization is achieving the outcome of talent sustainability

Leadership Strategy Plan Template

Executive Summary

The executive summary provides an overview of the results of the work done during phase 1 of the leadership strategy process, with a set of results from the discovery process and recommendations on the types of leadership solutions that can help the client address his or her leadership development needs to support the business strategy.

The Leadership Strategy Process

This section provides an overview of the leadership strategy process used to complete the work. Some of the key elements in this section are:

- Charter, mission, and membership of the team doing the work
- Methodology used
- Road map, steps, and process
- Communications process with the organization to ensure alignment

Leadership Strategy Discovery

This section of the plan provides an overview of the business, its strategy, and the strategic drivers that will determine the kinds of individual leadership needed to meet its business strategy. Then it focuses on current and future states of the organization's culture, talent, organizational design, and processes so that there is an integrated and systemic approach to developing the leadership and culture needed to succeed. Some of the data elements to be addressed are

- Description of the business—its products or services, industry, and market
- Current business challenges
- Business vision, strategy, and goals
- Strategic drivers for leadership development
- Leadership culture: current and future state, gap analysis
- Talent systems: current and future state, gap analysis
- Organizational design and processes: current and future state, gap analysis
- Summary gap analysis with implications for leadership development

Leadership Strategy Recommendations

This section of the plan builds on the analysis from the leadership strategy discovery analysis, especially the gap analysis, and provides a specific set of recommended leadership solutions for the client that will address the gaps from a systems perspective. One of the intentions of this section is to show the interconnectedness of the various elements and point the way toward a sequence of actions that senior leaders can take to implement these recommendations. It is the actual outline of the plan that can be implemented. Some of the possible leadership solutions could include custom or open enrollment leadership programs, executive team development and coaching, cultural transition or transformation processes, assessments, and organizational change and development. Elements that are covered in this section include

- Restatement of the business strategy
- The leadership development needed to achieve those goals

- Recommendations on cultural transition
- Recommendations on talent development and talent systems
- Recommendations on organizational design and processes
- Summary recommendations on the leadership development needed to achieve the business strategy

Leadership Strategy Implementation and Evolution

Based on the recommendations made in the leadership strategy recommendations phase, this section provides an implementation, transition, and transformation road map. Some of the elements that it can include are

- Goals of the implementation and transition strategy tied to direction, alignment, and commitment and evolution of leadership cultures
- Critical success factors
- Ownership strategy to address resistance to change
- Communications and engagement plan
- Taking it to the middle and the front lines
- Performance measures and evaluation process
- Ongoing learning and development

Appendixes

This final section of the plan provides graphs, charts, and other forms of data analysis generated during the discovery process. It also includes a summary of the communications and engagement process that was implemented to ensure alignment.

Appendix G

Action Learning Projects Criteria for Project Selection

The project involves a real organizational problem that needs to be addressed:

- It will contribute to the long-term viability of the organization if it is accomplished effectively.
- It's not simple and straightforward; it represents a challenge for the organization.
- The organization desires some tangible results.
- The team must use a diverse membership to approach this issue.
- The team must work across boundaries in the team and across the organization.

The project must be feasible:

- The competence exists in the group to address the problem: they have the ability, knowledge, and experience with the problem to address it.

The problem, task, or issue should not be a "puzzle":

- There are multiple possible satisfactory solutions, not just one right answer.

The project should be specific, time bound, and have a measurable impact:

- The team can generate a very specific and clear statement of the problem.
- The team has adequate time to do quality work, and they can finish the work in a reasonable amount of time.
- The team can produce a tangible result with a measurable outcomes.

The team can define boundaries of responsibility for the project:

- What exactly is the team's mandate:
  - To understand and isolate the causes of the problem?
  - To recommend solutions?
  - To experiment with solutions?
  - To implement solutions?
  - To evaluate solutions that have been implemented?

The project provides opportunities to learn:

- Team members can continue to learn about their own strategic thinking, acting, and influencing skills.
- The team learns about how to be a more effective strategic leadership team.
- The team can help the organization as a whole learn to be more strategic.

References

Advice on strategy: Quotes quotations. (n.d.). Retrieved from http://www .advice-onmanagement.com/advice_strategy.html

Ambrose, S. E. (1983). *Eisenhower: 1890–1952.* New York: Simon & Schuster.

Associated Press. (2004, May 16). Three die near Denver in I-70 girder collapse. *Gazette* (Metro), 27.

Baird, L., Holland, P., & Deacon, S. (1999, Spring). Learning from action: Imbedding more learning into the performance process fast enough to make a difference. *Organizational Dynamics*, pp. 19–31.

Banham, R. (1999, August). The revolution in planning. *CFO Magazine*, 46–56.

Bassi, L., & McMurrer, D. (2011). Training investment as a driver of stock prices [online]. *Training and Development in Australia, 37*(5), 4–5.

Beatty, K. (2003, January). Strategic leadership poll results. *CCL e-Newsletter.* Retrieved from https://www.ccl.org/CCLCommerce/news/newsletters /enewsletter/2003/JANdecpollresults.aspx?CatalogID=News&Catego ryID=Enewsletter(Newsletters)

Beatty, K., & Byington, B. (2010). Developing strategic leadership. In C. D. McCauley, E. Van Velsor, & M. N. Ruderman (Eds.), *The Center for Creative Leadership handbook of leadership development* (3rd ed., pp. 313–344). San Francisco: Jossey-Bass.

Beatty, K., & Smith, R. (2013). Developing high-impact teams to lead strategic change. In E. Salas, S. I. Tannenbaum, D. Cohen, & G. Latham (Eds.), *Developing and enhancing high-performance teamwork in organizations: Evidence-based best practices and guidelines* (pp. 154–181). San Francisco, CA: Jossey-Bass.

Beer, M., & Eisenstat, R. (2000). The silent killers of strategy implementation and learning. *Sloan Management Review, 41*(4), 29–40.

Bergen, P. (2012). *Sense and nonsense about Obama and Osama.* Retrieved from CNN.com/2012/08/29/opinion/bergen-obama-osama-books

Berlin, I. (1953). *The hedgehog and the fox: An essay on Tolstoy's view of history.* London: Weidenfeld & Nicolson.

Blue Horizons. (2007). *Horizon 21 Project report.* Maxwell AFB, AL: Air University Center for Strategy and Technology.

Blue Horizons. (2009). *The age of surprise: Implications of exponential change on Air Force strategy through 2035*. Maxwell AFB, AL: Air University Center for Strategy and Technology.

Blumberg, M., & Pringle, C. D. (1982). The missing opportunity in organizational research: Some implications for a theory of work performance. *Academy of Management Review, 7*(4), 560–570.

Bossidy, L., & Charan, R. (2002). *Execution: The discipline of getting things done.* New York, NY: Crown Business.

Brochet, F., Srinivasan, S., & Norris, M. (2013). *Neflix: Valuing a new business model.* Harvard Business School. Retrieved from www.hbr.org/product /netflix-valuing-a-new-business-model/an/113018-PDF-ENG

Campbell, A., & Alexander, M. (1997). What's wrong with strategy? *Harvard Business Review, 75*(6), 42–51.

Casciaro, T., & Lobo, M. S. (2005). Competence jerks, lovable fools, and the formation of social networks. *Harvard Business Review, 83*(6), 225–231.

Center for Creative Leadership. (2013). *Leadership strategy service model.* Greensboro, NC: Marshall, E., Reinhold, D., Martineau, J., Pasmore, B., Quinn, L., McGuire, J., Adkins, G., Dinwoodie, D. L.

Charan, R., Drotter, S., & Nobel, J. (2001). *The leadership pipeline: How to build the leadership-powered company.* San Francisco: Jossey-Bass.

Chatterjee, S., Carroll, E., & Spencer, D. (2010). *Netflix.* Richard Ivey School of Business Foundation. Retrieved from www.hbr.org/product/netflix /an/909M93-PDF-ENG

Chrobot-Mason, D., Ernst, C., & Feguson, J. (2012). *Boundary spanning as battle rhythm.* Retrieved from http://www.ccl.org/leadership/pdf/research /BoundarySpanningBattleRhythm.pdf

Collins, J. (2001). *Good to great.* New York, NY: Harper.

Collins J., & Hansen, M. T. (2011). *Great by choice: Uncertainty, chaos, and luck: Why some thrive despite them all.* New York, NY: HarperCollins.

Collis, D. J., & Rukstad, M. G. (2008). Can you say what your strategy is? *Harvard Business Review, 86*(4). Retrieved from www.hbr.org/product /can-you-say-what-your-strategy-is/an/R0804E-PDF-ENG

Cox, T. (1991). The multicultural organization. *Academy of Management Executive, 5*, 43–47.

Criswell, C., & Cartwright, T. (2010). *Creating a vision.* Greensboro, NC: Center for Creative Leadership, 2010.

Cunha, R. C., & Cooper, C. L. (2002). Does privatization affect corporate culture and employee wellbeing? *Journal of Managerial Psychology, 17*, 21–39.

DeRue, S. S., Nahrgang, J. D., Hollenbeck, J. R., & Workman, K. (2012). A quasi-experimental study of after-event reviews and leadership development. *Journal of Applied Psychology, 97*(5), 997–1015.

Digital Equipment Corporation. (2004, July 25). *Wikipedia.* Retrieved from http://en.wikipedia.org/wiki/Digital_Equipment_Corporation

Dinwoodie, D. (2005). Solving the dilemma: A leader's guide to managing diversity. *Leadership in Action, 25*(2), 3–6.

Dinwoodie, D. (2006). *Creating culturally competent firms.* Ashridge, UK: Management Center for Organizational Studies Annual Round Table.

Dinwoodie, D. (2007). *Liderazgo y diversidad. In 50 lecciones de management.* Barcelona: GRANICA.

Dinwoodie, D. (2011). *DCLP: A performance-oriented model to leading across differences and managing internationalization processes.* Birmingham, UK: Aston University.

Ernst, C., & Chrobot-Mason, D. (2011). *Boundary spanning leadership: Six practices for solving problems, driving innovation, and transforming organizations.* New York, NY: McGraw-Hill.

Ferris, G. R., Davidson, S. L., & Perrewe, P. L. (2010). *Political skill at work: Impact on work effectiveness.* Boston: Nicholas Brealey Publishing.

Fiorina, C. (2000, June 2). *Whole person leadership.* Commencement address at MIT, Cambridge MA. Retrieved from http://www.hp.com/hpinfo/execteam/speeches/fiorina/ceo_mit_commence.html

Floyd, S. W., & Wooldridge, B. (1996). *The strategic middle manager: How to create and sustain competitive advantage.* San Francisco, CA: Jossey-Bass.

Fortune's 20 most profitable companies. (2012). *Fortune, 165* (7), F29–F32.

Foschini Group. (2012). *Employment equity.* Retrieved from http://www.tfg.co.za/sustainability/employ_equity.asp

Gerstner, L. (2002). *Who says elephants can't dance?* New York, NY: HarperCollins.

Goldman, E. (2007). Strategic thinking at the top. *MIT Sloan Management Review, 48*(4), 75–81.

Hammond, J. S., Keeney, R. L., & Raiffa, H. (1998). The hidden traps in decision making. *Harvard Business Review, 76*(5), 47–58.

Haslam, S. A. (2001). *Psychology in organizations: The social identity approach.* London: Sage.

Haslam, S. A., Powell, C., & Turner, T. C. (2000). Social identity, self-categorization and work motivation: Rethinking the contribution of the group to positive and sustainable organizational outcomes. *Applied Psychology: An International Review, 49,* 319–339.

Hendricks, K. B., & Singhal, V. R. (1997). Does implementing an effective TQM program actually improve operating performance? Empirical evidence from firms that have won quality awards. *Management Science, 43*(9), 1258–1274.

Hofstede, G. H., Neuijen, B., Ohayv, D., & Sanders, G. (1990). Measuring organizational culture: A qualitative and quantitative study across twenty cases. *Administrative Quarterly, 35,* 286–316.

House, R. J., Hanges, P. J., Javidan, M., Dorfman, P. W., & Gupta, V. (2004). *Culture, leadership, and organizations: The GLOBE study of 62 societies.* Thousand Oaks, CA: Sage.

Hughes, R. L., Palus, C. J., Ernst, E., Houston, G. G., & McGuire, J. B. (2011), Boundary spanning across leadership cultures: A leadership strategy for the comprehensive approach. In E. Neal & L. Wells II (Eds.), *Capability development in support of comprehensive approaches: Transforming international civil-military interactions*. Washington, DC: NDU Press.

Iacocca, L., with Novak, W. (1984). *Iacocca: An autobiography*. New York, NY: Bantam.

Institute for Corporate Productivity. (2010). Developing agile leaders for the 21st century. *People and Strategy, 33*(4), 12–13.

Isaacson, W. (2011). *Steve Jobs*. New York, NY: Simon & Schuster.

Isern, J., Meaney M., & Wilson, S. (2009). Corporate transformation under pressure. *McKinsey Quarterly*, April 6–15.

Johansen, B. (2012). *Leaders make the future* (2nd ed.). San Francisco, CA: Berrett-Koehler Publishing.

Johnson, B. (1996). *Polarity management: Identifying and managing unsolvable problems*. Amherst, MA: HRD Press.

Kaplan, R. S., & Norton, D. P. (1996). *The balanced scorecard*. Boston: Harvard Business School Press.

Kates, A., & Downey, D. (2005). The challenges of general manager transitions. In R. B. Kaiser (Ed.), *Filling the leadership pipeline*. Greensboro, NC: Center for Creative Leadership.

Katz, D., Rosa, M., & Slavin, M. (2007). *So you want to be a franchisee, part II: Updated thoughts on the hotel franchising business*. Canadian Imperial Bank of Commerce World Markets.

Katzenbach, J. R. (1997). The myth of the top management team. *Harvard Business Review, 75*(6), 82–91.

Katzenbach, J. R. (1998). *Teams at the top: Unleashing the potential of both teams and individual leaders*. Boston, MA: Harvard Business School Press.

Keating, G. (2012). *Netflixed: The epic battle for America's eyeballs*. London: Penguin Books.

Kreiner, G. E., & Ashforth, B. E. (2004). Evidence towards an expanded model of organizational identification. *Journal of Organizational Behaviour, 25*, 1–27.

Lamoureux, K., Campbell, M., & Smith, R. (2009). *High impact succession management: Best practices, models and case studies in organizational talent mobility*. Bersin & Associates and Center for Creative Leadership.

Lazere, C. (1998, February). All together now: Why you must link budgeting and forecasting to planning and performance. *CFO Magazine*, 28–36.

Linkow, P. (1999). What gifted strategic leaders do. *Training and Development, 53*(7), 34–41.

Lombardo, M. M., & Eichinger, R. W. (1989). *Eighty-eight assignments for development in place: Enhancing the developmental challenge of existing jobs*. Greensboro, NC: Center for Creative Leadership.

Lynn, G. S., Morone, J. G., & Paulson, A. S. (1996). Marketing and discontinuous innovation: The probe and learn process. *California Management Review, 38*(3), 353–375.

McCall, M. W., Jr., Lombardo, M. M., & Morrison, A. M. (1988). *The lessons of experience: How successful executives develop on the job.* Lexington, MA: Lexington Books.

McCauley, C. D. (2006). *Developmental assignments: Creating learning experiences without changing jobs.* Greensboro, NC: Center for Creative Leadership.

McCauley, C. D., Palus, C. J., Drath, W. H., Hughes, R. L., McGuire, J. B., O'Connor, P.M.G., & Van Velsor, E. (2008). *Interdependent leadership in organizations: Evidence from six case studies.* Greensboro, NC: Center for Creative Leadership.

McCauley, C. D., Smith, R., & Campbell, M. (2007). *Talent sustainability framework.* Greensboro, NC: Center for Creative Leadership.

McGuire, J. B., & Rhodes, G. (2009). *Transforming your leadership culture.* San Francisco, CA: Jossey-Bass.

Michell, A. (2011). *Samsung Electronics and the struggle for leadership of the electronics industry.* San Francisco, CA: Jossey-Bass.

Mintzberg, H. (1987). Crafting strategy. *Harvard Business Review, 65*(4), 66–75.

Mintzberg, H. (1998). *Strategy safari.* New York: Free Press.

Montgomery, B. L. (1958). *Memoirs.* Cleveland, OH: World.

Montgomery, C. A. (2012, July). How strategists lead. *McKinsey Quarterly.* Retrieved from http://www.mckinsey.com/insights/strategy/how_strategists_lead

Morrison, J. J., & Aldrich, C. (2003). Simulations and learning revolutions: An interview with Clark Aldrich. *Technology Source.* Retrieved from http://technologysource.org/article/simulations_and_the_learning_revolution/

Nadler, D. A. (1996). Managing the team at the top. *Strategy and Business, 2,* 42–51.

Neilson, G. L., Martin, K. L., & Powers, E. (2008, June). The secrets to successful strategy execution. *Harvard Business Review,* 61–70.

Netflix. (2013, April 25). *Long-term view.* Retrieved from http://ir.netflix.com/long-term-view.cfm

Norton, M. I. (2009). The IKEA effect: When labor leads to love. *Harvard Business Review.* Retrieved from http://hbr.org/web/2009/hbr-list/ikea-effect-when-labor-leads-to-love

Ouwerkerk, J. W., Ellemers, N., & de Gilder, D. (1999). Group commitment and individual effort in experimental and organizational contexts. In N. Ellemers, R. Spears, & B. Doosje, *Social identity: Context, commitment, content.* Oxford: Blackwell.

Palus, C. J., & Horth, D. M. (2002). *The leader's edge: Six creative competencies for navigating complex challenges.* San Francisco, CA: Jossey-Bass.

Pasmore, W. (2009). *Developing a leadership strategy: A critical ingredient for organizational success*. Greensboro, NC: Center for Creative Leadership.

Petnaik, D. (2009, August 26). Crafting your own innovation strategy: The who, what, and how. *Fast Company*. Retrieved from http://www.fastcompany.com/1339764/crafting-your-own-innovation-strategy-who-what-and-how

Pfeffer, J. (1981). *Power in organizations*. Marshfield, MA: Pitman.

Porter, M. E., & Kramer, M. R. (2011). Creating shared value: How to reinvent capitalism—and unleash a wave of innovation and growth. *Harvard Business Review*. 89(1), pp. 62–77. Retrieved from http://hbr.org/product/creating-shared-value/an/R1101C-PDF-ENG

Powell, C., with Pirsico, J. (1995). *My American journey*. New York, NY: Random House.

Public papers of the presidents of the United States, Dwight D. Eisenhower, 1954: Containing the public messages, speeches, and statements of the presidents, January 1 to December 31, 1954. (1960). Item 182: The president's news conference of August 4, 1954 (p. 684). Washington, DC: Government Printing Office.

Reina, D. S., & Reina, M. L. (2006). *Trust and betrayal in the workplace: Building effective relationships in your organization* (2nd ed.). San Francisco, CA: Berrett-Koehler.

Richmond, B. (2000). *The "thinking" in systems thinking: Seven essential skills*. Waltham, MA: Pegasus Communications.

Schein, E. H. (1992). *Organizational culture and leadership*. San Francisco, CA: Jossey-Bass.

Senge, P. (1990). *The fifth discipline: The art and practice of the learning organization*. New York, NY: Doubleday.

Six aspects of political skill. (2007). *Leading Effectively*. Retrieved February 21, 2013, from http://www.ccl.org/leadership/enewsletter/2007/APRskill.aspx

Smith, R., & Campbell, M. (2010). C-suite challenges and the economic meltdown: What's next for senior leaders? *People and Strategy, 33*(4), 22–30.

Snowden, D. J., & Boone, M. E. (2007, November). A leader's framework for decision making. *Harvard Business Review*, 69–76.

Stewart, T. (1999, February/March). The status of communication today: Organizational change dominates internal communication activity. *Strategic Communication Management*, 22–25.

Storytelling that moves people: A conversation with screenwriting coach Robert McKee. (2003). *Harvard Business Review, 81*(6), 51–55.

Strategic management. (2013). *BusinessDictionary.com*. Retrieved from http://www.businessdictionary.com/definition/strategic-management.html

Syngenta. (2013). *Strategy*. Retrieved from http://www.syngenta.com/global/corporate/en/about-syngenta/Pages/Strategy.aspx

Tang, V., & Moore, C. (2009, October 1). *Transforming your organization: The Kone story*. Greensboro, NC: Center for Creative Leadership.

Tischler, L. (2005). Join the circus. *Fast Company, 96*, 52.

Torbert, B., and Associates. (2004). *Action inquiry: The secret of timely and transforming leadership*. San Francisco, CA: Berrett-Koehler.

Treacy, T., & Wiersema, F. (1995). *The discipline of market leaders*. Reading, MA: Addison-Wesley.

US Air Force Academy. (2013). *Curriculum handbook 2012–2013*. Colorado Springs: Author.

Van Velsor, E., McCauley, C. D., & Ruderman, M. N. (2010). *The Center for Creative Leadership handbook of leadership development* (3rd ed.). San Francisco, CA: Jossey-Bass.

Waldman, D. A. (1994). The contributions of total quality management to a theory of work performance. *Academy of Management Review, 19*(3), 510–536.

Wason, P. C. (1960). On the failure to eliminate hypotheses in a conceptual task. *Quarterly Journal of Experimental Psychology, 12*, 129–140.

Watson, T. J., Sr. (n.d.). *Quintessential quotes*. Retrieved from ibm.com/ibm/history/documents/pdf/quotes.pdf

Welch, J. (2003). *Jack: Straight from the gut*. New York, NY: Warner Business Books.

Wesley, D. (2012). *Netflix Inc.: Streaming away from DVDs*. London, ON: Richard Ivey School of Business Foundation. Retrieved from hbr.org/product/netflix-inc-streaming-away-from-dvds/an/W12850-PDF-ENG

West, M. A. (2002). Sparkling fountains or stagnant ponds: An integrative model of creativity and innovation implementation in work groups. *Applied Psychology: An International Review, 51*(3), 355–424.

Wheatley, M. J. (1992). *Leadership and the new science: Discovering order in a chaotic world*. San Francisco, CA: Berrett-Koehler.

Yip, J., Ernst, C., & Campbell, M. (2009). *Boundary spanning leadership: Mission Critical perspectives from the executive suite*. Greensboro, NC: Center for Creative Leadership.

Yukl, G. A. (2012). *Leadership in organizations* (8th ed.). Upper Saddle River, NJ: Prentice Hall.

Zauderer, D. G. (1992, Fall). Integrity: An essential executive quality. *Business Forum*, 12–16.

Index

About the Center for Creative Leadership

The Center for Creative Leadership (CCL) is a top-ranked, global provider of executive education that unlocks individual and organizational potential through its exclusive focus on leadership education and research. Founded in 1970 as a nonprofit, educational institution, CCL helps clients worldwide cultivate creative leadership—the capacity to achieve more than imagined by thinking and acting beyond boundaries—through an array of programs, products, and other services.

Ranked in the top ten in the *Financial Times* annual executive education survey every year since 2001, CCL is headquartered in Greensboro, North Carolina, with campuses in Colorado Springs, Colorado; San Diego, California; Brussels, Belgium; and Singapore. Supported by more than four hundred faculty members and staff, it works annually with more than twenty thousand leaders and two thousand organizations. In addition, twelve network associates around the world offer selected CCL programs and assessments.

CCL draws strength from its nonprofit status and educational mission, which provide unusual flexibility in a world where quarterly profits often drive thinking and direction. It has the freedom to be objective, wary of short-term trends, and motivated foremost by its mission—hence our substantial and sustained investment in leadership research. Although CCL's work is always grounded in a strong foundation of research, it focuses on achieving a beneficial impact in the real world. Its efforts are geared to be practical and action oriented, helping leaders and their organizations more effectively achieve their goals and vision. The desire to transform learning and ideas into action provides the impetus for CCL's programs, assessments, publications, and services.

Capabilities

CCL's activities encompass leadership education, knowledge generation and dissemination, and building a community centered on leadership. CCL is broadly recognized for excellence in executive education, leadership development, and innovation by sources such as *BusinessWeek*, *Financial Times*, the *New York Times*, and the *Wall Street Journal*.

Open-Enrollment Programs

Fourteen open-enrollment courses are designed for leaders at all levels, as well as people responsible for leadership development and training at their organizations. This portfolio offers distinct choices for participants seeking a particular learning environment or type of experience. Some programs are structured specifically around small group activities, discussion, and personal reflection, while others offer hands-on opportunities through business simulations, artistic exploration, team-building exercises, and new-skills practice. Many of these programs offer private one-on-one sessions with a feedback coach.

For a complete listing of programs, visit http://www.ccl.org /programs.

Customized Programs

CCL develops tailored educational solutions for more than one hundred client organizations around the world each year. Through this applied practice, CCL structures and delivers programs focused on specific leadership development needs within the context of defined organizational challenges, including innovation, the merging of cultures, and the development of a broader pool of leaders. The objective is to help organizations develop, within their own cultures, the leadership capacity they need to address challenges as they emerge.

Program details are available online at http://www.ccl.org /custom.

Coaching

CCL's suite of coaching services is designed to help leaders maintain a sustained focus and generate increased momentum toward achieving their goals. These coaching alternatives vary in depth and duration and serve a variety of needs, from helping an executive sort through career and life issues to working with an organization to integrate coaching into its internal development process. Our coaching offerings, which can supplement program attendance or be customized for specific individual or team needs, are based on our ACS model of assessment, challenge, and support.

Learn more about CCL's coaching services at http://www.ccl .org/coaching.

Assessment and Development Resources

CCL pioneered 360-degree feedback and believes that assessment provides a solid foundation for learning, growth, and transformation and that development truly happens when an individual recognizes the need to change. CCL offers a broad selection of assessment tools, online resources, and simulations that can help individuals, teams, and organizations increase their self-awareness, facilitate their own learning, enable their development, and enhance their effectiveness.

CCL's assessments are profiled at http://www.ccl.org /assessments.

Publications

The theoretical foundation for many of our programs, as well as the results of CCL's extensive and often groundbreaking research, can be found in the scores of publications issued by CCL Press and through the center's alliance with Jossey-Bass, a Wiley imprint. Among these are landmark works, such as *Breaking the Glass Ceiling* and *The Lessons of Experience*, as well as quick-read guidebooks focused on core aspects of leadership. CCL publications provide insights and practical advice to help individuals become more effective leaders, develop leadership training within organizations, address issues of change and diversity, and build the systems and strategies that advance leadership collectively at the institutional level.

A complete listing of CCL publications is available at http://www.ccl.org/publications.

Leadership Community

To ensure that the Center's work remains focused, relevant, and important to the individuals and organizations it serves, CCL maintains a host of networks, councils, and learning and virtual communities that bring together alumni, donors, faculty, practicing leaders, and thought leaders from around the globe. CCL also forges relationships and alliances with individuals, organizations, and associations that share its values and mission. The energy, insights, and support from these relationships help shape and sustain CCL's educational and research practices and provide its clients with an added measure of motivation and inspiration as they continue their lifelong commitment to leadership and learning.

To learn more, visit http://www.ccl.org/community.

Research

CCL's portfolio of programs, products, and services is built on a solid foundation of behavioral science research. The role of research at CCL is to advance the understanding of leadership and to transform learning into practical tools for participants and clients. CCL's research is the hub of a cycle that transforms knowledge into applications and applications into knowledge, thereby illuminating the way organizations think about and enact leadership and leader development.

Find out more about current research initiatives at http://www.ccl.org/research.

• • •

For additional information about CCL, please visit http://www.ccl.org or call Client Services at (336) 545-2810.